INTERNATIONAL DEVELOPMENT IN FOCUS

PEFA, Public Financial Management, and Good Governance

Jens Kromann Kristensen, Martin Bowen, Cathal Long,
Shakira Mustapha, and Urška Zrinski, Editors

Contents

CHAPTER 5   **PFM and Perceptions of Corruption   93**
Cathal Long

CHAPTER 6   **Revenue Administration Performance and Domestic Resource Mobilization   121**
Gundula Löffler, Cathal Long, and Zac Mills

Box

Figures

Tables

Preface

This book examines the interplay between public financial management (PFM) and other key aspects of governance in low- and middle-income countries, using the Public Expenditure and Financial Accountability (PEFA) framework and related data sets to measure the quality of PFM systems. The PEFA framework was developed on the premise that effective PFM institutions and systems play a crucial role in the implementation of national policies for development and poverty reduction. It is part of a broader set of initiatives aimed at strengthening public sector governance frameworks.

Governments and development partners have been using PEFA to support analysis of PFM since 2005. They have also used it to provide a baseline for reform initiatives and to inform action plans for improving performance. This book uses the PEFA assessment results to understand the impact of PFM performance on other governance initiatives.

The book is part of a project to improve the evidence base for understanding the impact of PEFA and PFM reforms with respect to political institutions, fragility, anticorruption, and revenue mobilization. The research was undertaken by the Overseas Development Institute (ODI) in close cooperation with the PEFA Secretariat.

The research seeks to strengthen the understanding of the relationship between political institutions, including forms and types of government, electoral systems, and political parties and the quality of PFM systems. It further explores the credibility of the budget and fiscal outcomes in fragile contexts and compares those to nonfragile contexts to highlight the role that PFM can play in environments with weak institutional capacity. The book also aims to disentangle the relationship between perceptions of corruption and PFM performance. Finally, it looks at the role of revenue administration in domestic resource mobilization and particularly at the credible use of penalties for noncompliance for improving tax performance.

The primary audience includes government officials, staff of bilateral and international organizations, researchers, and members of civil society involved in PFM reforms and other governance initiatives. This book contributes to discussions on the role of PFM in strengthening governance frameworks by offering a cross-country analysis to outline determinants and outcomes associated with better PFM performance. It also provides an overview of key debates on what constitutes a good PFM system, highlights which parts of the PFM system matter more for different governance initiatives, and attempts to quantify the impact of PFM reforms.

Acknowledgments

This book is an outcome of a joint project between the Public Expenditure and Financial Accountability (PEFA) Secretariat, the Overseas Development Institute (ODI), and the World Bank. It was produced under the overall guidance of Edward Olowo-Okere (Director, World Bank) and Adenike Sherifat Oyeyiola (Practice Manager, World Bank).

The research was led by Shakira Mustapha and Cathal Long of ODI. Joachim Wehner (London School of Economics and Political Science), Paolo de Renzio (ODI Senior Research Associate), and Zac Mills (ODI Research Associate) provided guidance on the research design and quality assurance of the four papers that constitute chapters 3 to 6. Zac Mills and Gundula Löffler (ODI) made significant contributions to chapter 6. Stephanie Sweet (ODI Research Associate) provided background research and analysis in support of chapter 2.

The book benefited from insights, comments, and reviews provided by ODI staff and associates, including Sierd Hadley, Tom Hart, Mark Miller, Roel Dom, and Simon Gill; World Bank staff, including Renaud Seligmann (Practice Manager), Manuel Vargas (Practice Manager), William Leslie Dorotinsky (Advisor), Verena Maria Fritz (Senior Public Sector Specialist), Srinivas Gurazada (Senior Financial Management Specialist), Love Emma Ghunney (Governance and Public Sector Specialist), and Lewis Hawke (former Head of the PEFA Secretariat); and Department for International Development staff, including Scott Caldwell, Rajesh Rajan, Mirza Jahani, and Alexander Hamilton.

This book was made possible by funding provided by the United Kingdom's Department for International Development.

The team thanks Elizabeth R. Forsyth for editing and revising the book and Janice Tuten for managing the production of the publication.

About PEFA

Public Expenditure and Financial Accountability (PEFA) is a partnership program initiated in 2001 by international development partners: the European Commission, International Monetary Fund, the World Bank, French Ministry of Foreign Affairs, Norwegian Ministry of Foreign Affairs, Swiss State Secretariat for Economic Affairs, and the United Kingdom's Department for International Development. In 2019, the Ministry of Finance of the Slovak Republic became a new partner of the program.

The PEFA program builds on the principles of the Strengthened Approach to Supporting Public Financial Management Reform, which is embodied in three components and closely aligned with the Paris Declaration on Aid Effectiveness, the Accra Agenda for Action, the Busan Partnership Agreement, and the Addis Ababa Action Agenda:

- A country-led agenda: a government-led reform program for which analytical work, reform design, implementation, and monitoring reflect country priorities and are integrated into governments' institutional structures

- A coordinated program of support from donors and international finance institutions in relation to analytical work, reform financing, and technical support for implementation

- A shared information pool on public financial management (PFM): information on PFM systems and their performance, which is commonly accepted by and shared among the stakeholders at country level, thus avoiding duplicative and inconsistent analytical work

The PEFA program produced the PEFA framework, which assesses the status of a country's PFM. It measures the extent to which PFM systems, processes, and institutions contribute to the achievement of desirable budget outcomes: aggregate fiscal discipline, strategic allocation of resources, and efficient service delivery. For more information about PEFA, visit www.PEFA.org.

The findings, interpretations, and conclusions expressed in this work do not necessarily reflect the views of the PEFA partners.

About the Authors and Editors

Martin Bowen is a Senior Public Sector Specialist at the Public Expenditure and Financial Accountability (PEFA) Secretariat. He has extensive experience in public financial management reform in more than 30 countries with various international organizations including the United Kingdom's Department for International Development, European Union, International Monetary Fund, U.S. Agency for International Development, and the World Bank, on long-term and short-term assignments. Martin also worked for 15 years with the Australian Department of Finance. He has a bachelor's degree in economics from the University of Leeds, United Kingdom, and a master's degree in international and community development from Deakin University, Australia.

Jens Kromann Kristensen is the Head of the Public Expenditure and Financial Accountability (PEFA) Secretariat. He has worked on a broad range of public financial management (PFM) reforms at the Danish Ministry of Finance, KPMG Risk Advisory Services, the Organisation for Economic Co-operation and Development (OECD), and the World Bank. He has experience from East Asia, Europe, and Sub-Saharan Africa working on PFM in high-, middle-, and low-income countries and in fragile and conflict-affected areas. He has a bachelor's degree and a master's degree in political science from the University of Copenhagen.

Gundula Löffler is a Senior Research Officer, Public Finance and Institutions, Overseas Development Institute (ODI). She specializes in institutional and governance reforms in low- and middle-income countries in the areas of taxation, fiscal decentralization, and intergovernmental relations. Prior to joining ODI, she was a researcher and consultant on fiscal decentralization and local taxation in Rwanda and other African countries. She also worked as a development adviser for the Gesellschaft für Technische Zusammenarbeit in the Arab Republic of Egypt, Germany, and the Syrian Arab Republic on participatory development, decentralization, urban management, and slum upgrading. She holds a PhD in public administration and development from New York University Wagner.

Cathal Long is a Research Fellow, Public Finance and Institutions, Overseas Development Institute (ODI). His research and advisory work focus on public finance reforms and service delivery in low-income countries, including Nepal, South Sudan, and Uganda. Before joining ODI, he was an ODI Fellow in the Ministry of Economic Planning and Development in Swaziland and previously worked in public sector accounting and audit in Ireland and the United Kingdom. He holds a master's degree in economics from University College Dublin and is an associate member of the Chartered Institute of Management Accountants.

Zac Mills is a Research Associate, Public Finance and Institutions, Overseas Development Institute (ODI). He specializes in public sector reforms and performance management tools to strengthen the links between planning, budgeting, and results. He previously worked eight years at the World Bank, most recently as a Governance Specialist in its Africa Region. He holds a master's degree in economics from the University of Sussex and a master's degree in international affairs from Carleton University.

Shakira Mustapha is a Research Fellow, Public Finance and Institutions, Overseas Development Institute (ODI). Her research interests cover public administration and development finance. Previously she worked with the government of Trinidad and Tobago in the Ministry of Trade and Industry as well as the Ministry of Planning and Sustainable Development on issues concerning economic diversification, and with various reform programs such as social safety nets and public financial management. She holds a master's degree in public and economic policy from the London School of Economics.

Urška Zrinski is Public Sector Specialist at the Public Expenditure and Financial Accountability (PEFA) Secretariat. She joined the Secretariat in October 2015 and has been working on the upgraded PEFA 2016 framework. She has been leading the Secretariat's efforts in promoting the use of PEFA to collect information on gender-responsive budgeting practices and is anchoring the Secretariat's research initiatives. Prior to joining the Secretariat, she was Chief Program Officer at the Center of Excellence in Finance, leading knowledge and learning programs for public finance officials in Southeast Europe. Urška holds a PhD from the University of Ljubljana and a master's degree from King's College London, University of London. Her research interests include on international development cooperation effectiveness, aid modalities, and the quality and use of public financial management systems.

Summary

The United Kingdom's Department for International Development (DFID) funded a research project to generate a robust evidence base for understanding the impact of Public Expenditure and Financial Accountability (PEFA) and public financial management (PFM) reforms. The purpose of the research project, based on the PEFA data set, was to understand how PEFA can be potentially utilized to shape policy development at the interface of PFM and other major relevant policy areas like anti-corruption, revenue mobilization, political economy analysis, and fragile states. Four research papers were produced to outline the relationship between PEFA, PFM, and the four selected policy areas. Additional papers on methodology, outlining the study approach and PEFA data set specifics, were produced to accompany the research project outputs. The Overseas Development Institute (ODI) was contracted to carry out the project work.

The research is based on the PEFA framework and methodology for assessing PFM performance and the data set that is generated from the PEFA assessments. The research quantified PEFA scores and aggregated them into overall scores, which required developing assumptions on weighting scores, measures, and assessments. The research acknowledges methodological limitations of using the PEFA data set, including the assumptions. In general, the research follows the approach taken by previous reseachers who have used PEFA data for quantitative analysis, but this does not eliminate the challenges that persist in transforming grades to numerical values and aggregating them. The time inconsistency issues and the limited number of observations also influenced the regression analysis using the PEFA data set. The team acknowledges that the PEFA data set was not designed for statistical analysis and that using it in quantitative regressions presents a series of econometric issues that cannot be fully resolved in this book, or in other papers that apply a similar approach.

The research report builds on general recognition that PFM is important for development and recognizes that there is limited evidence based on the nontechnical determinants of PFM performance, as well as the outcomes of a good PFM system. The report therefore aims to bridge some of this gap between theory and practice using data on PFM performance from PEFA assessments. The report undertakes a closer examination of the key debates on what constitutes a good PFM system by providing an overview of the PEFA framework, and the data set that is generated through PEFA assessments, including its strengths and weaknesses. This was done to enable the research team to undertake quantitative analysis of the relationship between PFM performance and other governance indicators and outcomes.

The report looks at the question of what shapes the PFM system in low- and middle-income countries by examining the relationship between political institutions and the quality of the PFM system. The report builds on the existing theoretical and empirical literature by refining and nuancing previous hypotheses on the relationship, retesting hypotheses using a larger sample, and testing new hypotheses. The report finds little evidence that these relationships hold in low- and middle-income country contexts and notes several relationships that are in fact counterintuitive. Although the report finds some evidence that having multiple political parties controlling the legislature is associated with better PFM performance, more generally, the report findings point to the need for further refinement and testing of the theories on the relationship between political institutions and PFM in low- and middle-income countries.

The report deals with the question of the outcomes of PFM systems, distinguishing between fragile and nonfragile states. Specifically, it explores whether the credibility of the budget and fiscal outcomes improve with better PFM performance using various definitions of fragility. The report findings are mixed. The report finds that better PFM performance is associated with more reliable budgets in terms of expenditure composition in fragile states, but not aggregate budget credibility. Moreover, in contrast to existing studies, it finds no evidence that PFM quality matters for deficit and debt ratios, irrespective of whether a country is fragile or not. The research study also concluded that there will be significant value in future research of conducting case studies on governments that have systematically met fiscal targets over a defined period of time.

The report also explores the relationship between corruption and PFM performance. The analysis is limited by the constraint that there is no cross-country measure of actual corruption, and the report is therefore reliant on corruption perceptions indexes as a proxy and the potential measurement error that comes with such an instrument. Nevertheless, the report finds strong evidence of a relationship between better PFM performance and better perceptions of corruption. It also finds that PFM reforms associated with better controls have a stronger relationship with better perceptions of corruption compared to PFM reforms associated with more transparency. However, it finds the magnitude of the relationships underwhelming when compared with the magnitude of the relationship between economic growth and perceptions of corruption. This is in line with the findings of other studies. The report findings suggest that PFM reform may be part of an effective anticorruption campaign, or that contexts where perceptions of corruption are improving are more amenable to PFM reform. However, there remains much scope for further research in this area that more tightly defines individual PFM measures to more relevant measures of corruption.

The last chapter of the report looks at the relationship between PEFA indicators for revenue administration and domestic resource mobilization. It focuses specifically on the credible use of penalties for noncompliance as a proxy for the type of political commitment that is necessary for improving tax performance. The analysis shows that countries that credibly enforce penalties for noncompliance collect more taxes on average. Because of the potential for measurement, further in-country research on the dynamics of penalties for noncompliance is warranted.

Abbreviations

BLNS	Botswana, Lesotho, Namibia, and Swaziland
CPIA	Country Policy and Institutional Assessment
DRM	domestic resource mobilization
GDP	gross domestic product
GRD	Government Revenue Dataset
ICRG	International Country Risk Guide
ICTD	International Centre for Tax and Development
IMF	International Monetary Fund
MDG	Millennium Development Goal
OBI	Open Budget Index
OECD	Organisation for Economic Co-operation and Development
OLS	ordinary least squares
PEFA	Public Expenditure and Financial Accountability
PER	Public Expenditure Review
PFM	public financial management
SDG	Sustainable Development Goal
SIDS	small island developing states
UNU WIDER	United Nations University World Institute for Development Economics Research
WGI	Worldwide Governance Indicators
WGI_COC	World Bank's Worldwide Governance Indicators for control of corruption
WLS	weighted least squares

1 Introduction: What Is PFM and Why Is It Important?

This publication is concerned with governance indicators and outcomes commonly associated with public financial management (PFM) performance. Our analysis is cross-country in focus and looks at both determinants and outcomes associated with better PFM performance using data from Public Expenditure and Financial Accountability (PEFA) assessments. This first chapter provides an overview of what PFM is and why it is important, its place within the context of international development, and the relevance of the findings in later chapters to the wider debate on PFM reform.

IMPORTANCE OF PFM

Commonly accepted frameworks

The term "public financial management" has only come into common use over the past 20 years, with a coherent and compact definition of PFM surprisingly absent in the literature (Allen, Hemming, and Potter 2013). Nevertheless, the PFM system is commonly described in terms of an annual budget cycle as illustrated in figure 1.1. This annual cycle aims to ensure that public expenditure is well planned, executed, accounted for, and scrutinized. It typically centers around the following key phases:

- *Budget formulation.* The budget is prepared with due regard to government fiscal policies, strategic plans, and adequate macroeconomic and fiscal projections.

- *Budget execution.* The budget is executed within a system of effective standards, processes, and internal controls, ensuring that resources are obtained and used as intended.

- *Accounting and reporting.* Accurate and reliable records are maintained, and information is produced and disseminated at appropriate times to meet decision-making, management, and reporting needs.

- *External security and audit.* Public finances are independently reviewed, and there is external follow-up on whether the executive has implemented the recommendations for improvement.

FIGURE 1.1
Annual budget cycle

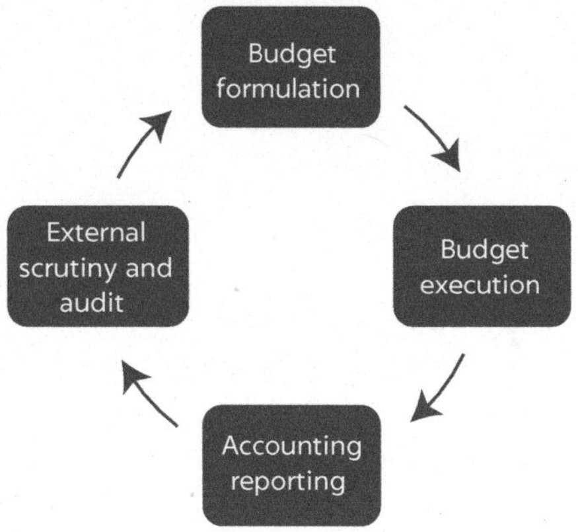

There is also general consensus around the objectives of the PFM system. Multiple authors have framed the PFM system around achieving the objectives of aggregate discipline, allocative efficiency, and operational efficiency (see, for example, Campos and Pradhan 1996; Schick 1998).

- The maintenance of aggregate fiscal discipline is the first objective of a PFM system and deals with the interaction between two variables: revenue and expenditure. It entails ensuring that aggregate levels of revenue and public spending are consistent with targets for the fiscal deficit and do not generate unsustainable levels of public borrowing.

- A PFM system should ensure that public resources are allocated to agreed strategic priorities and should spur reallocation from lesser to higher priorities—in other words, should ensure that allocative efficiency is achieved.

- The PFM system should ensure that operational efficiency is achieved, in the sense of achieving maximum value for money in the delivery of services.

Also common is the view that PFM is "instrumental" or a "means to an end" in the achievement of broader development objectives: state building, macroeconomic stability, efficient resource allocation, and service delivery (Welham, Krause, and Hedger 2013). However, although PFM does encompass the technical literature on budgeting, procurement, cash management, debt management, accounting, and auditing, a more contemporary view is that it is also part of the wider literature on systems of governance (Andrews et al. 2014). This view recognizes that PFM is also concerned with the policy-making process—that is, the interaction within and between technicians (economists, accountants, and auditors) and policy makers (cabinet members, parliamentarians, and advisers) in the formulation of fiscal policy.

This view is reflected in more contemporary definitions of PFM. For example, Cangiano, Curristine, and Lazare (2013) note that PFM "has broadened . . . to all aspects of managing public resources, including resource mobilization and debt management, with a progressive extension to the medium to long term implications and risks for public finances of today's policy decisions." More recently, Andrews et al. (2014) define PFM as "the way governments manage public resources (both revenue and expenditure) and the immediate and medium to long term impact of such resources on the economy or society." As such, "PFM has to do with both processes (how governments manage) and results (short, medium, and long term implications of financial flows)."

The PEFA Secretariat's definition captures much of this consensus, describing "good PFM" as "the linchpin that ties together available resources, delivery of services, and achievement of government policy objectives. If it is done well, PFM ensures that revenue is collected efficiently and used appropriately and sustainably" (PEFA Secretariat 2016).

At the same time, this framing remains ambivalent on the design of revenue and expenditure policies whose evaluation is generally left to those working in other fields. There remains a distinction between the field of "public finance," which focuses on "what to do" questions of policy, and "public financial management," which focuses more on "how to do" questions of implementation (Allen, Hemming, and Potter 2013).

The state's role in development

These PFM frameworks are cognizant of the role of the state in development through public spending. A key difference between today's Organisation for Economic Co-operation and Development (OECD) countries and developing countries is the size of the public sector in the overall economy, where tax and spending ratios are commonly in the range of 30 percent to 50 percent of gross domestic product (GDP). These ratios grew over time as OECD governments spent progressively more on health, education, social protection, and infrastructure. At the same time, these countries developed more sophisticated PFM systems, which were viewed as necessary to provide the required accountability mechanisms to raise taxes and debt to finance higher rates of expenditure. Later developing and less advanced economies have followed a similar trend, though without reaching similar levels of expenditure as a share of GDP.

Furthermore, successive global drives to increase the welfare of the citizens in developing countries have also included strengthening public expenditure systems and resource mobilization. For example, during the Millennium Development Goals (MDGs) era from 2000 to 2015, donors aimed to support more capable states by providing budget support to developing countries using country systems. Under the Sustainable Development Goals (SDGs), the international community is focusing significant attention on supporting developing countries to increase their budgets through domestic resource mobilization and access to private finance.

PFM as a means to achieving other desirable outputs and outcomes

To turn these laudable goals into a reality, there has been increasing recognition of the "instrumental" role PFM plays in delivering services on which human and economic development rely. For example, "Better payments systems and better cash management make it more likely that payments can be made on time, including for wages, transfers, operations and management, and investments" (World Bank 2012, 51). This link between inputs and service delivery outputs and outcomes led to the use of public expenditure tracking surveys (PETSs) that trace the actual flow of public funds in a program or a sector and establish the extent to which public funds and other resources reach service providers. Although different public services will require a different mix of these inputs, regular payment of staff salaries is likely to be critical to the delivery of all public services (Welham, Krause, and Hedger 2013; Welham et al. 2017).

PFM and development

However, both during the MDG era and now in the SDG era, donors seeking to promote state-led development through country PFM systems face a dilemma: many of the countries that they are seeking to support have extremely weak PFM systems. Indeed, early PETSs revealed large amounts of leakage in the flow of funds. This leakage exposes donor support to fiduciary risk or the more general risk that their support will have little impact. It has also led to an increase in technical support to improve PFM systems through reforms.

Conditionality has aimed to strengthen the PFM system in aid-recipient countries to help to ensure that aid is used effectively for the purposes intended (DFID 2009). This conditionality was particularly important with the shift toward budget support as an aid modality during the MDG era, with funds channeled directly to a recipient government's treasury account and thereafter executed using the country's own allocation, procurement, and accounting systems. Similarly, debt relief programs launched in the late 1990s and 2000s have been used as leverage to move the indebted country into a new mode of operations to ensure that resources freed up through debt relief are used to reduce poverty or increase growth. To meet aid conditionalities, countries have had to develop action plans to strengthen systems for public expenditure management.

The emergence of diagnostic tools for assessing PFM systems

However, during the MDG era, each donor was initially using its own diagnostic tool to assess whether it should provide budget support through country systems, creating a massive compliance burden for recipient countries. The Paris Declaration on Aid Effectiveness (2005) committed donors to implement harmonized diagnostic reviews and performance assessment frameworks in PFM.

The PEFA framework emerged as the instrument to harmonize these various diagnostic tools and, as a result, has become the most widely used assessment of PFM performance in low- and middle-income countries.

The PEFA framework was introduced with three goals in mind: (a) to strengthen the ability of governments to assess systems of public expenditure, procurement, and fiduciary management and contribute to a government-led reform agenda; (b) to support the development and monitoring of reform and capacity development programs and facilitate a coordinated program of support; and (c) to contribute to the pool of information on PFM.[1]

Since its launch in 2005, nearly 600 formal assessments (national and subnational) in 150 countries and territories have been undertaken and verified by the PEFA Secretariat. Today, most development partners use the PEFA framework as the basis for their diagnostics of PFM systems and assessment of associated fiduciary risks, especially to determine when to use country systems for individual operations. It has become the go-to measure of PFM.

Because of the international recognition of PEFA, there has also been a proliferation of other institutional diagnostics that largely replicate the approach and methodology of the PEFA framework. Most of these diagnostics focus on specific elements of the PFM system. Examples include the World Bank's Debt Management Performance Assessment (DeMPA) as well as the International Monetary Fund's Tax Administration Diagnostic Assessment Tool (TADAT) and Public Investment Management Assessment (PIMA).

Donor spending for strengthening PFM systems

Donors provide considerable financial support to PFM. Data from the OECD's Development Assistance Committee database shows a dramatic increase in disbursed funds for activities related to public sector financial management, which trebled from US$406 million in 2002 to US$1.3 billion in 2016 after peaking at roughly US$1.8 billion in 2011 (figure 1.2). This surge in financing has naturally led to questions about whether this spending is achieving the desired results.

RESEARCH CONTRIBUTION TO DISCUSSIONS ON PFM PERFORMANCE AND ISSUES IN PFM REFORM

While there is general recognition that PFM is important for development, there is limited empirical evidence on what determines "better" PFM performance and the outcomes associated with a "good" PFM system. This report seeks to bridge some of this gap between theory and practice using data on PFM performance from PEFA assessments.

FIGURE 1.2

Disbursements of overseas development assistance for public financial management (PFM) by all donors, 2002–16

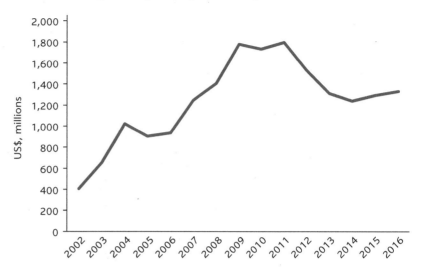

Source: OECD Creditor Reporting System.

In the next chapter, we undertake a closer examination of the key debates on what constitutes a good PFM system by providing an overview of the PEFA framework and the data set that is generated through PEFA assessments. This overview includes an analysis of the pros and cons of undertaking quantitative analysis using PEFA and similar governance indicators. Our aim is to address specific criticisms of the PEFA framework and similar diagnostic tools and to provide a guide to interpreting the analysis in the remaining chapters, including understanding its inherent strengths and weaknesses.

Chapters 3 to 6 examine the relationship between PFM performance and other indicators of governance. Across all four chapters, we try to tease out which parts of the PFM system matter more for different questions and attempt to quantify the impact of PFM reforms where relevant, albeit with important caveats.

In chapter 3 we investigate what shapes PFM systems in developing contexts by examining the relationship between political institutions and the quality of PFM systems. This chapter builds on the existing theoretical and empirical literature by refining and nuancing previous hypotheses on this relationship, retesting hypotheses using a larger sample, and testing new hypotheses. Much of this theoretical and empirical literature is based on observations for higher-income countries. We find little evidence that these relationships hold in low- and middle-income countries and note some counterintuitive relationships. Although we do find some evidence that having multiple political parties controlling the legislature is associated with better PFM performance more generally, our findings point to the need for further refinement and testing of the theories on the relationship between political institutions and PFM in low- and middle-income countries.

Chapter 4 assesses the outcomes of PFM systems, distinguishing between fragile and nonfragile states. Specifically, we explore whether the credibility of the budget and fiscal outcomes improves with better PFM performance using various definitions of fragility. Our findings are mixed. We find that better PFM performance is associated with more reliable budgets in terms of the composition of expenditures in fragile states, but not with aggregate budget credibility. Moreover, in contrast to existing studies, we find no evidence that PFM quality matters for deficit and debt ratios, irrespective of whether a country is fragile or not.

In chapter 5, we turn our attention to the relationship between corruption and PFM performance. Our analysis is limited by the constraint that there is no cross-country measure of actual corruption. We therefore use corruption perception indexes as a proxy, with the potential measurement error that comes with using such a blunt instrument. Nevertheless, we find strong evidence of a relationship between better PFM performance and better perceptions of corruption. We also find that PFM reforms associated with better controls have a stronger relationship with better perceptions of corruption than PFM reforms associated with more transparency. However, the magnitude of the relationship is underwhelming when compared with the magnitude of the relationship between economic growth and perceptions of corruption. This finding is in line with the findings of other studies. Our findings suggest that PFM reform may be part of an effective anticorruption campaign or that contexts where the perceptions of corruption are improving are more amenable to PFM reform. However, much scope remains for further research in this area to define individual PFM measures more tightly with more relevant measures of corruption.

We follow this advice in chapter 6 by looking at a more tightly defined relationship between domestic resource mobilization and revenue administration. We focus on the impact on tax performance of the credible use of penalties for noncompliance. This tool has become somewhat neglected from a research perspective, as more modern revenue administrations have shifted their focus toward voluntary compliance and taxpayer services. Our analysis shows that countries that credibly enforce penalties for noncompliance collect significantly more taxes on average. Because of the potential for measurement, further in-country research on the dynamics of penalties for noncompliance is warranted. This would allow for analysis of the individual responses of taxpayers to the use of penalties for noncompliance.

NOTE

1. See http://siteresources.worldbank.org/PEFA/Resources/PEFA-Signature-Proof.pdf.

REFERENCES

Allen, R., R. Hemming, and B. Potter. 2013. *The International Handbook of Public Financial Management*. London: Palgrave MacMillan. https://www.palgrave.com/gp/book/9780230300248.

Andrews, M., M. Cangiano, N. Cole, P. de Renzio, P. Krause, and R. Seligmann. 2014. "This Is PFM." CID Working Paper 285, Center for International Development, Harvard University, Cambridge, MA. https://www.hks.harvard.edu/centers/cid/publications/faculty-working-papers/pfm.

Campos, E., and S. Pradhan. 1996. "Budgetary Institutions and Expenditure Outcomes." Policy Research Working Paper 1646, World Bank, Washington, DC. http://documents.worldbank.org/curated/en/481221468774864173/.

Cangiano, M., T. Curristine, and M. Lazare. 2013. *Public Financial Management and Its Emerging Architecture*. Washington, DC: International Monetary Fund.

DFID (Department for International Development). 2009. "Implementing the UK's Conditionality Policy: A How-to Note." DFID, London.

PEFA (Public Expenditure and Financial Accountability) Secretariat. 2016. *Public Financial Management Performance Measurement Framework*. Washington, DC: PEFA Secretariat. https://pefa.org/sites/default/files/PEFA%20Framework_English.pdf.

Schick, A. 1998. *A Contemporary Approach to Public Expenditure Management*. Washington, DC: World Bank. http://documents.worldbank.org/curated/en/739061468323718599/pdf/351160REV0Contemporary0PEM1book.pdf.

Welham, B., T. Hart, S. Mustapha, and S. Hadley. 2017. *Public Financial Management and Health Service Delivery: Necessary, but Not Sufficient?* Report. London: Overseas Development Institute.

Welham, B., P. Krause, and E. Hedger. 2013. "Linking PFM Dimensions to Development Priorities." Working Paper 380, Overseas Development Institute, London.

World Bank. 2012. *Public Financial Management Reforms in Post-Conflict Countries: Synthesis Report*. Washington, DC: World Bank.

2 Measuring PFM Performance through PEFA: Approach and Methodology

In this chapter we provide an overview of the Public Expenditure and Financial Accountability (PEFA) framework and methodology for assessing public financial management (PFM) performance and the data set that is generated from these PEFA assessments. We present the methodological issues we encounter when using the data and how we deal with these issues in the chapters that follow.

The rest of the chapter proceeds as follows. First, we describe the PEFA framework, how it measures PFM performance, how it compares with other diagnostic tools, and how the framework has changed over time. We also describe descriptive statistics regarding the coverage and performance of our data set and provide a summary of the discussion. Then, we discuss the various approaches to quantifying PEFA scores for quantitative analysis and highlight common issues encountered when using these scores in regression analysis. We conclude by summarizing the key points.

THE PEFA FRAMEWORK AND DATA SET

The PEFA framework

The PEFA methodology has changed over time. The first PEFA framework was released in 2005, and updates followed in 2011 and 2016. These frameworks were developed to assess PFM performance at the national level. The framework has been applied at the subnational level as well. This report is based on a data set compiled from assessments using the national-level 2011 PEFA framework, which is the main focus of discussion in this chapter. However, we also discuss the 2005 and 2016 national-level PEFA frameworks given that some of the revisions are relevant to the analysis in subsequent chapters.

As discussed in chapter 1, the PFM system is commonly described in terms of the stages of the annual budget cycle, and a good PFM system is instrumental in supporting the objectives of aggregate fiscal discipline, strategic allocation of resources, and efficient delivery of services. This is the approach taken in the PEFA framework, which organizes key PFM processes into pillars and links process quality to budgetary

FIGURE 2.1

The public financial management (PFM) system according to the 2011 Public Expenditure and Financial Accountability (PEFA) framework

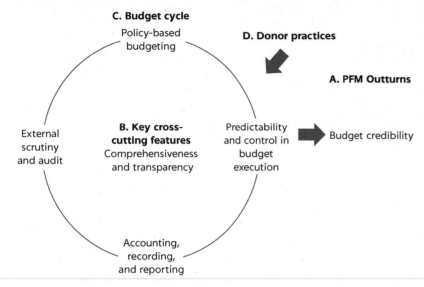

Source: PEFA Secretariat 2011.

outcomes. Figure 2.1 illustrates the PFM system as outlined in the 2011 PEFA framework. It includes four pillars corresponding to the phases of the budget cycle—policy-based budgeting; predictability and control in budget execution; accounting, recording, and reporting; and external scrutiny and audit—and one cross-cutting pillar on comprehensiveness and transparency (see box 2.1 for further discussion). In addition to well-aligned budget support from donors, improvements in these five core dimensions are expected to deliver budget credibility in the form of aggregate fiscal discipline, allocative efficiency, and operational efficiency (PEFA Secretariat 2011). The features of the budget cycle vary from country to country, but the outline is similar to what is found in most countries and what others have proposed.[i]

Measuring performance

Under each pillar of the 2011 PEFA framework are indicators of PFM performance (table 2.1). There are 28 performance indicators in total, denoted as PI-1 to PI-28, as well as three donor performance indicators, denoted as D-1 to D-3. Predictability and control in budget execution make up the largest pillar, with nine indicators (three of these indicators are related to tax administration and are the focus of chapter 6). Policy-based budgeting is the smallest pillar, with just two indicators. Under each PI are 1–4 dimensions that are assessed to determine the PI score. Each dimension measures performance against a four-point ordinal scale from D to A that captures levels of compliance with good practices in PFM. There are 76 dimensions within the 2011 framework, of which 5 are related to donor practices.

BOX 2.1

Public Expenditure and Financial Accountability (PEFA) 2011 pillars

1. *Credibility of the budget.* The budget is realistic and is implemented as intended.

2. *Comprehensiveness and transparency.* The budget and fiscal risk oversight are comprehensive, and fiscal and budget information is accessible to the public.

3. *Policy-based budgeting.* The budget is prepared with due regard to government policy.

4. *Predictability and control in budget execution.* The budget is implemented in an orderly and predictable manner, and there are arrangements for the exercise of control and stewardship in the use of public funds.

5. *Accounting, recording, and reporting.* Adequate records and information are produced, maintained, and disseminated to meet decision-making control, management, and reporting purposes.

6. *External scrutiny and audit.* Arrangements are operating for the scrutiny of public finances and follow-up by the executive.

Source: PEFA Secretariat 2011.

For example, under the policy-based budgeting pillar, PI-11 measures orderliness and participation in the annual budget process. Table 2.2 shows the minimum required for a country to score an A on each of the three dimensions under PI-11. In addition, the PEFA Secretariat regularly provides training for assessors carrying

TABLE 2.1 Number of pillars, indicators, and dimensions of the Public Expenditure and Financial Accountability (PEFA) framework

PILLAR	INDICATORS	DIMENSIONS
Credibility of the budget	4	6
Policy-based budgeting	2	7
Predictability and control in budget execution	9	29
Accounting, recording, and reporting	4	9
External scrutiny and audit	3	10
Comprehensiveness and transparency	6	10
Donor practices	3	5
Total	**31**	**76**

Source: PEFA Secretariat 2011.

TABLE 2.2 How to score an A on the three dimensions under PI-11—orderliness and participation in the annual budget process

DIMENSION AND SCORE	M2 SCORING METHOD: MINIMUM REQUIREMENTS
PI-11(i)—Existence of and adherence to a fixed budget calendar	
A	A clear annual budget calendar exists, is generally adhered to, and allows ministries, departments, and agencies (MDAs) enough time (at least six weeks from receipt of the budget circular) to complete their detailed estimates meaningfully and on time.
B	A clear annual budget calendar exists, but some delays are often experienced in its implementation. The calendar allows MDAs reasonable time (at least four weeks from receipt of the budget circular) so that most of them are able to complete their detailed estimates meaningfully and on time.
C	An annual budget calendar exists but is rudimentary, and substantial delays may often be experienced in its implementation. It allows MDAs so little time to complete detailed estimates that many fail to complete them in a timely manner.
D	A budget calendar is not prepared, OR it is generally not adhered to, OR the time allowed for MDAs' budget preparation is clearly insufficient to make meaningful submissions.
PI-11(ii)—Guidance on the preparation of budget submissions	
A	A comprehensive and clear budget circular is issued to MDAs, which reflects ceilings approved by the cabinet (or equivalent) prior to the circular's distribution to MDAs.
B	A comprehensive and clear budget circular is issued to MDAs, which reflects ceilings approved by the cabinet (or equivalent). This approval takes place after the circular is distributed to MDAs, but before MDAs have completed their submission.
C	A budget circular is issued to MDAs, including ceilings for individual administrative units or functional areas. The budget estimates are reviewed and approved by the cabinet only after they have been completed in all details by MDAs, thus seriously constraining the cabinet's ability to make adjustments.
D	A budget circular is not issued to MDAs, OR the quality of the circular is very poor, OR the cabinet is involved in approving the allocations only immediately before the submission of detailed estimates to the legislature, thus providing no opportunities for adjustment.
PI-11(iii)—Timely budget approval by the legislature	
A	The legislature has, during the last three years, approved the budget before the start of the fiscal year.
B	The legislature approves the budget before the start of the fiscal year, but a delay of up to two months has happened in one of the last three years.
C	The legislature has, in two of the last three years, approved the budget within two months of the start of the fiscal year.
D	The budget has been approved with more than two months delay in two of the last three years.

Source: PEFA Secretariat 2011.
Note: The M2 method is based on an approximate average of the scores for the individual dimensions of the Performance Indicator (PI); it is also referred to as the "averaging method." MDA = ministries, departments, and agencies.

FIGURE 2.2

Number of indicators in the Public Expenditure and Financial Accountability (PEFA) framework, by scoring methodology

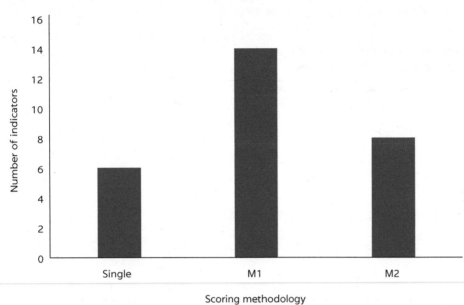

Note: M1 = weakest link method. M2 = averaging method.

out assessments, and the PEFA *Fieldguide* provides further guidance for assessors on the evidence that is required to assign a dimension score (see PEFA Secretariat 2012a). Nevertheless, the frequently asked questions that form part of the *Fieldguide* highlight the fact that at times assessors may find it difficult to apply the performance measurement framework easily and consistently. Moreover, because of the breadth of a PEFA assessment, performance measurement is generally carried out by a team of assessors, and some countries have established their own PEFA Secretariat and carry out self-assessments. These issues have raised concerns about quality control both within and across assessments. These issues are discussed in the context of recent changes in the PEFA framework and in the context of measurement error in this chapter.

To arrive at the PI scores, the assessor must combine the dimension scores using one of two methods referred to as method 1 (M1) and method 2 (M2). The scoring method is clearly prescribed for each of the indicators. Regardless of the method used, the first step in assigning a score to a PI is to score each of its dimensions separately based on the D through A ranking. For multidimensional indicators, where poor performance on one dimension of the indicator is likely to undermine the impact of good performance on other dimension(s) of the same indicator, assessors must apply the M1 method. Under this method, the indicator is assigned the score of the lowest dimension, but a "+" is added if one of the other dimension scores is higher. If a three-dimensional indicator scores two Ds and one C, then the indicator is assigned a D+ score. Because the score is determined primarily by the lowest score, the M1 method is also referred to as the "weakest link" method.

The M2 method is applied for some multidimensional indicators where a low score on one dimension of the indicator does not necessarily undermine the impact of higher scores on other dimensions of the same indicator. Because it applies equal weighting to each of the dimension scores within the PI, the M2 method is also referred to as the "averaging method." The PEFA framework provides conversion tables for two-, three-, and four-dimensional indicators. For our PI-11 example in table 2.2, a score of two Cs and one A would combine for a PI score of C+ under M1, but would be considered a B under M2, which is actually how PI-11 is assessed. Single-dimension indicators simply take the score of the single dimension and are not eligible for a "+" rating. As shown in figure 2.2, most indicators are scored according to the M1 methodology (the figure excludes donor indicators). The implications of the different scoring methodologies for quantitative analysis are discussed in chapter 3.

Framework comparability with other assessment frameworks

Although the scoring system, performance measures, and other aspects of the framework have been the subject of some criticism, other assessment frameworks apply similar methodologies, and PEFA remains the primary tool for measuring performance in PFM. Nevertheless, other tools exist for measuring aspects of PFM performance in more depth that are complementary rather than comparable to the PEFA framework. Some of these comparable and complementary tools are discussed further below.

Several diagnostic instruments are available to assess public expenditure, financial management, and procurement. Some broad diagnostic tools include the World Bank's Public Expenditure Reviews (PERs) and the International Monetary Fund's (IMF) Fiscal Transparency Evaluations (FTEs). Other comprehensive tools have been established by intergovernmental and nongovernmental organizations, including the International Budget Partnership's (IBP) Open Budget Survey and the Organisation for Economic Co-operation and Development's (OECD) Budget Practices and Procedures Database. Some diagnostics focus on specific PFM elements or institutions, including the World Bank's Debt Management Performance Assessment (DeMPA) for debt management, the IMF's Tax Administration Diagnostic Assessment Tool (TADAT) for tax administration, and the IMF's Public Investment Management Assessment (PIMA) for public investment. Last, development partners use other tools to make decisions on fiduciary risks, including, for example, the World Bank's Country Policy and Institutional Assessment (CPIA) indicators. Some of these tools are summarized in table 2.3.

TABLE 2.3 **Other diagnostic tools**

TOOL	DESCRIPTION	COMPARISON
World Bank Public Expenditure Review (PER)	PER assesses public expenditure policies and programs to provide governments with an external review of their policies in order to strengthen budget analysis and processes and achieve a better focus on growth and poverty reduction.	• Focuses mainly on upstream elements of public financial management • Lacks a standardized methodology • Provides an external review of public expenditure policies • Provides recommendations
International Monetary Fund Fiscal Transparency Evaluation (FTE)	FTE is based on the updated Fiscal Transparency Code and was developed in 2014 to replace the Fiscal Reports on the Observance of Standards and Codes (ROSCs). It is built around four pillars: (a) fiscal reporting, (b) fiscal forecasting and budgeting, (c) fiscal risk analysis management, and (d) resource revenue management.	• Analyzes the scale and sources of fiscal vulnerabilities (coverage of fiscal reports, quality of fiscal forecasts, and size of unreported contingent liabilities) • Accounts for strengths and weaknesses related to fiscal transparency • Yields a sequenced fiscal transparency action plan that helps to define reform priorities, including concrete and sequenced steps for addressing the main shortcomings in fiscal transparency
Organisation for Economic Co-operation and Development Recommendation of the Council on Budgetary Governance (RCBG)	RCBG sets out 10 principles that provide a concise overview of good practices across the full spectrum of budget activity.	• Aims to give practical guidance for designing, implementing, and improving budget systems • Subdivides each principle into 4–7 subprinciples—in total 48 subprinciples—that can be used as performance benchmarks
Open Budget Survey	This independent analysis and survey measures overall commitment of countries to transparency, specifically the availability and content of publicly available budget reports addressing (a) budget formulation, (b) legislative approval, (c) budget implementation, and (d) annual report and supreme audit institution.	• Focuses on the quality and public availability of budget documentation • Includes a set of quantifiable indicators • Allows comparison across countries • Tracks progress over time (conducted biennially) • Is prepared by a nongovernmental organization, the International Budget Partnership, using a network of independent researchers

continued

TABLE 2.3, *continued*

TOOL	DESCRIPTION	COMPARISON
World Bank Country Policy and Institutional Assessments (CPIAs)	CPIA-13 is part of an annual internal performance rating that measures the "quality of budgetary and financial management" along three dimensions: (a) comprehensive and credible budgeting linked to policy priorities; (b) effective financial management systems; and (c) timely and accurate accounting and fiscal reporting.	• Focuses on budget and financial management • Provides a quantifiable indicator • Allows comparison across countries • Tracks progress over time • May yield a subjective judgment and be affected by lending decisions

Sources: PEFA Secretariat 2018.

Despite the number of tools and instruments available, PFM performance is increasingly measured by PEFA. PEFA has several advantages over other frameworks. First, it is the most comprehensive measure of PFM to date, covering the entire budget cycle as well as other key PFM areas. Second, it is standardized so that it can be repeated and changes can be tracked over time. Third, it includes a narrative report that discusses qualitative evidence to complement the quantitative scores. Fourth, the PEFA Secretariat provides quality assurance to ensure that the standards are met consistently across countries and time. As a result, PEFA has the most coverage globally.

Moreover, PEFA tends to produce scores comparable to those of similar diagnostics (figures 2.3–2.5). CPIA-13 (CPIA indicator 13) data have been collected for longer than PEFA data and are generated annually for most low- and middle-income countries, but ratings are made publicly available only for countries receiving International Development Association lending. CPIA-13 is rated on a scale from 1 (worst) to 6 (best). General trends between the two data sets are the same. Low-income countries are underperforming compared with lower- and upper-middle-income countries. Likewise, Europe and Central Asia are performing better than the other regional groups, and Sub-Saharan Africa is performing the worst. However, the variations among income groups and regions are much smaller for CPIA-13 than for PEFA data. As mentioned previously, a disadvantage of the CPIA indicator is that it provides a single measure rather than a more disaggregated and detailed perspective on PFM performance, such as that provided by PEFA assessments. This narrow perspective is reflected in the narrow dispersion of averages, ranging from only 3.10 for low-income countries to 3.63 for upper-middle-income countries and from 3.17 for Sub-Saharan Africa to 3.79 for Europe and Central Asia.

FIGURE 2.3

Average Public Expenditure and Financial Accountability (PEFA) score, by country income level and region, most recent

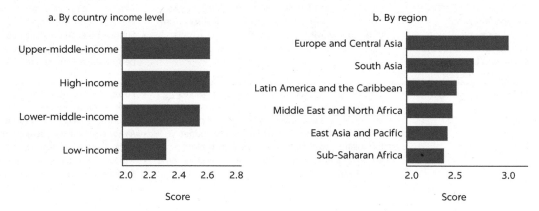

Sources: Data from https://www.pefa.org/ and https://databank.worldbank.org/source/world-development-indicators.

FIGURE 2.4

Average score on Country Policy and Institutional Arrangements indicator 13 (CPIA-13), by country income level and region, 2014

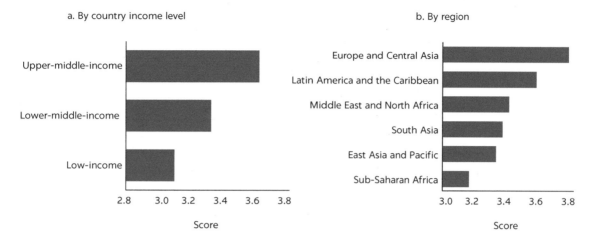

Sources: Data from https://databank.worldbank.org/source/worldwide-governance-indicators and https://databank.worldbank.org/source/world-development-indicators.

FIGURE 2.5

Average score on Open Budget Index (OBI), by country income level and region, 2015

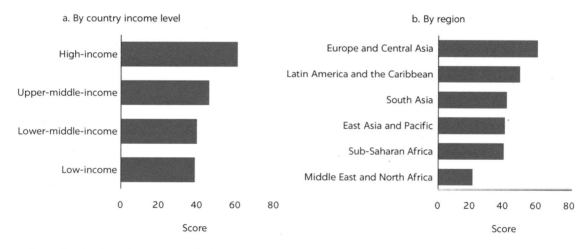

Sources: Data from https://www.internationalbudget.org/open-budget-survey/open-budget-index-rankings/ and https://databank.worldbank.org/source/world-development-indicators.

Another publicly available PFM-related indicator is the Open Budget Index (OBI) scores for budget transparency. The ratings (1–100) cover various years between 2006 and 2017, and components of the OBI are scored in a fashion similar to PEFA's M1 "weakest link" methodology. Like CPIA-13, global patterns are similar to PEFA, with low-income countries underperforming and the Europe and Central Asia region having a higher average than the rest. The main difference is the Middle East and North Africa region, which has the lowest average OBI score, but an overall score for PEFA and CPIA-13 in the middle of the other regions.

PEFA framework revisions

The data set we use in this report is based on the PEFA 2011 framework. The 2011 framework did not represent a significant departure from the 2005 framework, with the revision of just three indicators (PI-2, PI-3, and PI-19). As such, the data set includes assessments carried out under the 2005 framework that are comparable with assessments carried out under the 2011 framework. The 2016 framework represents a more significant revision (figure 2.6). The conceptual framework, though still based on the annual budget cycle, has been revised and now includes 7 pillars, 31 indicators, and 94 dimensions (figure 2.7). Whereas some indicators remain directly comparable, other indicators have been revised, dropped, or added, rendering them less comparable or, in some cases, incomparable. Moreover, the scoring guidance has been revised to clarify what constitutes a D score and to clarify issues that arose using the 2011 framework. However, the transition to the 2016 framework has been managed using a 2011 annex, whereby dual assessments are carried out using both the 2011 and 2016 frameworks. This treatment has had the benefit of generating one more wave of comparable assessments within the data set used in this report, which allows us to observe a larger sample of changes in PFM performance over time.

The upgrade was introduced to reflect evolution in the field of PFM and address shortcomings in the 2011 framework. It was developed with feedback from development partners, government officials, and other users and experts, as well as through public consultation. Significant changes between the 2011 and 2016 versions of the framework include the following:

- The addition of four new indicators

- The expansion and refinement of existing indicators

FIGURE 2.6

The public financial management (PFM) system according to the 2016 Public Expenditure and Financial Accountability (PEFA) framework

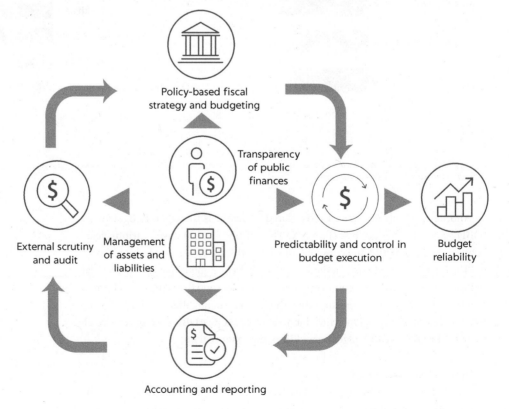

Source: PEFA Secretariat 2016.

FIGURE 2.7

Comparing the 2011 and 2016 Public Expenditure and Financial Accountability (PEFA) frameworks

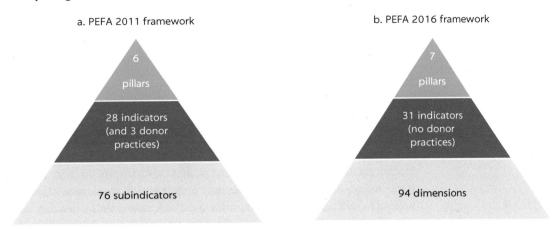

- Recalibration of baseline standards for good performance in many areas

- A stronger focus on transparency and internal financial control

- An expanded scope to include more coverage of central government performance

- Greater attention to noncash aspects of public finances.

Other changes were made in 2016:[2]

- Clearer and more consistent structure for reporting PEFA findings as well as improved terminology and measurement[3]

- Increased emphasis on the use of macrofiscal forecasts, the medium-term fiscal strategy and outlook, a medium-term perspective in expenditure budgeting, and the alignment of strategic plans with budget allocations

- Expansion of coverage of revenue administration to include both tax and nontax revenues

- Elimination of specific indicators of donor practices

- Application of a D score for all practices below the basic level of performance and where there is insufficient information to validate a higher score. D also replaces the NR (not rated) code used previously where there is insufficient information on an indicator.

The PEFA Secretariat has been reviewing assessments for quality since the launch of the framework in 2005; however, the decision to include proposed changes in the final assessment report rests with assessment managers, teams, and funding agencies. Prior to the introduction of PEFA Check—an official endorsement by the PEFA Secretariat—quality assurance was less standardized; therefore, the data from the assessments may be more susceptible to measurement error. PEFA Check sought to improve confidence in the findings of the PEFA assessment. This quality assurance process ensures the accuracy of supporting evidence and compliance with the PEFA methodology. PEFA Check indicates that the PEFA methodology was followed and fulfilled six formal criteria (PEFA Secretariat 2012b). Since its introduction in 2012, 85 out of 121 national assessments, or 70 percent, have received the PEFA Check.

But improvements to the 2016 framework for the quality assurance process also represent weaknesses in the 2011 framework and in assessments that were not quality assured. By extension, these weaknesses translate into weaknesses in our data set. In the next section, we provide further descriptive statistics from our data set.

The PEFA data set

Coverage of PEFA assessments

Our data set contains the scores from 307 PEFA assessments completed in 144 countries between June 2005 and March 2017. Per figure 2.8, almost all of today's low-income countries, lower-middle-income countries, and upper-middle-income countries have undertaken one or more assessments. In contrast, very few of today's high-income countries have undertaken an assessment. Moreover, some of today's higher-income countries undertook assessments when they were classified as lower income, which further biases the number of observations in the data set toward lower-income countries.

This lower-income-country bias inevitably leads to geographic bias within the data set. Coverage is almost complete across the world's poorest countries in South Asia and Sub-Saharan Africa, as highlighted in figure 2.9. Although the East Asia and Pacific and the Latin America and the Caribbean regions also have high coverage ratios, they are overrepresented by small island developing states (SIDS). Norway is the only high-income OECD country to have undertaken an assessment.

Frequency of PEFA assessments

Between 2006 and 2016, approximately 27 countries, on average, completed PEFA assessments annually. The overall number of countries carrying out assessments has declined from a peak of 37 in 2008 to 22 in 2016 (see figure 2.10). Repeat

FIGURE 2.8

Coverage of Public Expenditure and Financial Accountability (PEFA) assessments, by income classification, 2005–17

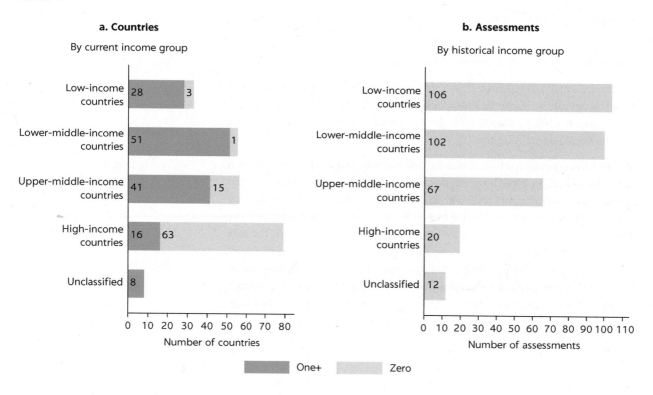

FIGURE 2.9

Coverage of Public Expenditure and Financial Accountability (PEFA) assessments, by region, 2005–17

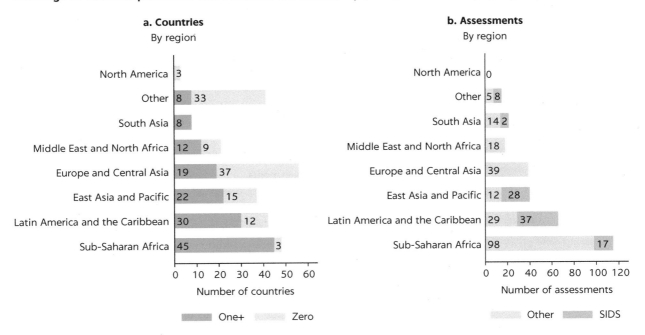

Note: SIDS = small island developing states.

FIGURE 2.10

Number of Public Expenditure and Financial Accountability (PEFA) assessments completed annually, 2005–17

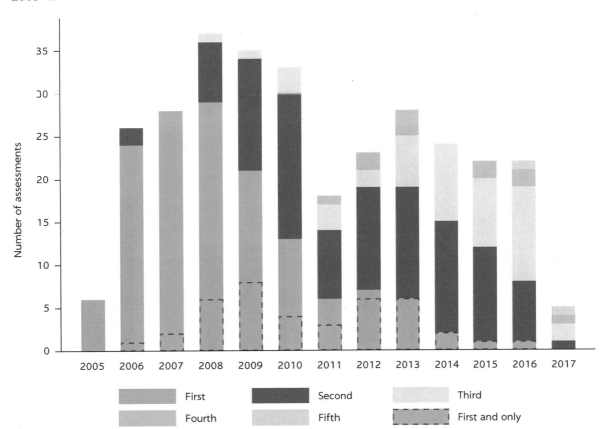

assessments now make up most assessments undertaken, although 40 of the 144 countries have yet to undertake a second assessment. While some of these countries may undertake repeat assessments in the future, more than a decade has passed since some countries carried out their *first and only* assessment, suggesting that they may be *one and done*. Of the 104 countries that have carried out at least one repeat assessment in our data set, 2 are on their fifth assessment, 9 are on their fourth assessment, and 35 are on their third assessment. The average length of time between assessments in our data set is 50 months (approximately four years), with the shortest time span between assessments being 9 months and the longest being 104 months.

Publication of PEFA assessments

Approximately 66 percent (202) of the assessments in the data set have been made publicly available through the PEFA Secretariat website. In some cases, the failure to publish is simply due to delays, while in others, the government has chosen not to publish the report. In addition, 30 assessments are drafts that have yet to be finalized, while a further 75 have been finalized but not published. The data set does not distinguish between an explicit decision not to publish and a failure to publish arising for more mundane reasons. Nevertheless, the standard time from draft to publication (six months to one year according to the PEFA Secretariat) suggests that few of the older assessments are likely to become publicly available whether they are draft or final. While some countries tend to publish all or none of their assessments, others choose to publish some but not others (figure 2.11). For example, 45 countries have made public all of their assessments, 13 have made none available, while 46 have chosen to make some but not others available. For countries that have carried out just one assessment, 18 have published, while 22 have not.

FIGURE 2.11

Publication of Public Expenditure and Financial Accountability (PEFA) assessments, by country, 2005–17

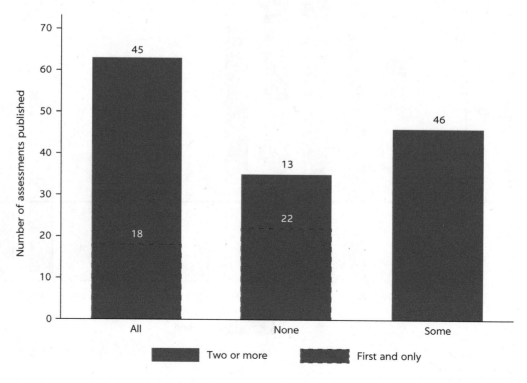

FIGURE 2.12

Number of Public Expenditure and Financial Accountability (PEFA) assessments, by lead organization, 2005–17

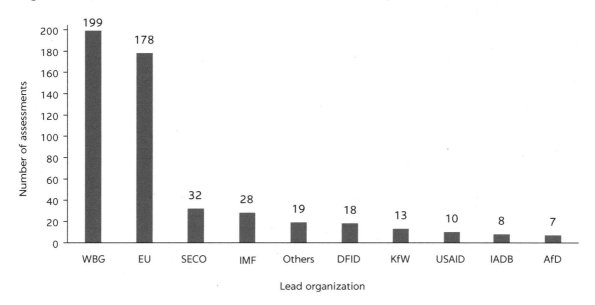

Source: PEFA Secretariat.
Note: WBG = World Bank Group. EU = European Union. SECO = Swiss State Secretariat for Economic Affairs. IMF = International Monetary Fund. DFID = U.K. Department for International Development. KfW = German Development Bank. USAID = U.S. Agency for International Development. IADB = Inter-American Development Bank. AfD = French Development Agency. Others include the Norwegian Agency for Development Cooperation (3), French Ministry of Foreign and European Affairs (3), African Development Bank (3), Asian Development Bank (3), Millennium Challenge Corporation (2), Australian Aid (2), Norwegian Ministry of Foreign Affairs (1), and German Development Agency (1).

Donor involvement in PEFA assessments

As discussed in chapter 1, one of the original objectives of the PEFA assessment was to coordinate donor assessments of PFM performance in the countries in which they provide financial and technical support. The seven PEFA partners continue to commission PEFA assessments, but an additional 33 international organizations have been involved in some capacity (figure 2.12). Almost 20 bilateral and multilateral development organizations have led PEFA assessments, with the European Union and the World Bank undertaking by far the most to date, followed by the IMF and the Swiss State Secretariat for Economic Affairs. As discussed earlier, a growing number of governments are managing the assessment process and writing the reports themselves.[4]

PFM performance

Using the conversion, weighting, and aggregation methods described in more detail in the next section, we observe an upward trend in the aggregate overall PEFA score over time, rising from an average of between C and C+ in 2006 to slightly above C+ in the 2016 (figure 2.13, panel a). But some variation is also evident in the median score across years and in the spread of the overall score within years (figure 2.13, panel b).

Some of the upward trend is because most assessments undertaken since 2010 have been repeat assessments, which have tended to produce higher overall scores on average than in previous years (figure 2.14). This finding is not surprising given the incentives associated with improving PFM performance and attracting donor financing. Nevertheless, the overall trend in year-on-year performance has been relatively slow moving and well below "good practice" A scores.

Lower-middle-income countries have contributed more to the improvement in average overall performance over time than low-income countries and

FIGURE 2.13

Average overall Public Expenditure and Financial Accountability (PEFA) score, 2005–17

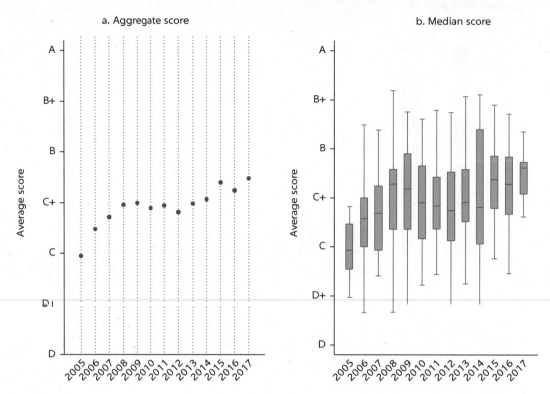

FIGURE 2.14

Average overall Public Expenditure and Financial Accountability (PEFA) score for first and repeat assessments, 2005–17

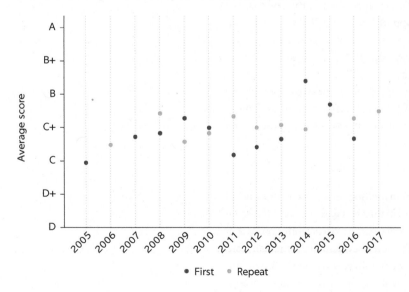

upper-middle-income countries, whose performance has been more stagnant (figure 2.15). In fact, since 2015 overall scores have been higher, on average, for lower-middle-income countries than for upper-middle-income countries.

Sub-Saharan Africa has been consistently the lowest-performing region, on average, while Europe and Central Asia has generally produced the highest average overall scores over time (figure 2.16). The average score for South Asia has climbed, although the sample is relatively small. Just 14 assessments have been undertaken by the 8 countries in South Asia over the sample period, compared with 115 by the 48 countries in Sub-Saharan Africa. The average overall performance of other regions has been more variable from year to year.

Over time, the external scrutiny and audit pillar has had consistently the worst average performance, while the cross-cutting comprehensiveness and transparency pillar has had the best performance. In recent years, there has been an upward trend in performance on the predictability and control in budget execution and policy-based budgeting pillars and a downward trend in performance on the accounting, recording, and reporting pillar. Over the long run, there are signs of improvement across all five pillars (figure 2.17).

Within pillar 1 (policy-based budgeting), countries have consistently performed better on PI-11 (orderliness and participation in the annual budget process) than on PI-12 (a multiyear perspective in fiscal planning, expenditure policy, and budgeting). Although performance on the latter has trended upward over time, while performance on the former has been relatively stagnant, a gap of 0.5 to 1.0 on the ordinal scale remains (figure 2.18).

Within pillar 2 (predictability and control in budget execution), there is an equally distinct upward trend for most indicators as well as distinct differences in performance across indicators (figure 2.19). On average, countries have performed best on PI-17 (recording and management of cash balances, debt, and guarantees) and worst on PI-21 (effectiveness of internal audit) on a fairly consistent basis, with a 1.0 to 1.5 differential in the ordinal scale. Average performance over time on the other indicators is more bunched, although countries tend to perform better on PI-16 (predictability in the availability of funds for commitment of expenditures) compared with indicators related to expenditure controls on payroll (PI-18), procurement (PI-19), and other expenditures (PI-20) which are the subject of discussion in chapter 5 on PFM and corruption.

On pillar 3 (accounting, recording, and reporting), PI-23 (availability of information on resources received by service delivery units) stands out as the indicator where performance is consistently poor on average and relatively stagnant over time (figure 2.20).

Although PI-25 (quality and timeliness of annual financial statements) has been fairly consistently the second worst-performing indicator, average annual performance has improved over time. In contrast, average annual performance for both PI-22 (timeliness and regularity of accounts reconciliation) and PI-24 (quality and timeliness of in-year budget reports) has barely changed over time.

As shown in figure 2.21, under pillar 4 (external scrutiny and audit), we observe a similar separation in performance across indicators, with countries performing better on PI-27 (legislative scrutiny of the annual budget law) and, to a lesser extent, on PI-26 (scope, nature, and follow-up of external audit) and scoring close to a D+ on average over time for PI-28 (legislative scrutiny of external audit reports). PI-26 has displayed a more discernible trend of improvement in average annual performance compared with the other two indicators over time.

FIGURE 2.15

Average overall Public Expenditure and Financial Accountability (PEFA) score, by historic income classification, 2005–17

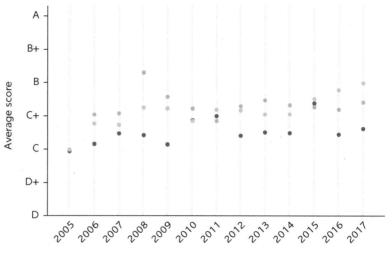

FIGURE 2.16

Average overall Public Expenditure and Financial Accountability (PEFA) score, by region, 2005–17

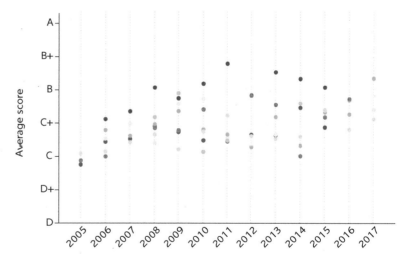

FIGURE 2.17

Average overall Public Expenditure and Financial Accountability (PEFA) score, by pillar, 2005–17

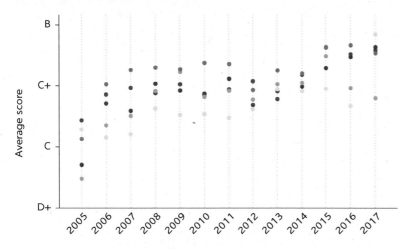

- Policy-based budgeting
- Predictability and control in budget execution
- Accounting, recording, and reporting
- External scrutiny and audit
- Comprehensiveness and transparency

FIGURE 2.18

Average Public Expenditure and Financial Accountability (PEFA) score on policy-based budgeting indicators, 2005–17

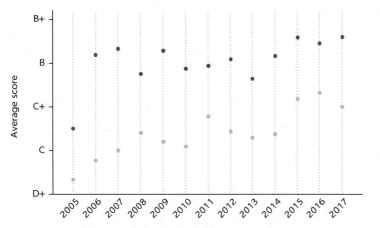

- PI-11—Orderliness and participation in the annual budget process
- PI-12—Multiyear perspective in fiscal planning, expenditure policy, and budgeting

Finally, for the cross-cutting pillar 5, we observe an upward trend in the average score for all six indicators from approximately 2011, which suggests that countries undertaking repeat assessments have improved on these indicators. But again, as shown in figure 2.22, we observe a fairly consistent hierarchy of scoring over time, with countries performing better on average on PI-5 (classification of the budget), PI-6 (comprehensiveness of information included in budget documentation), and PI-8 (transparency of intergovernmental fiscal relations), compared with PI-7 (extent of unreported government operations), PI-9 (oversight of aggregate fiscal risk from other public sector entities), and PI-10 (public access to key fiscal information).

The foregoing results suggest that it is easier to achieve better scores on some indicators than on others. Figure 2.23 shows the distribution of scores for the interquartile range by indicator—that is, scoring for the middle 50 percent of the distribution—further demonstrating that the distribution of some indicator scores is skewed. Notable examples are PI-22 and PI-23, where scores are concentrated in the D+ to C+ range, compared with PI-11 and PI-17, where scores are concentrated in the C+ to B+ range. For the purposes of statistical inference used in later chapters, it is preferable to have more normally distributed data.

Indeed, Andrews (2011) notes that it is easier to improve on some indicators than on others by changing the form of parts of the PFM system rather than how they function, which he describes as isomorphic mimicry. He notes that de jure, upstream, and concentrated functions of the PFM system are more amenable to isomorphic mimicry than de facto, downstream, and deconcentrated functions and characterizes each dimension of the PEFA 2011 framework in these terms. Using this characterization of the data, we construct indexes to compare relative performance. Panels a to c of figure 2.24 clearly show that performance is stronger on de jure, upstream, and concentrated dimensions on average over time compared with performance on de facto, downstream, and deconcentrated dimensions, respectively. However, performance on the latter has also trended up over time, in line with the trend in overall performance in panel d, implying that functional dimensions have also improved over time.

Summing up

The PEFA framework has changed over time, with the most significant changes occurring between the 2011 and 2016 frameworks. Nevertheless, the framework remains based on the annual budget cycle, the scoring methodology has remained broadly similar, and therefore the data across assessments remain comparable. However, in using the data, which are based predominantly on the 2011 framework, it is important to be cognizant of the revisions made in 2016, as they represent weaknesses in our data. These weaknesses include poor coverage of some PFM functions, lack of clarity on the scoring of some dimensions, and issues regarding quality assurance of assessments. All of these issues have been addressed in the 2016 framework revisions but remain pertinent when using the data set, particularly with respect to earlier assessments.

We have also noted that many other PFM diagnostic tools cover similar areas and use similar scoring methodologies to PEFA. These include the CPIA and OBI assessments, which produce comparable findings to PEFA assessments. Other diagnostics, including PERs and Public Expenditure Tracking Surveys (PETSs), should be viewed as complementary, more in-depth analyses. The main strength of PEFA over similar assessments is its breadth of coverage, which has made it the most frequently used PFM diagnostic tool globally, with repeat assessments allowing PFM performance to be tracked over time. Nevertheless, several biases are evident in the data set, with poorer regions and smaller countries overrepresented compared with higher-income regions and larger countries. The former may be driven by donor engagement in these countries, with donors still commissioning the vast majority of assessments. The latter may be explained somewhat by the fact that larger countries have switched their attention to carrying out subnational PEFA assessments. A final analytical concern is the lack of variation in performance, both across countries and across time, which is discussed in more detail in the following section.

FIGURE 2.19

Average Public Expenditure and Financial Accountability (PEFA) score on predictability and control in budget execution indicators, 2005–17

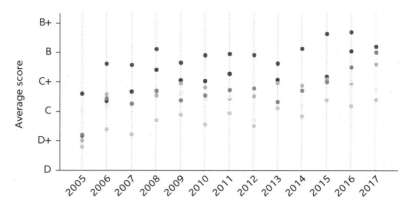

- PI-16—Predictability in the availability of funds for commitment of expenditures
- PI-17—Recording and management of cash balances, debt, and guarantees
- PI-18—Effectiveness of payroll controls
- PI-19—Competition, value for money, and controls in procurement
- PI-20—Effectiveness of internal controls for nonsalary expenditure
- PI-21—Effectiveness of internal audit

FIGURE 2.20

Average Public Expenditure and Financial Accountability (PEFA) score on accounting, recording, and reporting indicators, 2005–17

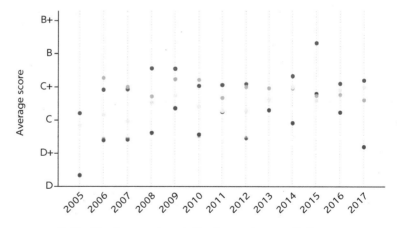

- PI-22—Timeliness and regularity of accounts reconciliation
- PI-23—Availability of information on resources received by service delivery units
- PI-24—Quality and timeliness of in-year budget reports
- PI-25—Quality and timeliness of annual financial statements

FIGURE 2.21

Average Public Expenditure and Financial Accountability (PEFA) score on external scrutiny and audit indicators, 2005–17

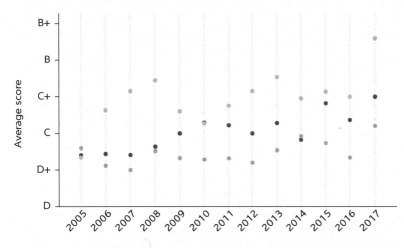

- PI-26—Scope, nature, and follow-up of external audit
- PI-27—Legislative scrutiny of the annual budget law
- PI-28—Legislative scrutiny of external audit reports

FIGURE 2.22

Average Public Expenditure and Financial Accountability (PEFA) score on comprehensiveness and transparency indicators, 2005–17

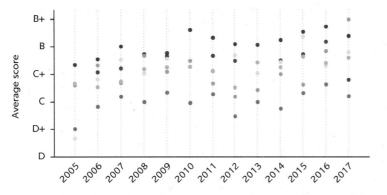

- PI-5—Classification of the budget
- PI-6—Comprehensiveness of information included in budget documentation
- PI-7—Extent of unreported government operations
- PI-8—Transparency of intergovernmental fiscal relations
- PI-9—Oversight of aggregate fiscal risk from other public sector entities
- PI-10—Public access to key fiscal information

ISSUES IN QUANTIFYING AND ANALYZING PFM PERFORMANCE

As noted in the previous section, PEFA dimension and indicator scores are based on an ordinal scale from D to A. Unlike performance assessments such as the OBI, a PEFA assessment carries no overall score. However, this has not stopped researchers from quantifying and aggregating PEFA assessment scores to investigate their relationships with other indicators. The main advantage of quantifying and aggregating the assessment scores is to facilitate the analysis and comparison of PFM performance across a large sample of countries and over time.

This report is no different in this regard. Chapters 3–6 all convert PEFA scores to numerical values to investigate the relationship between aspects of PFM performance and other governance indicators. In this section, we explain the conversion, weighting, and aggregation methodologies used in subsequent chapters and their limitations. We also discuss other limiting factors associated with using PEFA assessment scores for quantitative analysis.

Quantifying PEFA scores

The PEFA Secretariat has noted that there is no scientific method for conversion and aggregation, which requires assumptions about the weighting to be applied to scores, measures, and assessments (PEFA Secretariat 2009). With respect to scores, numerical conversion requires a judgment about the distance between the ordinal rankings D to A (that is, should progressing from C to B carry the same weighting as improving from B to A?). With respect to measures, there is a question of whether some dimensions, indicators, or pillars are more important than others. And with regard to assessments, there is a need to consider whether some assessments should be assigned lower importance or disregarded because of concerns over the quality of the assessment. As discussed in chapter 1, issues of quality may arise because of biases generated by assessment teams and a lack of quality assurance over some assessments. There are also related questions over how to treat missing data.

Initially, the PEFA Secretariat made no recommendations on how to undertake conversion and aggregation aside from appealing to researchers to document the reasons for their assumptions (PEFA Secretariat 2009). Recently, the PEFA Secretariat has recommended converting indicators using the methodology employed in de Renzio (2009).[5] However, in general, researchers have tended to take

FIGURE 2.23

Distribution of Public Expenditure and Financial Accountability (PEFA) scores, by indicator

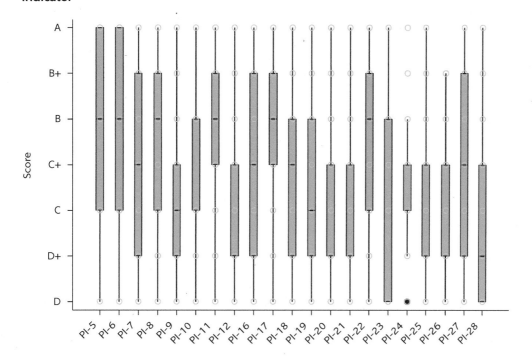

FIGURE 2.24

Analysis of Public Expenditure and Financial Accountability (PEFA) performance on form versus function, 2005–17

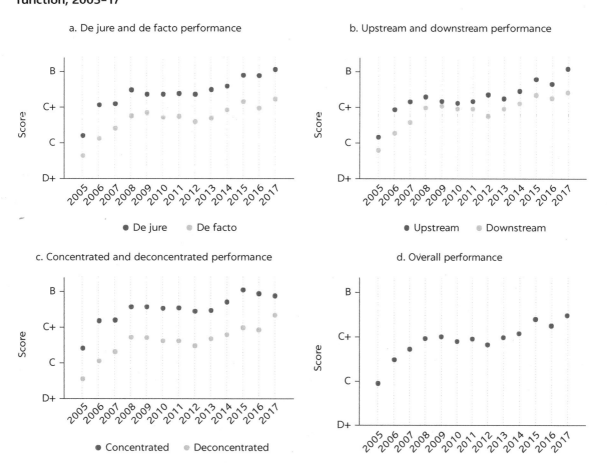

a. De jure and de facto performance

b. Upstream and downstream performance

c. Concentrated and deconcentrated performance

d. Overall performance

TABLE 2.4 **Numerical conversion of Public Expenditure and Financial Accountability (PEFA) scores**

PEFA SCORE	NUMERICAL VALUE
A	4.0
B+	3.5
B	3.0
C+	2.5
C	2.0
D+	1.5
D	1.0

Source: de Renzio 2009.

the PEFA framework as they find it, using only limited subjective judgment. As such, most research has applied equal weights to the distance between scores, weighted either indicators or dimensions with equal importance, and treated all assessments with equal status. This report does not diverge significantly from previous research in this respect.

Weighting scores

The standard approach of researchers has been to convert the categorical PEFA scores D to A to numerical values 1 to 4, as shown in table 2.4 (see, for example, de Renzio 2009). This approach is sometimes applied to dimension scores and sometimes to indicator scores, depending on the assumptions related to calculating an aggregate score. For the individual dimension and indicator scores, the implied assumption is that the same level of effort is required to move from D to C, from C to B, and from B to A. Andrews (2009) provides an alternative approach to scoring individual dimensions, assigning dummy variables to separate lower scores (that is, assigning a 0 to D or C) from higher scores (that is, assigning a 1 to a B or A). This conversion methodology is used and discussed further in chapter 6, where we examine the effect of individual tax administration dimensions on domestic resource mobilization. However, the analysis in chapters 4 to 6 is based either on an overall score or on composite scores and therefore requires numerical conversion to make aggregation possible. Following previous studies, we make the assumption of equal weights between categorical scores.

Weighting measures

de Renzio (2009) pioneered the approach to quantifying and aggregating PEFA assessment scores and investigating their relationship with other indicators, including income, aid dependency, population, and governance indicators. The conversion method he uses involves assigning numerical values from 1 to 4 to the ordinal scale from D to A for each indicator (table 2.4) and calculating an overall score as the average for the 28 indicators. He excludes the three indicators of donor practice because of the possible bias to the overall score of the "country PFM system performance" and because of the number of missing values for these indicators.

Subsequent studies using PEFA data have taken a slightly more nuanced approach to calculating an overall PEFA assessment score depending on their research question. In an evaluation of donor support to PFM in low- and middle-income countries, de Renzio, Andrews, and Mills (2010) calculate their overall score based on indicators PI-5 to PI-28. They justify the exclusion of PI-1 to PI-4 on the basis that these are indicators of outcome rather than indicators of PFM quality per se. Similarly, Haque, Knight, and Jayasuriya (2012) omit both the PI-1 to PI-4 and the D-1 to D-3 indicators from their analysis of PFM in the Pacific to avoid "results being biased by macroeconomic factors or the different practices of development agencies operating in different countries." Investigating the drivers and effects of PFM performance, Fritz, Sweet, and Verhoeven (2014) further omit indicators PI-13 to PI-15, which measure the quality of tax administration, to obtain an overall score that covers "the quality of PFM systems on the expenditure side." Fritz, Verhoeven, and Avenia (2017) take the same approach in a study on the political economy of PFM reform experiences.

Another difference between these studies is the choice of whether to aggregate the scores for indicators or their underlying dimensions. Aggregating indicators recognizes the M1 "weakest link" scoring methodology and gives equal weighting to each indicator. Aggregating dimensions disregards the M1 "weakest link" scoring methodology and gives equal weighting to each dimension. de Renzio, Andrews, and Mills (2010) do the latter, justifying the decision on the basis of fully exploiting the information underlying indicators as well as avoiding the downward bias associated with the M1 "weakest link" scoring methodology. Both Fritz, Sweet, and Verhoeven (2014) and Fritz, Verhoeven, and Avenia (2017) aggregate an overall score using the converted indicator scores.

In this report, we borrow from these previous methodologies, adding our own nuances. Like Fritz, Sweet, and Verhoeven (2014), we exclude the revenue administration indicators because our research questions in chapters 4, 5, and 6 are more relevant to the expenditure side of PFM. However, we follow the example of de Renzio, Andrews, and Mills (2010) by disregarding the M1 "weakest link" scoring methodology and aggregating on the basis of dimension rather than indicator scores. But our approach to aggregation is slightly more nuanced. As described in figure 2.25, it involves three aggregation steps in calculating an overall score. Our justification for this approach is that it provides an equal weighting to each of the pillars of the 2011 PEFA framework, rather than ascribing more importance to phases of the budget cycle that have more indicators.

Nevertheless, we investigate the implications of calculating the overall score in different ways. Table 2.5 describes four slightly different ways of calculating the

FIGURE 2.25

Calculating an overall Public Expenditure and Financial Accountability (PEFA) score

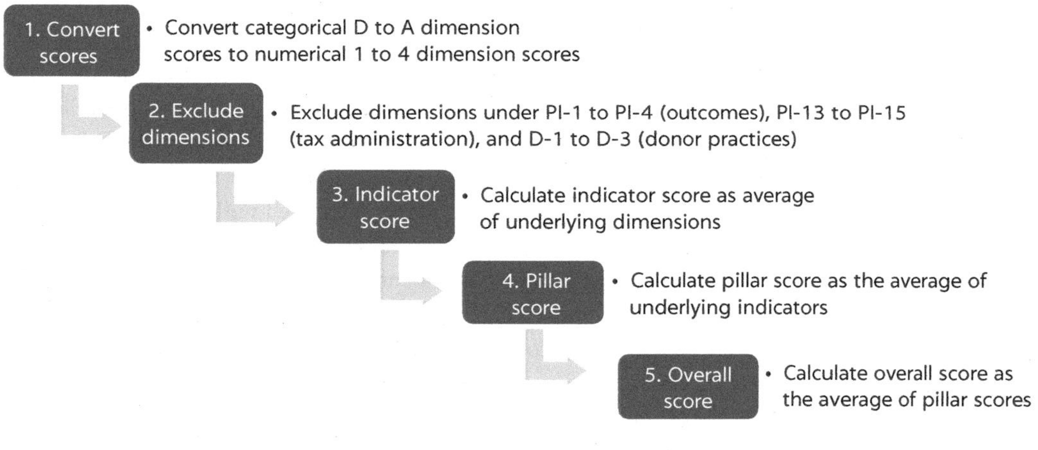

TABLE 2.5 **Summary statistics for different methodologies for calculating an overall score**

METHOD	DESCRIPTION	ASSUMPTION	COUNT	MEAN	VAR	SD	MIN	MAX
1i	The average of indicators (for example, Fritz, Sweet, and Verhoeven 2014)	Indicators carry equal weight; M1 scoring is incorporated	307	2.400	0.247	0.497	1.306	3.548
1ii			307	2.417	0.236	0.485	1.333	3.500
2i	The average of dimensions (for example, de Renzio, Andrews, and Mills 2010)	Dimensions carry equal weight; M1 scoring is disregarded	307	2.475	0.237	0.487	1.360	3.600
2ii			307	2.501	0.226	0.475	1.393	3.609
3i	The average of indicators, first calculated as the average of underlying dimensions	Indicators carry equal weight; M1 scoring is disregarded	307	2.487	0.249	0.499	1.304	3.647
3ii			307	2.509	0.237	0.487	1.344	3.649
4i	The average of pillars, first calculated as the average of indicators or as the average of dimensions	Pillars carry equal weight; M1 scoring is disregarded	307	2.488	0.232	0.482	1.333	3.626
4ii			307	2.475	0.239	0.489	1.324	3.611

Note: All calculations exclude PI-1 to PI-4 and D-1 to D-3. (i) = tax administration indicators or dimensions are included. (ii) = tax administration indicators are excluded.

TABLE 2.6 **Correlations between different methodologies for calculating an overall score**

METHOD	1i	1ii	2i	2ii	3i	3ii	4i	4ii
1i	1.0000							
1ii	0.9921	1.0000						
2i	0.9734	0.9637	1.0000					
2ii	0.9665	0.9722	0.9900	1.0000				
3i	0.9800	0.9712	0.9902	0.9837	1.0000			
3ii	0.9731	0.9775	0.9824	0.9925	0.9928	1.0000		
4i	0.9626	0.9570	0.9737	0.9730	0.9813	0.9797	1.0000	
4ii	0.9673	0.9553	0.9806	0.9708	0.9850	0.9760	0.9972	1.0000

overall score. Method 1, following Fritz, Sweet, and Verhoeven (2014), recognizes the M1 "weakest link" scoring methodology and gives equal weight to the indicators. Methods 2, 3, and 4 are all variations that disregard the M1 "weakest link" scoring methodology. Method 2 is simply an average of the dimensions, following de Renzio, Andrews, and Mills (2010), and so provides equal weighting to each dimension. Method 3 gives equal weight to indicators through a two-step calculation. Method 4, our preferred method, gives equal weight to pillars through a three-step calculation.

As expected, the first methodology provides the lowest scores due to the downward bias of the M1 "weakest link" scoring methodology. Nevertheless, all four scoring methodologies provide approximately similar summary statistics. The largest difference between mean scores excluding tax administration indicators is 0.092 or 3 percent between method 1ii and method 3ii. Standard deviations and variances are also similar across methodologies. Moreover, as shown in table 2.6, all four scoring methodologies are highly correlated with one another, at the 95 percent level or higher. As such, the question of which to use for the purposes of statistical analysis is a question of judgment as to the weighting of the constituent parts of the PEFA framework. In this report, we base our calculation of the overall score on the view that all four stages of the budget cycle and the cross-cutting theme of transparency as represented by the pillars of the PEFA 2011 framework should carry an equal weighting.

A fundamental problem with the relatively equal weighting applied to dimensions and indicators in all of these methodologies is the issue of form over function. Some PEFA dimensions measure form (often categorized as de jure) as opposed to function (de facto) (see Andrews 2009). Ronsholt (2011) contrasts de jure dimension PI-11(i), where "a C score is attained as long as an annual budget calendar exists, even though there may be substantial delays in implementation, with not enough time allowed to budget entities to complete detailed estimates" compared with de facto dimension PI-12(i), where a C score "requires that two-year forecasts of fiscal aggregates are actually produced on a rolling annual basis." De facto dimensions are frequently correlated with upstream and concentrated[6] activities as opposed to downstream and deconcentrated activities. Andrews (2009) estimates that de jure, upstream, and concentrated dimensions account for 41 percent, 25 percent, and 41 percent of PEFA dimensions, respectively, noting that progress on these dimensions has been slower for African countries. Hadley and Miller (2016) raise concerns that, given the donor-recipient dynamics associated with PEFA scores, recipient countries may engage in "gaming" by targeting easier-to-move indicators.

These issues provide further justification for providing equal weighting to the pillars of the PEFA 2011 framework rather than to indicators or dimensions. Moreover, although the overall score is used throughout the chapters that follow, we also formulate hypotheses based on individual dimensions, individual indicators, and composites of indicators. This discussion follows the example of more recent research examining specific questions using specific PEFA dimensions. For example, Knack, Biletska, and Kacker (2017) focus on PI-18 to investigate the effect of better procurement practices on corruption. Similarly, Ricciuti, Savoia, and Sen (2016) use tax administration dimensions to investigate the effect of political institutions on fiscal capacity.

Weighting assessments

Several interrelated issues arise with respect to the weighting of assessments. These issues include how to treat missing values, how to treat earlier assessments, and how to assure the quality of assessments. In general, we seek to maximize the sample by retaining as many assessments as possible. Nevertheless, we ascribe more importance to more recent assessments.

The validity of converting categorical scores to numerical scores and then aggregating is also affected by missing data for some dimensions. With regard to the 2011 PEFA framework, data may be missing for three reasons: the data were NA (not applicable to the context), NU (not used for the assessment), or NR (not rated due to insufficient information). The revised 2016 methodology ascribes missing values to NA and NU categories and assigns a D score when sufficient information is not available to establish actual performance (equivalent to NR under the 2011 framework). Therefore, researchers using the 2011 framework data set generally assign a D score to an NR score and missing values to NA and NU scores.

However, according to discussions with the PEFA Secretariat, prior to the introduction of the 2016 guidance, assessors may have ascribed NR scores unsystematically. Therefore, we assign NR scores as missing values rather than D scores. Similarly, earlier assessments carried out under the 2005 framework include missing values for dimensions that were added through the introduction of the 2011 framework. The effect of the missing values for some dimensions is that, when multidimensional indicator scores are aggregated (as described above), the missing dimension value assumes the value of the other dimensions. This implies an upward bias if the dimension would have been assessed at a lower score and a downward bias if the dimension would have been assessed at a higher score. As most missing values apply to earlier assessments, in the chapters that follow we construct samples that focus on a country's most recent assessments rather than pooling observations.

Analyzing PFM performance

In the chapters that follow, we employ regression analysis to examine the relationship between PFM performance and political institutions, budget credibility, corruption, and domestic resource mobilization (DRM). In general, we use ordinary least squares (OLS), but also use weighted least squares (WLS) and panel estimators where the data are amenable.[7] However, our research design, data, and estimators suffer from inherent problems, including endogeneity and limited sample size. The extent to which these problems can be and are addressed in the next four chapters is discussed below, along with the implications for interpreting the results.

In the chapters that follow, we generally estimate equations in the form of equation (2.1):

$$Y_i = \alpha + \beta X_i + \gamma Z_i + \varepsilon_i, \tag{2.1}$$

where Y_i is our dependent variable, X_i is our explanatory variable with estimated coefficient β, Z_i is a control variable with estimated coefficient γ, α is the estimated constant term, and ε_i is the estimated error term. Furthermore, we generally use PEFA scores as our explanatory variable, apart from chapter 4, where we use PEFA scores as the dependent variable. Technically, endogeneity refers to a situation where the explanatory variable and the estimated error term are correlated. This presents a problem for our estimated coefficients because least squares estimation works on the assumption of no endogeneity. When this assumption is violated, least squares estimation may produce biased results. In other words, relationships may be estimated to be higher or lower than their true relationships. Endogeneity concerns can arise because of omitted variable bias, measurement error, and simultaneity, all of which are present to varying degrees in the chapters that follow.

Omitted variable bias arises when the estimated equation is poorly specified. For example, in chapter 5, although we hypothesize that there is a relationship between corruption and PFM, we also recognize that corruption is not wholly explained by PFM, and some of the factors influencing corruption may be unobservable. To deal with this issue, we include control variables based on the existing literature on the relationship. However, adding control variables reduces the degrees of freedom available to estimate the parameters' variability. To circumvent omitted variable bias arising from unobservable factors, we estimate the relationship over time using panel estimators. This method is possible with our data set because of the presence of repeat assessments. However, it is a valid method for dealing with omitted variable bias only when the suspected omitted variable is not expected to change over the sample period. For example, panel estimators are a good way of dealing with the fact that "culture" is often an important but unobservable determinant of corruption that changes only slowly over time.

Measurement error is another potential source of bias in each of the chapters that follow. As discussed previously, measurement error in our PEFA variables may arise from incorrect weighting of the scores, measures, and assessments. As noted previously, we assume equal weights on the distance between scores that may not reflect the "true" level of effort required to improve from D to C compared with improving from C to B and so forth. Measures have been given relatively equal weighting in calculating both the overall score and composite scores within some of the chapters. In chapter 6, we avoid the weighting issue associated with aggregation by examining the relationship between DRM and specific PEFA dimensions related to tax administration. However, this approach does not fit the research design across all chapters, so measurement error due to the biases associated with aggregation remains a concern in chapters 4, 5, and 6.

Of course, measurement error may also arise in our dependent variables. This is of particular concern in chapter 5, which investigates the relationship between PFM and corruption using perceptions of corruption as a proxy for the latter. This approach has been criticized for not capturing corruption accurately. Similarly, in chapter 6, which investigates the relationship between PFM and DRM, our ratio of tax to gross domestic product may induce bias because there are inconsistencies in the treatment of subnational revenues. To address these concerns, we also use alternative variables as robustness tests when possible and appropriate.

Measurement error may also arise because of inconsistency in scoring across assessments. As discussed above, the PEFA Secretariat has been reviewing the quality of assessments since the launch of the framework in 2005; however, the decision to include proposed changes rests with assessment managers, teams, and funding agencies. To strengthen the quality of PEFA reports, the PEFA Secretariat introduced a quality assurance system (the PEFA Check). However, this was only done in 2012, and, although compliance is improving, it is far from perfect. As a result, there may be measurement errors within some assessments. We attempt to circumvent the issue at least partially by focusing on the most recent country assessments. We also maximize the sample size where feasible to reduce the risk of measurement error biasing our estimated coefficients.

In addition, concerns regarding measurement error arise because of time inconsistencies between PEFA variables and other variables of interest. These concerns may arise because of potential inconsistencies relating to the "date of assessment" within the data set. While a PEFA assessment provides an evidence-based analysis of PFM performance at a specific point, it takes four to five months to conduct the assessment and prepare a draft report (PEFA Secretariat 2012a). Although two assessments may have a date of assessment of June 2010, the evidence may represent 2006–08 in one country and 2007–09 in the other country. These concerns are generally addressed by matching the PEFA score to three-year moving averages for the year of the assessment and the previous two years for other variables in the studies. For example, if the PEFA score is for 2015, the associated variable takes the average value for 2013, 2014, and 2015.

Simultaneity bias, or reverse causality, arises when the direction of causality between the dependent and explanatory variable is unclear. Taking the example of PFM and corruption once again, while we argue that "better PFM" can reduce corruption, it is equally plausible that lower levels of corruption allow for "better PFM" or that both are jointly determined by other factors such as country income level. Methods to address endogeneity concerns arising from simultaneity are beyond the scope of this research and the sample size of the data set.

Biases in our sample with respect to income levels, geography, and donor influence, discussed in the previous section, are pertinent issues for regression analysis. Although our data set includes more than 307 assessments in 144 countries, in the chapters that follow the number of usable observations falls because of the unavailability of other data required to address the research questions. For example, in chapter 5, which investigates the relationship between corruption and PFM, the sample size falls to 99 in our cross-sectional regression analysis. Moreover, not all countries have completed repeat assessments, reducing the sample size of our panel estimations further. As such, although the data set is the most comprehensive source of data on PFM performance to date, sample size remains a limiting factor, and the robustness of the results in later chapters needs to be interpreted in this light.

Summing up

Quantifying PEFA scores and aggregating them into overall scores require assumptions on weighting scores, measures, and assessments. There is no theoretical or scientific basis for these assumptions. In general, we follow the approach taken by previous researchers who have used PEFA data for quantitative analysis, but this does not eliminate the significant challenges that persist in transforming number grades to numerical values. We also note that, from a statistical perspective, differing methodologies for calculating the overall score are highly correlated with one another, so the choice of methodology is largely academic.

We also note that significant endogeneity concerns arise when using PEFA data. Although we attempt to circumvent some of these problems, others are beyond the scope of this research and data set. Consequently, estimated coefficients in the results section of later chapters may be biased, which would affect the integrity of the results. They should be interpreted as indicators of the direction of the relationship rather than as actual effects.

Furthermore, the time inconsistency issues and the limited number of observations further compound the challenges of regression analysis with PEFA data. These issues are further exacerbated for the panel regressions that use repeated PEFA assessments.

Overall, it is worth emphasizing that the PEFA assessments were not designed for statistical analysis and that using them in quantitative regressions presents a series of econometric issues that cannot be fully resolved in this book, or in other papers that apply a similar approach.

NOTES

1. See, for example, Andrews et al. (2014) for a somewhat different illustration and description of the PFM cycle.
2. See https://pefa.org/pefa-2016-faqs.
3. See https://www.adb.org/sites/default/files/publication/384381/governance-brief-31.pdf and https://pefa.org/pefa-2016-faqs.
4. As of today, 115 governments have been involved (PEFA Secretariat 2010).
5. See https://pefa.org/sites/default/files/Transfer%20of%20PEFA%20Scores%20into%20numerical%20values_1.pdf.
6. With respect to the number of actors involved.
7. Although other research using the PEFA data set has sometimes used maximum likelihood estimators, it has frequently produced similar results to OLS (see, for example, Haque, Knight, and Jayasuriya 2012). We therefore found no justification for their use in this study.

REFERENCES

Andrews, M. 2009. "Isomorphism and the Limits to African Public Financial Management Reform." HKS Faculty Research Working Paper RWP09-012, John F. Kennedy School of Government, Harvard University, Cambridge, MA. https://dash.harvard.edu/handle/1/4415942.

———. 2011. "Which Organizational Attributes Are Amenable to External Reform? An Empirical Study of African Public Financial Management." *International Public Management Journal* 14 (2): 131–56. doi: 10.1080/10967494.2011.588588.

Andrews, M., M. Cangiano, N. Cole, P. de Renzio, P. Krause, and R. Seligmann. 2014. "This Is PFM." CID Working Paper 285, Center for International Development, Harvard University, Cambridge, MA. https://www.hks.harvard.edu/sites/default/files/centers/cid/files/publications/faculty -working-papers/285_Andrews_This+is+PFM.pdf.

de Renzio, P. 2009. "Taking Stock: What Do PEFA Assessments Tell Us about PFM Systems across Countries?" Working Paper 302, Overseas Development Institute, London. https://www.odi.org /sites/odi.org.uk/files/odi-assets/publications-opinion-files/4359.pdf.

de Renzio, P., M. Andrews, and Z. Mills. 2010. *Evaluation of Donor Support to Public Financial Management (PFM) Reform in Developing Countries*. Final Report. London: Overseas Development Institute. www.odi.org.uk.

Fritz, V., S. Sweet, and M. Verhoeven. 2014. "Strengthening Public Financial Management: Exploring Drivers and Effects." Policy Research Working Paper 7084, World Bank, Washington, DC. http://econ.worldbank.org.

Fritz, V., M. Verhoeven, and A. Avenia. 2017. *Political Economy of Public Financial Management Reforms: Experiences and Implications for Dialogue and Operational Engagement*. Washington, DC: World Bank. http://documents.worldbank.org/curated/en/349071468151787835 /Strengthening-public-financial-management-exploring-drivers-and-effects.

Hadley, S., and M. Miller. 2016. *PEFA: What Is It Good For? The Role of PEFA Assessments in Public Financial Management Reform*. London: Overseas Development Institute. https://www.odi.org /sites/odi.org.uk/files/resource-documents/10484.pdf.

Haque, T. A., D. S. Knight, and D. S. Jayasuriya. 2012. *Capacity Constraints and Public Financial Management in Small Pacific Island Countries*. Washington, DC: World Bank. http://econ.worldbank.

Knack, S., N. Biletska, and K. Kacker. 2017. "Deterring Kickbacks and Encouraging Entry in Public Procurement Markets: Evidence from Firm Surveys in 88 Developing Countries." Policy Research Working Paper 8078, World Bank, Washington, DC. https://openknowledge.worldbank.org /bitstream/handle/10986/26950/WPS8078.pdf?sequence=1&isAllowed=y.

PEFA (Public Expenditure and Financial Accountability) Secretariat. 2009. *Issues in Comparison and Aggregation of PEFA Assessment Results over Time and across Countries*. Washington, DC: PEFA Secretariat. https://pefa.org/sites/default/files/asset/study_document /NoteonAggregationandComparisonofPEFAratingsfinal-EN-May13.pdf.

———. 2010. "The PEFA Framework: Five Years of Successful Implementation." PEFA Secretariat, Washington, DC. http://siteresources.worldbank.org/PEFA/Resources/PEFA-Signature -Proof.pdf.

———. 2011. *Public Financial Management Performance Measurement Framework*. Washington, DC: PEFA Secretariat. https://pefa.org/sites/default/files/PMFEng-finalSZreprint04-12_1.pdf.

———. 2012a. *Fieldguide*. Washington, DC: PEFA Secretariat. http://siteresources.worldbank.org /PEFA/Resources/PEFAFieldguide.pdf.

———. 2012b. *Good Practices in Applying the PFM Performance Measurement Framework: Guidance for Assessment Planners and Managers*. Final Report. Washington, DC: PEFA Secretariat. https://pefa.org/sites/default/files/attachments/Good%20Practices%20in%20Applying%20 the%20PEFA%20Framework%20revised%20June%207_2012_0.pdf.

———. 2016. *Public Financial Management Performance Measurement Framework*. Washington, DC: PEFA Secretariat. https://pefa.org/sites/default/files/PEFA%20Framework_English.pdf.

———. 2018. *Stocktake of PFM Diagnostics 2016*. Washington, DC: PEFA Secretariat. https://pefa.org /research-impact/stocktake-pfm-diagnostic-tools-2016.

Ricciuti, R., A. Savoia, and K. Sen. 2016. "How Do Political Institutions Affect Fiscal Capacity? Explaining Taxation in Developing Economies." ESID Working Paper 59, European Social Innovation Database, University of Manchester. https://papers.ssrn.com/sol3/papers.cfm?abstract_id=2835498.

Ronsholt, F. E. 2011. *Are Public Financial Management Systems Improving in Low and Middle Income Countries? A Preliminary Analysis Based on Data from PEFA Assessments in 32 Countries.* Washington, DC: PEFA Secretariat. www.pefa.org.

3 Political Institutions and PFM Performance

SHAKIRA MUSTAPHA

This chapter investigates the extent to which political institutions are associated with public financial management (PFM) performance. Using cross-country data on PFM performance from the Public Expenditure and Financial Accountability (PEFA) data set, we find no evidence in support of theoretical propositions that ex ante legislative budgetary institutions are stronger in presidential systems or majoritarian systems. We also find no evidence that having a more programmatic political party system is associated with better systems for strategic budgeting or better institutions for overseeing the handling of public finances. We do, however, find some evidence that having multiple political parties controlling the legislature is associated with better PFM systems—overall and ex ante legislative budgetary powers.

INTRODUCTION

Practitioners active in the field of public sector reform have long recognized that reform is far from a purely technocratic exercise whereby technical solutions based on best practices can be transferred easily from one country to the next irrespective of context. This is perhaps more pertinent in the field of PFM, where reforms affect the budget, an inherently political process that entails politicians allocating scarce resources to competing priorities (Von Hagen and Harden 1995; Weingast, Shepsle, and Johnsen 1981). In addition to the "public politics" of negotiating trade-offs, there are the "private politics" of special interests engaging in rent seeking and pursuing political advantage (Dorotinsky and Pradhan 2007). Analysis of the political economy of PFM suggests that actors with incentives to obstruct reforms are a more critical bottleneck than weak capacity (Bunse and Fritz 2012; Keefer 2011). Political incentives to reforming the PFM system often stem from the wider political and institutional environment.

Most of the existing theoretical and empirical literature on the political and institutional determinants of PFM performance comes from countries that are already at an advanced stage of economic development (Lienert 2005; Wehner 2010; Wehner and de Renzio 2013). In this chapter, we use this literature to formulate hypotheses relating to the form of government, electoral system, pro-grammatic parties, and divided government and then use the PEFA data set to probe whether hypotheses developed with reference to high-income countries travel to other contexts. This is important given that formally similar institutions can have quite different "real-life" implications and consequences in high- versus low- and middle-income countries, as described by North, Wallis, and Weingast (2006) and Rodrik, Subramanian, and Trebbi (2002). Although a few papers have sought to do this using the PEFA data set (de Renzio 2009; Fritz, Sweet, and Verhoeven 2014; Fritz, Verhoeven, and Avenia 2017), we add value to the discussion in three ways. First, we focus on the relationship between political institutions and specific elements of the PFM system rather than the entire PFM system. Second, we retest some hypotheses from previous studies using a larger sample size. Third, we consider two additional characteristics, specifically the electoral system and divided government.

The analysis presented in this chapter seeks to assess the advantages and disadvantages of using the PEFA data set to deepen our understanding of the contextual factors that can influence the potential scope for PFM reforms in a given country. This is important given the increasing recognition of the importance of good PFM for the effectiveness of the state. Good PFM not only supports fiscal discipline and macroeconomic stability but also is critical for effectively delivering the services on which human and economic development rely. For these reasons, many donors consider PFM to be a priority.

The chapter is laid out as follows. We begin with a brief overview of relevant literature and the hypotheses to be tested. We then describe the variables and data sources used in the analysis, some basic bivariate analysis, and the empirical models to be tested. This is followed by a presentation and discussion of the results of the econometric analysis.

LITERATURE REVIEW

Several studies have used the PEFA data set to investigate country characteristics associated with strengthening the overall PFM system. Of the political and institutional variables considered to date, state fragility and political instability have been found to have a statistically significant negative correlation with the quality of PFM systems (Andrews 2010; de Renzio, Andrews, and Mills 2011; Fritz, Sweet, and Verhoeven 2014; Fritz, Verhoeven, and Avenia 2017). The argument is that political stability is a prerequisite for developing and improving institutions because, in its absence, capacity tends to be very weak, informality predominant, and political will lacking. In contrast, the link between PFM quality and other political variables such as forms of government and democracy level is much less compelling, with studies often finding either weak (in magnitude and statistical significance) or no relationship.

This chapter adds value to this existing literature in the following ways. First, we focus exclusively on political and institutional contextual factors that are likely to influence the incentives of politicians to reform specific elements of the PFM system, such as legislative budgetary powers, strategic budgeting, and accountability structures. Notably, we use the literature on higher-income countries (Lienert 2005; Wehner 2010) to formulate our hypotheses and use the PEFA data set to probe whether hypotheses developed with reference to Organisation for Economic Co-operation and Development (OECD) countries apply to other contexts. Second, although we consider the association between the quality of the aggregate PFM system and each of these macropolitical or institutional factors, we do not consider all PFM elements individually. Instead, we limit our focus to those areas for which the theoretical relationship with certain political and institutional variables tends to be more compelling and for which the required data are available. This approach has three advantages:

1. It allows us to retest previous variables—for example, form of government—that were found to be weak or statistically insignificant in previous studies that focused on explaining the performance of the aggregate PFM system or very broad PFM pillars.

2. It allows us to consider a wider set of political and institutional variables than those that have been considered to date—for example, electoral system and divided government.

3. It makes it easier to assess the plausibility of the underlying causal arguments by focusing on specific elements of the PFM system rather than the entire system. Our theoretical propositions are as follows:

Forms of government

According to Posner and Park (2007) legislatures in OECD countries tend to have a stronger role in presidential systems than in Westminster-style parliamentary systems, where the executive often dominates.[1] Lienert (2005) contends that in presidential systems "the legislature is a powerful agenda-setter and decision-maker." For a sample of 28 (mostly) high-income countries, he examines the linear relationship between an index of legislative budgetary powers and an index of separation of political power. He finds that the legislative authority to shape the size of the annual budget is strong in a presidential form of government and particularly weak in countries with Westminster parliamentary systems. Using a multiple ordinary least squares (OLS) regression, Wehner (2005) finds no evidence of an inherent difference in legislative budgetary powers between presidential[2] and nonpresidential systems for a sample of 43 national legislatures in OECD countries. Similarly, for a sample of 43 (mostly) low- and middle-income countries, de Renzio (2009) finds no statistically significant relationship between the overall quality of the PFM system (as measured by PEFA) and the form of government after controlling for other factors, including democracy.

One reason for these contradictory results is that the sample size may be too small and lacking in variation to uncover these relationships. Another reason is that the hypothesis may be too broad. Although presidential systems often create a separation of powers allowing a greater role for the legislature in the management of public finances, this role may not translate immediately into improvements in the overall quality of the PFM system, because of other factors beyond the legislature's scope of control, such as technical capacity. We are therefore interested primarily in the relationship between the political system and the parts of the PFM system that are specific to the role of the legislature. We further distinguish between the role of the legislature in ex ante budgeting and ex post oversight, because these tend to differ depending on the type of political system.[3] Our first hypothesis is that countries with presidential regimes are likely to allow the legislature to be more involved in the management of public finances.

Hypothesis 1:
Countries with presidential regimes are more likely to have an incentive to develop PFM systems that allow for more legislative involvement in the management of public finances, especially ex ante.

Electoral systems

The type of electoral system also shapes legislative behavior. The argument is as follows. Plurality or majoritarian rule is geared toward holding politicians accountable, and proportional representation is geared toward representing different voters in the legislative process (Persson and Tabellini 2005). This means that in plurality systems, it is possible for the voters to identify who is responsible for policy decisions and to oust officeholders whose performance they find deficient. Politicians in majoritarian systems are therefore more likely to face sharper individual incentives to please their territorially defined constituencies than politicians under proportional elections (Persson and Tabellini 2005) and thus will have incentive to push for a greater role in formulating the budget. In contrast, politicians under a majoritarian system are likely to have less interest in exercising oversight ex post since they might not be able to hold any minister closely associated with the president to account and doing so may have limited relevance for their chances of reelection.

Although there are several empirical studies on the relationship between the electoral systems and fiscal outcomes (Addison 2013; Persson and Tabellini 2005; Von Hagen 2002), there is none exploring the relationship between electoral systems and the quality of PFM institutions. The first set of studies generally finds that overall government spending and deficits are smaller in majoritarian countries, supporting the idea that the design of electoral rules entails a trade-off between accountability and representation. Our second hypothesis is that countries with a majoritarian electoral system are more likely to allow the legislature to be more involved in the management of public finances.

Hypothesis 2:
Countries where legislators are elected under a majoritarian electoral system are more likely to have an incentive to develop PFM systems that allow for more legislative involvement in the management of public finances, especially ex ante.

Divided government

The dispersion of political power among different political parties in the government may also be associated with the quality of the PFM system. Divided government is defined as "the absence of simultaneous same-party majorities in the executive and legislative branches of government" (Elgie 2001). According to this definition, divided government in parliamentary regimes takes the form of minority government (Wehner 2005).

The study of divided versus single-party governments on PFM systems has been confined largely to OECD countries. Wehner (2010), for example, found that divided government is associated with greater legislative financial scrutiny in a sample of 30 OECD countries. The underlying argument is that, in countries experiencing protracted spells of divided government, legislatures have an incentive to champion reforms to strengthen their capacity for scrutiny in order to have the means to challenge executive-led fiscal policy. Our hypothesis is therefore that divided governments are associated with higher-quality legislative involvement in the management of public finances.

Hypothesis 3:
Countries with divided governments are more likely to have an incentive to develop PFM systems that allow a higher quality of legislative involvement in the management of public finances, ex ante and ex post.

Programmatic parties

Cruz and Keefer (2012) argue that, when politicians are not collectively organized, particularly into programmatic political parties, they have weak incentives to pursue broad public policies that rely on a well-functioning administration. They further contend that, in the absence of programmatic parties, politicians are less able to act collectively to demand that the executive implement transparent and rule-bound administrative practices. They support their argument using the ratings of 511 World Bank public sector reform loans in 109 countries as the dependent variable in a logistic regression.

Fritz, Sweet, and Verhoeven (2014) apply these insights to examine the relationship between programmatic parties and the quality of public financial management (as measured by a country's most recent PEFA), finding a relationship of potentially substantial impact, though of weak statistical significance for a sample of 102 countries. In fact, the authors conclude that the relationship is "significantly weaker compared to the relationship between the presence of programmatic parties and the success of World Bank projects supporting public sector reforms that Cruz and Keefer (2012) report and more likely to be influenced by which countries are included and how specific countries and parties are coded." In contrast, a revised version of the paper (Fritz, Verhoeven, and Avenia 2017) that uses all PEFA observations for each country, including repeat assessments, finds that programmatic parties appear to have a positive and strong impact on PFM quality. However, when using the World Bank's Country Policy and Institutional Assessment indicator 13 (CPIA-13) as the proxy for PFM performance, programmatic parties no longer appear as a significant factor.

Here, instead of looking solely at the quality of the overall PFM system, we focus on the relationship between the programmatic party variable and specific elements of the PFM system that are likely to be of particular salience to politicians organized into programmatic parties: (a) strategic budgeting; (b) internal audit; (c) accounting, recording, and reporting; and (d) external audit.

Programmatic political parties provide electorates with meaningful choice over policies by reaching out to them through coherent political programs (Cheeseman et al. 2014). Politicians belonging to such parties therefore have an incentive to support reforms to ensure that systems are in place to link high-level policy decisions to the PFM system to maintain credible stances on broad public policies. These high-level policy decisions may include the overall fiscal strategy and the allocation of resources in line with politically determined priorities. However, in countries where political parties do not campaign on a coherent policy program, politicians are less likely to have an incentive to develop systems that would allow the budget to be used as a planning tool for achieving the government's policy goals. They may even be averse to such systems, which can undermine their ability to allocate resources according to their own private interests. Our fourth hypothesis is therefore that countries with programmatic political parties are more likely to develop higher-quality strategic budgeting as a feature of their PFM systems.

Hypothesis 4:
Countries with programmatic political parties are more likely to have an incentive to develop PFM systems for strategic budgeting.

Countries with programmatic parties should also prefer financial management systems that allow them to monitor the possible diversion of financial resources away from their priorities. These systems might include higher-quality arrangements for accounting and reporting, internal audit, and external audit. Weaknesses in these areas allow for leakages and other corrupt practices that would undermine the credibility of the electoral commitments of a programmatic party. If such a party does not govern according to its programmatic platform, it could be held accountable in the next electoral round (Cheeseman et al. 2014). Our fifth hypothesis is therefore that countries with programmatic political parties are likely to have higher-quality accountability mechanisms for their PFM.

Hypothesis 5:
Countries with programmatic political parties are more likely to have an incentive to develop PFM systems that allow for higher-quality accountability mechanisms.

DATA AND ANALYSIS

Quality of the PFM system

Our primary measure of the quality of PFM systems is based on the PEFA data set as described in chapter 2. We exclude countries with missing scores on several dimensions when measuring the quality of the overall PFM system[4] or specific elements. In addition to measuring the aggregate PFM system, we also compute measures of specific elements of the PFM system that are relevant to our theoretical propositions. Given that we are looking at specific elements rather than the overall PFM system, we use the M1 scoring methodology where applicable. These elements are as follows:

- *Legislative budgetary powers (budget preparation)*. Average of scores of the following PEFA indicators: PI-6, comprehensiveness of information included in budget documentation (submitted to the legislature for scrutiny and approval), and PI-27, legislative scrutiny of the annual budget law.

- *Legislative budgetary powers (execution and evaluation)*. Score of the following PEFA indicator: PI-28, legislative scrutiny of external audit reports.

- *Strategic budgeting*. Average of scores of the following four PEFA dimensions: PI-12(i), preparation of multiyear fiscal forecasts and functional allocations; PI-12(ii), scope and frequency of debt sustainability analysis; PI-12(iii), existence of sector strategies with multiyear costing of recurrent and investment expenditure; and PI-12(iv), links between investment budgets and forward expenditure estimates.

- *Internal audit*. Average of scores of the following PEFA dimensions and indicators: PI-18(iv), existence of payroll audits, and PI-21, effectiveness of internal audit.

- *Accounting, recording, and reporting*. Average of scores of the following PEFA dimensions and indicators: PI-22(i)–(ii), timeliness and regularity of accounts reconciliation; PI-23, information at service delivery level; PI-24, quality and timeliness of in-year budget reports; and PI-25, quality and timeliness of annual financial statements.

- *External audit*. Score of the following PEFA indicator: PI-26, scope, nature, and follow-up of external audit.

We also use the World Bank's CPIA-13, which measures the quality of budgetary and financial management as a robustness check. The correlation between CPIA-13 and the aggregate PEFA score is quite high at 0.775.

Political characteristics

Measuring forms of government

To test whether the form of government affects the quality of the PFM system and legislative budgeting more specifically, we use the Inter-American Development Bank's Database of Political Institutions (2015) to construct a dummy variable for presidential governments that is equal to 1 for systems with unelected executives, with presidents who are elected directly or by an electoral college, or with no prime minister.[5] In systems with both a prime minister and a president, we consider the following factors to categorize the system:

a. *Hold veto power.* President can veto legislation and the parliament needs a super-majority to override the veto.

b. *Appoint prime minister.* President can appoint and dismiss prime minister, other ministers, or both.

c. *Dissolve parliament.* President can dissolve parliament and call for new elections.

The system is presidential if (a) is true or if (b) and (c) are true.[6] Governments are parliamentary (PRES 1 = 0) when the legislature elects the chief executive or if that assembly or group can recall him or her.

We also consider a more straightforward classification that is based solely on whether the government in democratic countries[7] can be removed by a legislative majority during its constitutional term in office (also known as a confidence requirement). According to the literature (Persson and Tabellini 2005), systems in which governments cannot be removed by the assembly are coded as "presidential" (PRES 2 = 1), while systems in which they can be removed are coded as nonpresidential (PRES 2 = 0).[8]

Measuring electoral systems

Our most basic measure is a simple classification of the electoral formula into "majoritarian," "mixed," or "proportional" electoral rules using the Varieties of Democracy Institute's V-Dem database, resulting in a binary indicator (dummy) variable, majoritarian.[9] More precisely, countries electing their lower house exclusively by plurality rule in the year of the PEFA assessment[10] are coded as MAJ = 1 and 0 otherwise.

Measuring divided government

Our measure of divided government is based on the degree of fragmentation of the legislature (Divided govt 1). The divided party control of legislature index from the V-Dem database assesses the extent to which legislative chambers are controlled by different political parties. Extreme positive values represent "divided party control," intermediate values signify "unified coalition control," and extreme negative values signify "unified party control." This variable is available for 46 countries in our sample, with observations for at least six years (inclusive) prior to the year of the earliest or most recent PEFA assessment.[11] We calculate a 10-year average of this variable for these countries.

As an alternative measure, we construct a divided government index, which is the ratio of years in which the government did not command a legislative majority in the lower house (Divided govt 2). It covers the 10-year period immediately before the year of the country's most recent PEFA assessment. We consider the fraction of seats held by all government parties[12] using the Database of Political Institutions (2015), giving a score of 0 when the government held more than 50 percent of seats in that year and otherwise 1. We then compile the index by summing across the 10 years for each country and dividing by 10. Possible index values therefore range between 0 (never minority government) and 1 (always minority government). According to the data, 45 out of the 101 countries for which this measure is available had experience with minority government at some point during the 10-year period considered.

Measuring programmatic parties

The "programmatic parties" variable is constructed in a manner similar to that of Cruz and Keefer (2012) and Fritz, Sweet, and Verhoeven (2014), both of which assume that a party is programmatic if it has a specific political orientation (right, left, or center) using variables from the Database of Political Institutions (2015). However, where applicable, we consider the three largest government parties and the largest opposition party, weighing each party by its share of seats in the legislature, and sum these values across the four parties.[13] Our second measure is unweighted and is the fraction of parties in a country that are programmatic (either left, right, or center). Both measures therefore range from 0 to 1. Although programmatic parties exist in several middle-income countries, they are rather rare in low-income environments. Of the 124 countries in our sample, 105 countries have a measure of programmatic parties: 31 are low-income countries (weighted average of 0.29), 42 are lower-middle-income countries (weighted average of 0.42), and 32 are upper-middle-income countries (weighted average of 0.62).

Bivariate analysis

As a first step, we use the Spearman rank coefficients to see the extent to which our data confirm previous findings from the literature as well as some of our hypotheses. Of the two nonbinary political variables considered, only the programmatic party system measure (unweighted) has a weak but statistically significant positive relationship with the quality of the overall PFM system (at the 10 percent level) (see table 3.1). Regarding the specific elements of the PFM system, the programmatic party system measure (weighted and unweighted) has a weak but statistically significant positive relationship with legislative budgetary powers—overall and ex ante. The divided government variable is positively and weakly associated with only one specific PFM element—ex ante legislative budgetary powers.

Concerning the relationship between the form of government and the quality of the PFM system, we do not find a statistically significant difference in the means between presidential and nonpresidential governments with regard to the quality of the overall PFM system as well as legislative budgetary powers (ex ante and ex post).

However, contrary to our expectations, we do find that nonmajoritarian electoral systems have better-quality PFM systems—overall and ex ante legislative budgetary—relative to majoritarian ones, with the difference statistically significant at the 5 percent and 1 percent level, respectively. Majoritarian systems, however, perform better on average with respect to ex post legislative budgetary systems (at the 5 percent level).

TABLE 3.1 **Spearman rank coefficients for nonbinary macropolitical variables**

VARIABLE	OVERALL PUBLIC FINANCIAL MANAGEMENT	STRATEGIC BUDGETING	LEGISLATIVE BUDGETARY POWERS	EX ANTE LEGISLATIVE BUDGETARY POWER	EX POST LEGISLATIVE BUDGETARY POWER	INTERNAL AUDIT	ACCOUNTING, RECORDING, AND REPORTING	EXTERNAL AUDIT
	(1)	(2)	(3)	(4)	(5)	(6)	(7)	(8)
Weighted program (5 yr)	0.1236	0.0939	0.1869*	0.1775*	0.0487	0.1467	0.0211	0.0651
Unweighted program (5 yr)	0.1779*	0.1325	0.1918*	0.2152**	−0.0013	0.0951	0.0129	0.0753
Divided govt 1 (10 yr)	0.1532	−0.0130	0.0727	0.1311	−0.1114	0.0478	0.1303	0.1084
Divided govt 2 (10 yr)	0.1864	0.2191	0.1681	0.2831*	−0.0091	0.1164	0.1746	0.1404

*** $p<0.01$, ** $p<0.05$, * $p<0.10$

Overall, simple bivariate statistics do not provide strong evidence in support of our theoretical propositions. However, these tests might not be very informative, because the countries included in our sample are heterogeneous and the quality of their PFM systems are potentially influenced by some important factors that may obscure the impact of the macropolitical variables. We therefore take an econometric approach.

ESTIMATION APPROACH

In this section, we test our hypotheses using multivariate analysis to understand how these and our other variables jointly affect PFM quality. Given the mostly cross-sectional nature of our data, the standard econometric method to be used is OLS regression, the limitations of which are discussed in chapter 2.

- *Cross-sectional regressions.* For these models, we exploit cross-country variation in the quality of PFM in low- and middle-income countries as measured by their most recent PEFA assessment.[14] We regress each country's PEFA score on a five-year lagged average (unless stated otherwise) of the other variables (depending on data availability) prior to the year of the most recent PEFA assessment for the country.

- *First-differences method.* Although one of the political and institutional features is relatively fixed, some features exhibit within-country variation, specifically with regard to programmatic parties. The measure of divided government is also likely to vary across time, but an insufficient number of observations prevents its use for this method. In order to understand patterns of institutional change as well as to control for possible time-invariant omitted variables, we run a first-differences regression model for countries with repeat PEFA assessments. However, we cannot run a fixed-effects estimation because of the varying time interval between PEFA assessments across countries. Instead, we compute the absolute change in PEFA scores and the absolute change over the same period in the variables capturing country characteristics. This approach allows us to relate changes in PFM quality to changes in these country characteristics. Specifically, we are asking if characteristics change within a country, then how much is PFM quality expected to change on average?

Apart from the variables of interest—"quality of PFM systems" (dependent variable) and "macropolitical variables" (independent variable)—some other independent variables are included in the analysis. They represent other country-specific factors that have been identified in previous studies as influencing the level and change in the quality of the PFM system (de Renzio, Andrews, and Mills 2011; Fritz, Sweet, and Verhoeven 2014). To avoid the trap of "garbage-can" regressions, we only include variables that have tended to be statistically significant in previous analyses, and that have a strong theoretical foundation. This includes variables such as gross domestic product (GDP) per capita, GDP growth, resource dependence, population size,[15] and political stability. Their theoretical relationship with the PFM system is as follows:

- *Income level.* Income is likely to be strongly associated with a wide range of variables that would enable better PFM systems such as financial, human, and technical resources. Citizens in higher-income countries may also have a higher demand for outcomes associated with a well-functioning PFM system, such as better fiscal performance and public service delivery.

- *Economic growth.* Higher rates of recent growth are expected to facilitate institutional improvements through their impact on resource availability and possibly growing expectations of what government ought to achieve.

- *Resource dependency.* Resource dependency may undermine the quality of a PFM system in several ways. It can weaken the social contract and accountability between citizens and state elites and create greater incentives for lack of transparency in the management of public funds. In addition, volatile revenues due to commodity price shocks and other types of fiscal shocks might negatively affect budget planning and execution.

- *Population size.* A large population may be associated with more resources (financial and human) as well as a greater need for advanced PFM systems. Similarly, larger states may find the cost of centralized PFM systems to be low and their return on investment high.

- *Political stability.* Politically unstable countries find it more challenging to carry out PFM reforms because of weak capacity, widespread informality, and lack of political will.

We also included dummies for colonial heritage, specifically Anglophone and Francophone dummies, although previous studies found them not to have significant effects (de Renzio, Andrews, and Mills 2011). However, we included these variables because cross-national commonalities may be due to institutional replication from colonial powers transferring institutional features to their colonies; once in place, these institutions may be resistant to change (Acemoglu, Johnson, and Robinson 2001; Lienert 2003). Andrews (2010) also found some preliminary evidence that colonial heritage may matter for the quality of certain elements of the PFM system, with Francophone countries substantially lagging other groups[16] in external audit and legislative audit review. Wehner (2005), in contrast, found that British colonial heritage is negatively associated with legislative budget capacity. The summary statistics of these variables are presented in annex 3A, table 3A.1.

The cross-sectional model, across countries, is estimated as follows:

$$Y_i = \beta_0 + \beta_1 X_i + \beta_2 Z_i + \varepsilon. \tag{3.1}$$

The first-differences model focusing on within-country changes over time is as follows:

$$Y_{it} = \beta_0 + \beta_1 X_{it} + \beta_2 Z_{it} + \delta_i + \varepsilon_{it}, \tag{3.2}$$

where i indexes countries, Y is the dependent variable of interest (PFM performance), X is the political institutional variable, Z is a matrix of socioeconomic and political macro-level variables, δ is fixed effects, and ε is the error term. These equations are estimated using OLS.

RESULTS

Forms of government

Contrary to our hypothesis, we do not find that countries with presidential systems have better PFM systems. This finding is similar to de Renzio (2009), who found a negative (though statistically insignificant) coefficient on his presidential dummy variable when looking at correlates of the PEFA overall score. Using our broad definition of presidential government in table 3.1, we find that having a presidential regime is negatively associated with the overall quality of the PFM system as well as legislative budgetary powers—overall, ex ante, and ex post. However, none of these coefficients is statistically significant in table 3.2, even when we control for a country's democracy level (annex 3A, table 3A.2).[17] Nevertheless, in line with earlier studies and our expectations, we find that larger population size, lower reliance on natural resources, and greater political stability are generally associated with better PFM quality, albeit at different confidence levels in columns 1–3 in table 3.2. Notably, when we consider more narrow PFM definitions, the fit of the model declines, falling from almost 50 percent in column 1, when we investigate the determinants of the overall PFM system, to as low as 7 percent in column 4, when we measure only ex post legislative budgetary powers. In the case of the latter, only the economic growth variable is statistically significant at the 10 percent level, with faster-growing economies tending to have stronger systems for ex post legislative involvement in the budget process.

Using our more simplistic classification of forms of democratic government (Pres 2) in table 3.3 also produces results contrary to our hypothesis, although the negative relationship between the presidential dummy and overall PFM quality is now statistically significant at the 1 percent level in column 1. Furthermore, contrary to our hypothesis that presidential systems are relatively strong ex ante, the

TABLE 3.2 **Cross-sectional analysis for presidential regimes vs. nonpresidential regimes and other country characteristics**

VARIABLE	OVERALL PUBLIC FINANCIAL MANAGEMENT (1)	LEGISLATIVE BUDGETARY POWERS (2)	EX ANTE LEGISLATIVE BUDGETARY POWERS (3)	EX POST BUDGETARY POWERS (4)
Pres 1	−0.0820	−0.0471	−0.0118	−0.129
	(0.105)	(0.127)	(0.143)	(0.242)
GDP per capita (log)	0.0542	0.00746	0.0114	−0.0224
	(0.0511)	(0.0756)	(0.0886)	(0.116)
GDP growth	0.00295	0.0164	−0.0121	0.0658*
	(0.0164)	(0.0258)	(0.0280)	(0.0392)
Resource	−0.209**	−0.324**	−0.357**	−0.236
	(0.102)	(0.130)	(0.162)	(0.202)
Population (log)	0.122***	0.112***	0.161***	0.0128
	(0.0296)	(0.0423)	(0.0438)	(0.0703)
Political stability	0.191***	0.206**	0.240*	0.123
	(0.0664)	(0.0996)	(0.121)	(0.143)
Former French colony	−0.528***	−0.512***	−0.764***	−0.0790
	(0.144)	(0.167)	(0.191)	(0.269)
Former British colony	−0.335***	−0.203	−0.327**	0.0374
	(0.0982)	(0.132)	(0.150)	(0.220)
Constant	0.574	1.022	0.818	1.699
	(0.634)	(0.855)	(0.889)	(1.411)
Observations	79	76	77	78
R-squared	0.486	0.331	0.412	0.077

Note: Robust standard errors are in parentheses.
*** $p<0.01$, ** $p<0.05$, * $p<0.1$

TABLE 3.3 **Alternative definition of democratic presidential regimes**

VARIABLE	OVERALL PUBLIC FINANCIAL MANAGEMENT	LEGISLATIVE BUDGETARY POWERS	EX ANTE LEGISLATIVE BUDGETARY POWERS	EX POST BUDGETARY POWERS
	(1)	(2)	(3)	(4)
Pres 2	−0.259***	−0.214	−0.252	−0.171
	(0.0954)	(0.132)	(0.156)	(0.187)
GDP per capita (log)	0.124**	0.000	0.135	−0.288**
	(0.0568)	(0.0842)	(0.111)	(0.121)
GDP growth	0.0280	0.0580*	0.0595*	0.0454
	(0.0203)	(0.0294)	(0.0352)	(0.0432)
Resource	−0.349***	−0.460**	−0.404*	−0.512**
	(0.125)	(0.178)	(0.241)	(0.195)
Population (log)	0.0938***	0.0546	0.0851*	−0.00257
	(0.0304)	(0.0360)	(0.0496)	(0.0661)
Political stability	0.0444	−0.0636	−0.113	0.0297
	(0.0822)	(0.0966)	(0.132)	(0.147)
Former French colony	−0.325*	−0.484**	−0.356	−0.764***
	(0.187)	(0.229)	(0.288)	(0.238)
Former British colony	−0.290***	−0.347**	−0.501***	−0.0501
	(0.107)	(0.134)	(0.172)	(0.216)
Constant	0.285	1.818**	0.671	4.261***
	(0.619)	(0.893)	(1.202)	(1.336)
Observations	63	60	61	62
R-squared	0.529	0.380	0.436	0.174

Note: Robust standard errors are in parentheses.
*** $p<0.01$, ** $p<0.05$, * $p<0.1$

coefficient for ex ante legislative powers in column 3 is negative, but not statistically significant.

Electoral system

Contrary to our theoretical proposition, but in line with our bivariate analysis, a majoritarian electoral system is not associated with greater legislative budgetary powers during budget formulation, as shown in column 3 of table 3.4. In fact, although the coefficient is not statistically significant at conventional levels, it is negative rather than the expected positive.

Divided government

Using our first measure of divided government, we find that more divided party control of the legislature is associated with better PFM systems—overall (at the 1 percent level in column 1 of table 3.5) and for specific elements related to legislative powers (at the 10 percent and 1 percent level, respectively, of columns 2–3 in table 3.5). The size of the coefficient is also largest for ex ante budgetary powers (0.32).

Conversely, using our more simplistic measure, we find that having a more divided government is associated with a lower quality of the overall PFM system (as shown in column 1 of table 3.6) as well as specific elements relating to legislative budgetary powers (as shown in columns 2–4). However, none of these coefficients is statistically significant at conventional levels, with the exception of ex post budgetary

TABLE 3.4 **Cross-sectional analysis for majoritarian vs. nonmajoritarian systems and other country characteristics**

VARIABLE	OVERALL PUBLIC FINANCIAL MANAGEMENT (1)	LEGISLATIVE BUDGETARY POWERS (2)	EX ANTE LEGISLATIVE BUDGETARY POWERS (3)	EX POST BUDGETARY POWERS (4)
Maj	–0.0293	0.0454	–0.0988	0.331
	(0.105)	(0.151)	(0.162)	(0.219)
GDP per capita (log)	0.0654	0.00378	–0.0153	0.0418
	(0.0461)	(0.0745)	(0.0894)	(0.107)
GDP growth	–0.00435	0.0144	–0.00875	0.0366
	(0.0170)	(0.0283)	(0.0287)	(0.0414)
Resource	–0.185*	–0.281**	–0.380**	–0.0676
	(0.0949)	(0.130)	(0.152)	(0.190)
Population (log)	0.123***	0.0964**	0.116***	0.0652
	(0.0258)	(0.0397)	(0.0441)	(0.0644)
Political stability	0.230***	0.234**	0.223*	0.254*
	(0.0657)	(0.0970)	(0.120)	(0.141)
Former French colony	–0.402***	–0.434**	–0.632***	–0.0613
	(0.120)	(0.167)	(0.187)	(0.224)
Former British colony	–0.243**	–0.222	–0.362**	0.0808
	(0.107)	(0.157)	(0.174)	(0.240)
Constant	0.429	1.290*	1.832**	0.179
	(0.523)	(0.771)	(0.861)	(1.270)
Observations	92	86	90	88
R-squared	0.472	0.310	0.374	0.138

Note: Robust standard errors are in parentheses.
*** $p<0.01$, ** $p<0.05$, * $p<0.1$

powers in column 4. Ultimately, the difference between the results presented in table 3.5 and those in table 3.6 may be due to sample size: the number of observations in table 3.6 is more than twice the number of observations in table 3.5.

Programmatic parties

Contrary to expectations, we find a negative relationship between how programmatic the party system is and the quality of the aggregate PFM system as well as specific elements (table 3.7). This negative relationship, however, is only statistically significant at the 10 percent level in column 4, when the dependent variable is the quality of accounting, recording, and reporting. Moving from having a party system that is completely nonprogrammatic to one that is completely programmatic is associated with a decrease of 0.28 for accounting, recording, and reporting. Notably, the magnitude of the programmatic party coefficient increases to 0.38 when we use an unweighted programmatic party measure in column 6. Ultimately, both results are counter to our proposition that, in a political system in which parties have clear policy agendas, politicians are more likely to have an incentive to demand systems that can provide information on the cost of programs and the use of resources to ensure that resources are allocated to their priorities. Our results differ from those of Fritz, Sweet, and Verhoeven (2014), because both of our measures of programmatic parties and overall PFM quality are different.

TABLE 3.5 Cross-sectional analysis for partisan fragmentation and other country characteristics

VARIABLE	OVERALL PUBLIC FINANCIAL MANAGEMENT (1)	LEGISLATIVE BUDGETARY POWERS (2)	EX ANTE LEGISLATIVE BUDGETARY POWERS (3)	EX POST BUDGETARY POWERS (4)
Divided govt 1	0.264***	0.196*	0.321***	−0.0487
	(0.0939)	(0.111)	(0.116)	(0.184)
GDP per capita (log)	0.0125	−0.0856	−0.0562	−0.158
	(0.0860)	(0.117)	(0.121)	(0.196)
GDP growth (5 yr)	0.0295	0.0103	−0.00969	0.0362
	(0.0230)	(0.0393)	(0.0320)	(0.0593)
Resource	−0.345**	−0.330	−0.438**	−0.160
	(0.139)	(0.195)	(0.212)	(0.275)
Population (log)	0.124**	0.202**	0.251***	0.124
	(0.0514)	(0.0734)	(0.0717)	(0.126)
Political stability (5 yr)	0.245*	0.412**	0.397**	0.466
	(0.122)	(0.177)	(0.168)	(0.275)
Former French colony	−0.324**	−0.297	−0.243	−0.155
	(0.156)	(0.220)	(0.242)	(0.374)
Former British colony	−0.126	−0.0743	−0.222	0.233
	(0.127)	(0.218)	(0.220)	(0.335)
Constant	0.827	0.551	0.111	1.304
	(0.760)	(1.050)	(1.114)	(1.816)
Observations	42	39	41	40
R-squared	0.591	0.395	0.523	0.164

Note: Robust standard errors in parentheses.
*** p<0.01, ** p<0.05, * p<0.1

TABLE 3.6 Cross-sectional analysis using alternative measure of divided government

VARIABLE	OVERALL PUBLIC FINANCIAL MANAGEMENT (1)	LEGISLATIVE BUDGETARY POWERS (2)	EX ANTE LEGISLATIVE BUDGETARY POWERS (3)	EX POST BUDGETARY POWERS (4)
Divided govt 2	−0.0476	−0.206	−0.0635	−0.468**
	(0.106)	(0.161)	(0.187)	(0.226)
GDP per capita (log)	0.0793*	−0.00495	0.0272	−0.0584
	(0.0441)	(0.0690)	(0.0842)	(0.0899)
GDP growth (5 yr)	−0.00694	0.000785	−0.0198	0.0291
	(0.0171)	(0.0288)	(0.0300)	(0.0416)
Resource	−0.196**	−0.248*	−0.296**	−0.166
	(0.0927)	(0.127)	(0.147)	(0.188)
Population (log)	0.117***	0.132***	0.159***	0.0753
	(0.0274)	(0.0425)	(0.0444)	(0.0657)
Political stability (5 yr)	0.196***	0.257**	0.235*	0.272*
	(0.0662)	(0.102)	(0.119)	(0.143)
Former French colony	−0.414***	−0.473***	−0.637***	−0.142
	(0.110)	(0.145)	(0.169)	(0.226)
Former British colony	−0.244***	−0.247*	−0.401***	0.0861
	(0.0902)	(0.130)	(0.141)	(0.203)
Constant	0.425	0.932	0.775	1.239
	(0.536)	(0.769)	(0.835)	(1.173)
Observations	98	92	96	94
R-squared	0.437	0.316	0.374	0.108

Note: Robust standard errors are in parentheses.
*** p<0.01, ** p<0.05, * p<0.1

TABLE 3.7 **Cross-sectional analysis for programmatic party systems using other country characteristics**

VARIABLE	OVERALL PUBLIC FINANCIAL MANAGEMENT	STRATEGIC BUDGETING	INTERNAL AUDIT	ACCOUNTING, RECORDING, AND REPORTING	EXTERNAL AUDIT	ACCOUNTING, RECORDING, AND REPORTING
	(1)	(2)	(3)	(4)	(5)	(6)
Programmatic (w)	−0.176	−0.0703	0.0811	−0.283*	−0.0932	
	(0.119)	(0.160)	(0.159)	(0.156)	(0.230)	
Programmatic (uw)						−0.376**
						(0.163)
GDP per capita (log)	0.0825**	−0.0669	−0.122*	0.162***	0.0691	0.172***
	(0.0414)	(0.0533)	(0.0646)	(0.0610)	(0.0837)	(0.0607)
GDP growth (5 yr)	−0.00834	−0.0358	−0.0624**	−0.00211	0.0338	−0.00461
	(0.0164)	(0.0243)	(0.0244)	(0.0258)	(0.0359)	(0.0253)
Resource	−0.208**	−0.224*	−0.0654	−0.0313	−0.252	−0.0569
	(0.0904)	(0.114)	(0.132)	(0.122)	(0.173)	(0.124)
Population (log)	0.123***	0.0585	0.147***	0.112***	0.108*	0.119***
	(0.0270)	(0.0477)	(0.0466)	(0.0411)	(0.0586)	(0.0408)
Political stability (5 yr)	0.226***	0.0795	0.304***	0.268***	0.131	0.276***
	(0.0661)	(0.0880)	(0.0918)	(0.0839)	(0.125)	(0.0803)
Former French colony	−0.424***	−0.257*	−0.293*	−0.590***	−0.431***	−0.600***
	(0.0989)	(0.134)	(0.153)	(0.155)	(0.163)	(0.155)
Former British colony	−0.251***	−0.0933	−0.0396	−0.542***	0.155	−0.566***
	(0.0835)	(0.136)	(0.126)	(0.125)	(0.193)	(0.123)
Constant	0.377	2.338***	1.289	−0.203	−0.157	−0.298
	(0.513)	(0.817)	(0.924)	(0.817)	(1.087)	(0.810)
Observations	101	104	103	104	102	104
R-squared	0.464	0.110	0.194	0.375	0.193	0.387

Note: Robust standard errors are in parentheses. uw = unweighted; w = weighted.
*** p<0.01, ** p<0.05, * p<0.1

TABLE 3.8 **First-differences analysis with absolute change in programmatic party measure**

VARIABLE	OVERALL PUBLIC FINANCIAL MANAGEMENT	STRATEGIC BUDGETING	INTERNAL AUDIT	ACCOUNTING, RECORDING, AND REPORTING	EXTERNAL AUDIT
	(1)	(2)	(3)	(4)	(5)
Absolute change in programmatic	−0.292	−0.521	0.0970	0.294	−0.116
	(0.230)	(0.426)	(0.385)	(0.357)	(0.489)
Absolute change in GDP per capita	0.504	0.454	0.562	0.517	1.364*
	(0.338)	(0.520)	(0.564)	(0.525)	(0.701)
Absolute change in population	0.885	−0.111	2.807***	0.703	0.542
	(0.541)	(0.814)	(0.903)	(0.841)	(1.098)
Absolute change in political stability	0.342***	0.563***	0.207	0.154	−0.0561
	(0.122)	(0.188)	(0.204)	(0.190)	(0.248)
Time between assessments	−0.00552	0.0188	−0.0354	−0.0138	−0.000479
	(0.0166)	(0.0253)	(0.0277)	(0.0258)	(0.0339)
Observations	77	65	76	77	72
R-squared	0.359	0.309	0.247	0.073	0.205

Note: Standard errors are in parentheses.
*** p<0.01, ** p<0.05, * p<0.1

We also test this hypothesis using a first-differences model in table 3.8. This model uses the absolute change in the PEFA-based measure of PFM quality as the dependent variable. The coefficients of the absolute change in the political variable of interest—programmatic parties (weighted) in table 3.8—are not statistically significant at conventional levels. The number of years between assessments also appears to have no statistical correlation with the change in PFM quality. However, both an increase in population size and political stability tend to be associated with a small improvement in PFM quality in some models in table 3.8 at varying confidence levels. For example, in column 3, a 1 percent increase in total population size is associated with an increase in the internal audit score by 0.03.

We also find no statistically significant relationship between the change in our macropolitical variables and the change in our alternative measure of PFM quality, CPIA-13 average (as shown in annex 3A, table 3A.4). However, in these models, the absolute change in GDP per capita is positively associated with a small improvement in the CPIA score at the 10 percent level. More specifically, a 1 percent increase in GDP per capita is associated with an improvement in the CPIA score of 0.0035.

DISCUSSION

Summary of results

Our analysis shows that, with the exception of divided government, our macropolitical variables generally have a weak or no relationship with the quality of the PFM system (as measured by PEFA and CPIA) when we control for other country characteristics. In fact, to a large extent, we find no evidence in support of our theoretical propositions that the ex ante legislative budgetary institutions are stronger in presidential systems or majoritarian systems, with the sign of the coefficient in the opposite direction from what we predicted. Similarly, we find no evidence that having a more programmatic political party system is associated with better systems for strategic budgeting or better institutions for overseeing the handling of public finances. This lack of evidence in favor of our hypotheses, especially those developed on the basis of the experience of higher-income countries, may be because formally similar political institutions may function differently in low- and middle-income countries for reasons discussed below. We find that more divided party control of the legislature (Divided govt 1) is associated with better PFM systems—overall and specific elements related to legislative budgetary powers, especially ex ante at the 1 percent level. We also find the following weak—and counterintuitive—relationships:

- A *presidential regime* (as defined in terms of a confidence requirement) is negatively associated with the quality of the overall PFM system (at the 1 percent level).

- A *more divided government* (defined in terms of whether the government had a legislative majority in the lower house) is negatively associated with ex post legislative budgetary powers (at the 5 percent level).

- A *more programmatic party system* is associated with a lower quality of accounting, recording, and reporting (at the 10 percent level).

Furthermore, when we exploit within-country variation in our first-differences models, we find no statistically significant correlation between the absolute change in our measure of programmatic parties and the absolute change in the quality of the overall PFM system or specific elements. However, a larger population size and political stability are generally associated with an improvement in the quality of the PFM system overall and for specific elements.

Limitations of the study

The lack of a clear empirical relationship between these macropolitical variables and PFM quality should not be interpreted to mean that these factors do not have a strong predetermining effect on the quality of the PFM system and thus should be disregarded when designing PFM reforms for the following four reasons.

First, our PEFA-based measure of PFM quality is not without limitations, as noted in chapter 2. This weakness is currently insurmountable given the absence of other available indicators for measuring the quality of PFM systems (overall and most elements) with the coverage and timeliness required for regression analysis.

Second, our measure of the political variables may also be subject to measurement error or be an imperfect proxy for the characteristics they are intended to capture. For example, although we have improved on the programmatic party measure that has been adopted in previous studies by considering the share of seats in the legislature, this measure is less precise than other empirical work investigating the effect of programmatic party systems. Wantchekon (2003), for example, distinguishes between electoral platforms based on clientelism as opposed to the ones based on public policy (public goods) in Benin. Moreover, although the political and institutional variables used in this chapter are relatively well defined for high-income countries, they may not be reliable in some low- and middle-income countries, because they focus on formal aspects of democratic institutions that do not necessarily reflect the actual exercise of political power in these contexts. Informal institutions, such as family and kinship structures, traditions, and social norms, play a critical role in many political systems; and it may be misleading to examine the political incentives for reforms only through the lens of the formal institutions captured by the variables used in this chapter. As Rodrik, Subramanian, and Trebbi (2002, 24) conclude on the question of formal institutions and development, "Desirable institutional arrangements have a large element of context specificity, arising from differences in historical trajectories, geography, and political economy or other initial conditions." Hence, whether or not institutions lead to better PFM systems is as much a question of the incentive and enforcement mechanism of the institutions themselves as the environment in which the institution operates.

Third, for each of the macropolitical variables, the fit of the model is generally lower when we investigate the correlates of specific elements of the PFM system compared with when we look at the quality of the overall PFM system. For example, the country variables used in the regression models in table 3.3 jointly account for only 7 percent of the variation in PFM quality across countries in column 4 as compared with 49 percent when the PEFA-based measure of quality of the overall PFM system is the dependent variable in column 1.

Finally, our first-differences models only consider a relatively short time period, with the average time between a country's first and most recent PEFA assessment being 6.5 years. The lack of a statistically significant coefficient on the change in the programmatic party variable is therefore not surprising given that this variable shows little variation over time compared with the change in other country characteristics considered, specifically income and population size.

Next steps

Given the limitations of quantitative analysis to generate insight into the political incentives for PFM reforms, further research is needed to inform how PFM reforms should be calibrated to country context. This research may not necessarily be empirical, but it might use a country's PEFA score as one of the key selection criteria when undertaking case studies. For example, a group of countries that are highly similar in most respects including their formal political features, but that perform quite differently in regard to their PEFA scores, could be investigated for possible reasons for this divergence, including the interaction between formal and informal institutions. Similarly, because most countries have had repeat PEFA assessments, we can also identify countries that are mostly similar, including similar initial PEFA scores, but that subsequently diverged on the basis of their most recent PEFA assessment.

Furthermore, given that most studies in this area have focused on macropolitical variables, another potential area of research is to investigate the relationship between features of the microinstitutional environment and the quality of the PFM system. An example of a more microinstitutional feature is the degree of fragmentation of central finance functions. Such a study can be beneficial for two reasons. First, these institutional features can typically be adjusted more easily than high-level political variables and thus can potentially be altered as part of a PFM reform strategy if a convincing argument can be made. Second, the relationship between microfactors and PFM quality may be more direct than one with macropolitical characteristics, and thus causality may be more easily inferred.

Moreover, some of the existing research that has used the PEFA data set to measure PFM improvements has suggested that the existing quantitative analysis needs to be complemented by qualitative research. Qualitative research is envisaged to provide a more comprehensive understanding of the role of specific contexts, the role of different stakeholders and their motivations in pursuing PFM reforms, and how this influences the results and impact of reforms (Andrews 2010; de Renzio 2009; Fritz, Verhoeven, and Avenia 2017).

Finally, the growing number of subnational PEFA assessments and growing popularity of decentralization reforms can provide another research opportunity for assessing the extent to which certain political and institutional characteristics may explain differences in the quality of the PFM system. Ultimately, significant scope remains for using PEFA assessments to gain a greater understanding of the determinants of PFM quality, but further work is needed to overcome the challenges to using PEFA scores for statistical analysis.

ANNEX 3A STATISTICAL TABLES

TABLE 3A.1 **Summary statistics**

VARIABLE	OBSERVATION	MEAN	STANDARD DEVIATION	MINIMUM	MAXIMUM
PEFA-based measures					
Overall PFM quality	129	2.53	0.48	1.42	3.55
Strategic budgeting	129	2.19	0.62	1.00	3.75
Legislative budgetary powers	129	2.51	0.63	1.00	4.00
Legislative budgetary preparation	128	2.86	0.72	1.00	4.00
Legislative audit	121	1.81	0.85	1.00	4.00
Internal audit	129	2.07	0.63	1.00	4.00
Accounting, recording, and reporting	129	2.38	0.69	1.00	3.70
External audit	124	2.10	0.80	1.00	3.50
Macropolitical variables					
Program. parties (5 yr avg)	105	0.41	0.35	0	1.00
Weighted program. parties (5 yr avg)	105	0.37	0.35	0	1.00
Divided govt 1 (10 yr avg)	101	0.22	0.32	0	1.00
Divided govt 2 (10 yr avg)	46	−0.36	0.74	−1.57	1.65
Political stability (5 yr avg)	124	−0.38	0.92	−2.79	1.45
Socioeconomic variables					
GDP per capita (5 yr avg)	120	6,384	4,899	614	18,163
GDP growth (5 yr avg)	121	4.60	2.63	−0.16	11.59
Population (5 yr avg)	121	33,000,000	113,000,000	10,338	1,180,000,000

TABLE 3A.2 **Cross-sectional analysis for presidential regimes vs. nonpresidential regimes controlling for democracy level and other country characteristics**

VARIABLE	OVERALL PUBLIC FINANCIAL MANAGEMENT (1)	LEGISLATIVE BUDGETARY POWERS (2)	EX ANTE LEGISLATIVE BUDGETARY POWERS (3)	EX POST BUDGETARY POWERS (4)
Pres 1	−0.125	−0.112	−0.0197	−0.302
	(0.108)	(0.132)	(0.156)	(0.239)
Democracy	−0.0291	−0.0438	−0.00528	−0.123**
	(0.0184)	(0.0353)	(0.0386)	(0.0476)
GDP per capita (log)	0.0529	0.00497	0.0112	−0.0239
	(0.0502)	(0.0774)	(0.0893)	(0.113)
GDP growth	0.000630	0.0125	−0.0125	0.0565
	(0.0164)	(0.0277)	(0.0288)	(0.0374)
Resource	−0.229**	−0.355***	−0.361**	−0.327*
	(0.0999)	(0.127)	(0.165)	(0.186)
Population (log)	0.127***	0.120***	0.161***	0.0332
	(0.0298)	(0.0428)	(0.0446)	(0.0673)
Political stability	0.230***	0.264**	0.247*	0.292*
	(0.0738)	(0.111)	(0.128)	(0.155)
Former French colony	−0.554***	−0.554***	−0.769***	−0.196
	(0.146)	(0.173)	(0.195)	(0.258)

continued

TABLE 3A.2, *continued*

VARIABLE	OVERALL PUBLIC FINANCIAL MANAGEMENT	LEGISLATIVE BUDGETARY POWERS	EX ANTE LEGISLATIVE BUDGETARY POWERS	EX POST BUDGETARY POWERS
	(1)	(2)	(3)	(4)
Former British colony	−0.339***	−0.210	−0.328**	0.0131
	(0.0975)	(0.129)	(0.152)	(0.213)
Constant	0.758	1.302	0.852	2.441*
	(0.634)	(0.865)	(0.893)	(1.419)
Observations	79	76	77	78
R-squared	0.499	0.354	0.412	0.166

Note: Robust standard errors are in parentheses.
*** p<0.01, ** p<0.05, * p<0.1

TABLE 3A.3 Cross-country regression using Country Policy and Institutional Arrangements indicator 13 (CPIA-13)

VARIABLE	(1)	(2)	(3)	(4)	(5)	(6)	(7)
Pres 1	−0.147						
	(0.122)						
Pres 2		−0.216					
		(0.153)					
Maj			−0.213				
			(0.147)				
Programmatic_w				0.0142			
				(0.193)			
Programmatic_uw					0.00567		
					(0.199)		
Divided govt 1						0.207	
						(0.183)	
Divided govt 2							−0.0417
							(0.159)
ln GDP per capita (5 yr)	0.0515	0.283**	0.0523	0.0651	0.0651	−0.0843	0.0586
	(0.0807)	(0.129)	(0.0806)	(0.0817)	(0.0829)	(0.161)	(0.0811)
GDP growth (5 yr)	−0.0370	0.0199	−0.0284	−0.0438	−0.0439	−0.0482	−0.0438
	(0.0261)	(0.0357)	(0.0260)	(0.0267)	(0.0268)	(0.0628)	(0.0275)
Resource	−0.320**	−0.349	−0.273*	−0.292*	−0.291*	−0.430	−0.307*
	(0.150)	(0.245)	(0.157)	(0.154)	(0.154)	(0.260)	(0.155)
ln population (5 yr)	0.195***	0.148***	0.201***	0.186***	0.186***	0.183*	0.188***
	(0.0470)	(0.0524)	(0.0435)	(0.0436)	(0.0443)	(0.0979)	(0.0445)
Political stability	0.373***	0.271**	0.406***	0.389***	0.390***	0.186	0.382***
	(0.0920)	(0.135)	(0.0882)	(0.0887)	(0.0900)	(0.195)	(0.0885)
Former French colony	−0.383***	−0.124	−0.315**	−0.376***	−0.377***	0.0480	−0.396***
	(0.146)	(0.322)	(0.151)	(0.141)	(0.142)	(0.257)	(0.147)
Former British colony	−0.251**	−0.173	−0.0926	−0.190	−0.190	0.0943	−0.200
	(0.120)	(0.139)	(0.171)	(0.132)	(0.131)	(0.258)	(0.136)
Constant	0.525	−0.982	0.301	0.446	0.446	1.675	0.500
	(0.789)	(1.116)	(0.753)	(0.761)	(0.770)	(1.603)	(0.768)
Observations	118	71	110	117	117	40	114
R-squared	0.376	0.459	0.401	0.372	0.372	0.290	0.373

Note: Robust standard errors are in parentheses.
*** p<0.01, ** p<0.05, * p<0.1

TABLE 3A.4 **First-differences model using absolute change in Country Policy and Institutional Arrangements indicator 13 (CPIA-13)**

VARIABLE	MODEL 1 (1)	MODEL 2 (2)
Absolute change programmatic_w	−0.0749	
	(0.201)	
Absolute change programmatic_uw		−0.0605
		(0.178)
Absolute change GDP per capita (log)	0.348*	0.353*
	(0.191)	(0.190)
Absolute change population (log)	−0.576	−0.593
	(0.359)	(0.363)
Absolute change political stability	0.0795	0.0820
	(0.107)	(0.108)
Observations	110	110
R-squared	0.050	0.050

Note: Standard errors are in parentheses.
*** $p<0.01$, ** $p<0.05$, * $p<0.1$

NOTES

1. Legislative powers are arguably weakest under the Westminster system, where the executive leadership is drawn from the parliament and where the legislature is politically obligated to support the government.

2. Based on data from the Central Intelligence Agency (2003).

3. For example, the Westminster model is often weak ex ante. The U.K. Parliament abdicates the right of financial initiative to the executive. In contrast, the U.S. Congress is strong ex ante, with a complex system of specialized committees in both houses to make budgetary decisions with the support of extensive analysis from the Congressional Budget Office. Conversely, the Westminster model is relatively strong ex post, whereas the U.S. Congress conducts less ex post scrutiny, with no public accounts committee or equivalent (Pelizzo, Stapenhurst, and Olson 2006).

4. When looking at the overall quality of the PFM system, we exclude five countries with 10 or more missing scores for PEFA dimensions: Fiji, Lebanon, Myanmar, Nauru, and Uruguay.

5. This definition excludes countries with a communist government system. For the database, see https://mydata.iadb.org/Reform-Modernization-of-the-State/Database-of-Political -Institutions-2015/ngy5-9h9d.

6. If no information or ambiguous information is available on factors (a), (b), and (c), then if sources mention the president more often than the prime minister, the system is considered presidential (Estonia, the Kyrgyz Republic, Romania).

7. A regime is considered a democracy if the executive and the legislature are directly or indirectly elected by popular vote, multiple parties are allowed, there is de facto existence of multiple parties outside of the regime, there are multiple parties within the legislature, and there has been no consolidation of incumbent advantage (for example, unconstitutional closing of the lower house or extension of the incumbent's term by postponing of subsequent elections).

8. Nonpresidential systems include countries in which the head of state is popularly elected for a fixed term in office.

9. For the V-Dem database, see https://www.v-dem.net/en/data/data-version-8/.

10. For countries missing observations for the year of the PEFA assessment, we use the most recent observation three years before or after the PEFA assessment.

11. Data are available for 11 countries before the earliest PEFA assessment and 35 countries before the most recent PEFA assessment.

12. Calculated by dividing the number of government seats by total (government plus opposition plus nonaligned) seats.

13. We consider four political parties: the three largest government parties and the largest opposition party.
14. Ukraine is the exception across all models, with the PEFA scores from 2012 used instead of those from the most recent 2016 assessment because of the large number of missing indicator scores in the latter.
15. We do not control for being a small island state given that population size and small island dummy are highly correlated (−0.71) in our sample.
16. Relative to Anglophone countries and those of Portuguese heritage in Africa.
17. Democracy level is measured using the Freedom House's level of democracy index.

REFERENCES

Acemoglu, D., S. Johnson, and J. A. Robinson. 2001. "The Colonial Origins of Comparative Development: An Empirical Investigation." *The American Economic Review* 91 (5): 1369–1401. http://www.jstor.org/stable/2677930.

Addison, D. 2013. "The Quality of Budget Execution and Its Correlates." Policy Research Working Paper 6657, World Bank, Washington, DC.

Andrews, M. 2010. "How Far Have Public Financial Management Reforms Come in Africa?" HKS Faculty Research Working Paper RWP10-018, John F. Kennedy School of Government, Harvard University, Cambridge, MA.

Bunse, S., and V. Fritz. 2012. "Making Public Sector Reforms Work: Political and Economic Contexts, Incentives, and Strategies." Policy Research Working Paper 6174, World Bank, Washington, DC.

Central Intelligence Agency. 2003. *The World Factbook.* Washington, DC: Central Intelligence Agency.

Cheeseman, N., J. P. Luna, H. Kitschelt, D. Paget, F. Rosenblatt, K. Sample, S. Toro, J. Valladares Molleda, S. van der Staak, and Yi-ting Wang. 2014. *Politics Meets Policies: The Emergence of Programmatic Political Parties.* Stockholm: International IDEA.

Cruz, C., and P. Keefer. 2012. "Programmatic Parties and the Politics of Bureaucratic Reform." University of California, Santa Cruz; World Bank, Washington, DC.

de Renzio, P. 2009. "Taking Stock: What Do PEFA Assessments Tell Us about PFM Systems across Countries?" ODI Working Paper 302, Overseas Development Institute, London.

de Renzio, P., M. Andrews, and Z. Mills. 2011. "Does Donor Support to Public Financial Management Reforms in Developing Countries Work? An Analytical Study of Quantitative Cross-Country Evidence." ODI Working Paper 329, Overseas Development Institute, London.

Dorotinsky, W., and S. Pradhan. 2007. "Exploring Corruption in Public Financial Management." In *The Many Faces of Corruption: Tackling Vulnerability at the Sector Level,* edited by J. E. Campos and S. Pradhan. Washington, DC: World Bank.

Elgie, R., ed. 2001. *Divided Government in Comparative Perspective.* Oxford: Oxford University Press.

Fritz, V., S. Sweet, and M. Verhoeven. 2014. "Strengthening Public Financial Management: Exploring Drivers and Effects." Policy Research Working Paper 7084, World Bank, Washington, DC. http://documents.worldbank.org/curated/en/349071468151787835 /Strengthening-public-financial-management-exploring-drivers-and-effects.

Fritz, V., M. Verhoeven, and A. Avenia. 2017. *Political Economy of Public Financial Management Reforms: Experiences and Implications for Dialogue and Operational Engagement.* Washington, DC: World Bank. https://openknowledge.worldbank.org/handle/10986/28887 License: CC BY 3.0 IGO.

Keefer, P. 2011. "Collective Action, Political Parties, and Pro-Development Public Policy." Policy Research Working Paper 5676, World Bank, Washington, DC.

Lienert, I. 2003. "A Comparison Between Two Public Expenditure Management Systems in Africa." IMF Working Paper WP/03/2, Washington, DC. https://www.imf.org/external/pubs/ft/wp /2003/wp0302.pdf.

———. 2005. "Who Controls the Budget: The Legislature or the Executive?" IMF Working Paper 05/115, International Monetary Fund, Washington, DC.

North, D., J. Wallis, and B. Weingast. 2006. "A Conceptual Framework for Interpreting Recorded Human History." NBER Working Paper 12795, National Bureau of Economic Research, Cambridge, MA.

Pelizzo. R., R. Stapenhurst, and D. Olson. 2006. "The Role of Parliaments in the Budget Process." Research Collection School of Social Sciences Paper 84, Singapore Management University.

Persson, T., and G. Tabellini. 2005. *Economic Effects of Constitutions*. Cambridge, MA: MIT Press.

Posner, P., and C. Park. 2007. "Role of the Legislature in the Budget Process: Recent Trends and Innovations." *OECD Journal on Budgeting*, 7 (3). https://www.oecd.org/gov/budgeting/43411793.pdf.

Rodrik, D., A. Subramanian, and F. Trebbi. 2002. "Institutions Rule: The Primacy of Institutions over Geography and Integration in Economic Development." IMF Working Paper, International Monetary Fund, Washington, DC.

Von Hagen, J. 2002. "Fiscal Rules, Fiscal Institutions, and Fiscal Performance." *Economic and Social Review* 33 (3): 263–84.

Von Hagen, J., and I. J. Harden. 1995. "Budget Processes and Commitment to Fiscal Discipline." *European Economic Review* 39 (3–4): 771–79.

Wantchekon, L. 2003. "Clientelism and Voting Behavior: Evidence from a Field Experiment in Benin." *World Politics* 55 (April): 399–422. https://www.princeton.edu/~lwantche/Clientelism_and_Voting_Behavior_Wantchekon.

Wehner, J. 2005. "Legislative Arrangements for Financial Scrutiny: Explaining Cross-National Variation" in *The Role of Parliaments in the Budget Process*, edited by Ricardo Pelizzo, Rick Stapenhurst, and David Olson, 2–17. World Bank, Washington D.C. http://siteresources.worldbank.org/PSGLP/Resources/TheRoleofParliamentsintheBudgetProcess.pdf.

———. 2010. *Explaining Cross-National Patterns in Legislatures and the Budget Process: The Myth of Fiscal Control*. London: Palgrave Macmillan.

Wehner, J., and P. de Renzio. 2013. "Citizens, Legislators, and Executive Disclosure: The Political Determinants of Fiscal Transparency." *World Development* 41 (C): 96–108.

Weingast, B. R., K. A. Shepsle, and C. Johnsen. 1981. "The Political Economy of Benefits and Costs: A Neoclassical Approach." *Journal of Political Economy* 89 (4): 642–64.

4 Budget Credibility, Fiscal Outcomes, and PFM Performance in Fragile and Nonfragile Countries

SHAKIRA MUSTAPHA

In this chapter, we explore whether the credibility of the budget and fiscal outcomes improve with the quality of the public financial management (PFM) system in fragile and nonfragile states. Using a cross-sectional multiplicative interaction model, we exploit the variation in PFM quality as measured by Public Expenditure and Financial Accountability (PEFA) indicators and outcomes across countries. Our results are mixed. We find that, controlling for other determinants of credibility, better PFM quality is associated with more reliable budgets in terms of expenditure composition in fragile states, but not with aggregate budget credibility. Moreover, in contrast to existing studies, we find no evidence that PFM quality matters for fiscal outcomes—such as deficit and debt ratios—irrespective of whether a country is fragile or not. This is despite controlling for other key determinants of fiscal outcomes and running several robustness checks.

INTRODUCTION

The literature on PFM reforms has grown extensively in recent years; as a result, we now know much more about the effectiveness of PFM reforms than we did a decade ago. But significant gaps in knowledge remain. One such gap pertains to the outcomes of PFM reforms in "fragile states"—countries that either recently experienced conflict or have weak institutional capacity. This chapter aims to address this void by examining possible links between the quality of the PFM system as measured by PEFA indicators and outcomes such as budget credibility and fiscal outcomes in fragile states.

Building or rebuilding fiscal institutions in fragile states is generally perceived as an important part of state building (Boyce and O'Donnell 2007; Ghani, Lockhart, and Carnahan 2005; World Bank 2011b). The underlying logic is that, if a state cannot tax reasonably or spend responsibly, a key element of statehood is missing because it would be unable to deliver basic goods and services as well as manage expenditure in a manner that its citizens regard as effective and equitable. Although the evidence on what works when it comes to strengthening PFM systems in fragile states is growing (Fritz 2012; IMF 2017a; Williamson 2015), much less is known about the actual effects of these improved systems in these environments. Traditionally, a sound PFM system supports aggregate control, prioritization, accountability, and efficiency in the management of public resources and delivery of services. However, PFM systems in fragile states, even those conforming to "best practice," may fail to function as expected because of a crippling combination of factors that often leaves these states stuck in a "capability trap" (Pritchett and de Veijer 2011). Low human capacity, lack of physical infrastructure, and persistence of parallel informal systems are some of the factors that can impair the proper functioning of a well-designed PFM system in a fragile state.

This chapter investigates this wider question regarding whether PFM reforms can produce the desired outcomes in fragile states. From a political economy perspective, evidence that a well-functioning PFM system can be linked to tangible results even in fragile environments is important to convince decision makers in these countries to commit to these reforms. Furthermore, focusing on building sound fiscal institutions in fragile states may bring relatively high returns. For example, even though the development of effective budget institutions takes time and resources, these requirements tend to be much smaller than those needed for more general institutional improvements (Deléchat et al. 2015). Here we consider both a narrow and a broad definition of fragility because, although fragile states share some broad common characteristics, they are all different in their own ways. Context matters and needs to be understood.

We focus on understanding the impact of the PFM system on budget credibility and fiscal discipline in fragile states for two reasons. First, credibility and discipline are often the first and foremost concern in many low- and middle-income countries, with any efforts to address the other PFM objectives—strategic allocation of resources and efficient delivery of services—coming next. In addition, various macroeconomic goals and national objectives for development and public service delivery are also easier to achieve when funds are disbursed as allocated. As a result, a credible budget is seen as a priority for many fragile states. According to the former president of Liberia, Ellen Johnson Sirleaf, "Perhaps our greatest fiscal challenge lies in focusing the expenditure of cash inflows from domestic revenue and from donors on established priorities. The better we can manage our public finances, the better we can deliver on our poverty reduction and job creation agenda" (World Bank 2011a, 3).

Achieving fiscal discipline also tends to be a priority for fragile states. Better fiscal outcomes are expected to widen the fiscal space, providing room to meet pressing development needs as well as the ability to respond to adverse shocks by running expansionary fiscal policies and therefore mitigating the impact of shocks on the population (Gelbard et al. 2015). This improvement can, in turn, enhance state legitimacy as well as avoid or minimize the risk of relapse to conflict. A second reason for focusing on budget credibility and fiscal outcomes relates to data availability. Measuring other PFM outcomes such as efficient service delivery or corruption tends to require special studies or imperfect proxies (see chapter 5 on PFM and corruption). In investigating the interaction between fragility and the effects of the PFM system, it is therefore reasonable to look first at budget credibility and fiscal outcomes.

Using a cross-country interactive regression model and a PEFA-based measure of PFM quality, we find mixed evidence regarding the relationship between PFM quality and budget credibility in fragile states, depending on the definitions of credibility and fragility used. On the one hand, better PFM quality is associated with better budget credibility—aggregate and compositional—in nonfragile states. More important, although this relationship with aggregate budget credibility generally becomes insignificant in fragile states, there is some evidence that a positive and statistically significant relationship persists in fragile states when we look at compositional budget credibility and adopt the World Bank's definition of fragility. Better systems for predictability and control in budget execution, in particular, are associated with a higher level of composition credibility in fragile states. On the other hand, there is no evidence that the quality of the overall PFM system matters for fiscal outcomes in both fragile and nonfragile states. However, given that estimating the impact of budget institutions on fiscal performance is plagued by several identification challenges—such as reverse causality and omitted variable bias as well as potential limitations with the PEFA data set—results should be treated as preliminary.

The remainder of the chapter is structured as follows. We begin by summarizing the literature on the effects of budget institutions on budget credibility and fiscal outcomes before describing how we measure the key variables of interest and our empirical strategy. We then outline and discuss our results.

LITERATURE REVIEW

In this section, we first consider the broader literature concerning the track record of PFM reforms with regard to improving budget credibility and fiscal outcomes and then focus on these same outcomes in fragile states specifically. Although most studies find evidence that a stronger PFM system is associated with a more credible budget and better fiscal outcomes, very little can be gleaned from the existing literature about the achievements of PFM reforms in fragile states.

PFM system and budget credibility

We assume that a credible budget is one that displays minimal deviation from approved allocations, in aggregate and in composition. The budgets in most low- and middle-income countries deviate considerably from budget plans recognized for some time, with Wildavsky and Caiden (1980) identifying the numerous political and technical challenges that affect the ability of poor countries to manage budgets effectively. Schick (1998) also has classified various types of harmful budgeting practices in low- and middle-income countries that contribute to unreliable budgets. These practices include unrealistic budgeting that authorizes more spending than the government can mobilize; hidden budgeting, where the real priorities are known only to a narrow clique within government; and deferred budgeting, where real spending patterns are obscured by the generation of arrears (Schick 1998, 36).

Deviating from budget plans, however, is not necessarily deliberate, with unforeseen budgetary pressures often requiring unplanned expenditures. This is ultimately due to the inherent uncertainty of budgeting. When the assumptions made during preparation of the budget do not materialize, perhaps because of a macroeconomic shock or natural disaster, difficult questions on how to choose between competing priorities can reemerge. Where budgets are overly rigid, there is a risk that spending will be locked into choices made in the past when the world looked very different. At the other extreme, where budgets are constantly remade, the whole credibility of the budget process is undermined.

The few empirical papers that explore the relationship between the quality of the PFM system and these budget deviations generally find that a better PFM system is associated with a more credible budget after controlling for other variables. Using data on expenditure deviations extracted from PEFA reports for a small sample of 45 countries, Addison (2013) finds that compositional accuracy improves with the quality of the PFM system,[1] but that the correlation between aggregate expenditure deviations and the capacity for PFM is small.[2] Using an ordered logit model and looking specifically at expenditure deviations in the health and education sectors for a sample of 73 countries, Sarr (2015) finds that a more transparent budgetary system[3] increases the likelihood of having a credible and reliable budget.[4] Similarly, Fritz, Sweet, and Verhoeven (2014) find that better PFM systems are associated with a higher rate of overall budget execution for 102 countries and with a more credible budget for 97 countries, meaning that sector allocations are aligned with original allocations. Although the sample is largest for Fritz, Sweet, and Verhoeven (2014), the model controls only for gross domestic product (GDP) per capita, which increases the likelihood of omitting key predictors, which can sometimes bias the coefficients of included variables.

PFM system and fiscal outcomes

A good PFM system is essential for achieving aggregate fiscal discipline by restraining expenditures. Theoretically, unless regulated by strong institutional arrangements, the deficit (and debt) bias inherent in the political process will lead to an unsustainable fiscal position in the form of excessive expenditures, deficits, and debt levels. This bias has been studied extensively in the literature as the product of two distinct but interrelated theoretical phenomena. The first is the common-pool resource problem (Weingast, Shepsle, and Johnsen 1981) that arises when the various decision makers involved in the budgetary process compete for public resources and fail to internalize the current and future costs of their choices. The second pertains to information asymmetry and incentive incompatibilities—the agency phenomenon—between the government and voters. This phenomenon leads to rent seeking in which politicians appropriate resources for themselves at the cost to citizens (Persson and Tabellini 2000). Strong PFM systems such as a top-down approach to planning the budget can mitigate this tendency to overspend by ensuring that the budgetary consequences of policy decisions are considered appropriately. Strong accountability mechanisms and supporting structures that comprehensively and transparently monitor and enforce budget decisions can minimize the agency problem (Hallerberg, Strauch, and von Hagen 2004; Hallerberg and von Hagen 1999; Ljungman 2009).

Although many factors affect the behavior of public finances, most of the empirical work confirms a relationship between better PFM systems and a more sustainable fiscal balance, albeit with various caveats and nuances. This evidence covers different time periods, geographic regions, and countries with varying political setups and income levels and generally involves constructing indexes of budget institutions. See Hallerberg and Yläoutinen (2010), von Hagen (1992), and von Hagen and Harden (1996) for Europe; Perotti and Kontopoulos (2002) for Organisation for Economic Co-operation and Development (OECD) countries; Alesina et al. (1999), and Filc and Scartascini (2007) for Latin America; Prakash and Cabezón (2008) for

39 Sub-Saharan African heavily indebted countries; Dabla-Norris et al. (2010) for 65 low-income and middle-income countries; and Gollwitzer (2011) for 40 African countries. Several studies explore the relationship between specific aspects of the PFM system and fiscal discipline. For example, by exploiting within-country variation for a panel of 181 countries over the period 1990–2008, Vlaicu et al. (2014) find that fiscal discipline improves after the adoption of a medium-term expenditure framework.

In contrast, Fritz, Sweet, and Verhoeven (2014), using a PEFA-based measure of the quality of the PFM system and controlling only for per capita income, find that a stronger PFM system is not associated with lower deficits for 56 countries.[5] However, the limited number of observations makes it more difficult to establish statistical relationships. In fact, the coefficient, though statistically insignificant, is negative rather than the expected positive. The lack of relationship with deficit levels may also be related to the time period, with many PEFA assessments undertaken as part of the process toward debt relief and during the global financial crisis, which has prompted larger deficits in many countries, including those with stronger PFM systems.

PFM system in fragile countries

Reforms to improve public financial management have been high on the agenda in fragile states for both governments and donors alike. Although there is a growing body of evidence that these reforms improve the quality of the PFM system (Fritz 2012; IMF 2017a; Williamson 2015), much less is known about whether these reforms achieve their ultimate objectives of improving the credibility of the budget as well as fiscal outcomes. In fact, a qualitative study of eight fragile countries found no clear relationship between overall progress made on strengthening PFM systems and processes and achievements on budget credibility (World Bank 2012). The authors conclude that outcomes like budget credibility are substantially influenced by political incentives and considerations and that these can fluctuate and change in negative directions, even where PFM systems as such are improved. In addition, although fiscal deficits have been controlled across the eight case studies, a clear caveat is that current stability does not necessarily imply long-run fiscal sustainability, because grants from development partners still play a significant role in funding public expenditures. To our knowledge, no quantitative study has looked at the relationship between the PFM system and these outcomes in fragile states.

The literature also suggests some plausible reasons why PFM reforms may not have the desired impact in fragile states:

- *Low human capacity.* The effectiveness of formal systems is likely to be weakened by the low human capacity in fragile settings. Emigration, the absence or deterioration of the education system, distorted incentives, and clientelistic appointments are likely to contribute to this low capacity. At the same time, there is great competition for the few skilled staff from other strategic areas in the government or from donors to manage in-country projects.

- *Weak physical capacity and basic operating systems and processes to make budgetary institutions function.* This feature may be heavily dependent on the nature of the conflict and the emerging political settlement. Physical infrastructure may need to be developed or rebuilt, the banking system may have extremely limited reach, and basic systems and processes may need to be established or reestablished. In Liberia, for example, human resource capacity constraints as well as power and connectivity problems hamper the functioning of the PFM system, particularly the usefulness of the Integrated Financial Management Information System.

- *Persistent parallel, informal systems and practices based on personalized arrangements.* Such systems and practices ensure that formal systems for PFM remain functionally weak, painfully slow and unreliable, illegitimate, and widely corrupted (Levi and Sacks 2009).

Following from this literature, we test the following two hypotheses.

DATA AND ANALYSIS

Measuring PFM quality

Our primary measure of the quality of PFM systems is the set of indicators developed under the PEFA initiative using the 2005 and 2011 versions of the framework. PEFA is the most comprehensive attempt thus far to construct a framework to assess the quality of budget systems and institutions across countries and over time. The 2011 framework comprises 28 indicators that assess institutional arrangements at all stages of the budget cycle, together with cross-cutting dimensions and indicators of budget credibility. Before the 2016 revision, it also included three additional indicators of donor practice. The PEFA data set, however, is not without limitations, including limited availability of time-series data; inconsistent time period of PEFA assessments (between countries and within countries); the fact that some PEFA 2011 indicators measure processes rather than PFM functionality; and potential sample selection bias, with PEFA assessments being largely donor driven. Our findings should therefore be interpreted in the context of these limitations.

We worked with a data set that included the results of 307 PEFA assessments completed in 144 countries between June 2005 and March 2017. Several countries were subsequently excluded from our sample because of limited availability of other relevant data. Our main regression models included observations ranging from 93 to 116 countries (see annex 4A for country coverage).

In order to transform PEFA scores into the dependent variable to be used in our empirical analysis, we followed a series of steps. First, we only considered indicators that cover the quality of PFM systems on the expenditure side. We therefore excluded PI-1 through PI-4, which measure PFM outcomes; indicators PI-13 to PI-15, which cover transparency and effectiveness of tax administration; and D-1 to D-3, which are donor-related indicators. This allowed us to compare our results to previous studies that have also tended to focus on expenditure management. Moreover, although the donor-related indicators are likely to affect the credibility of the budget, especially in aid-dependent countries, we excluded these indicators given data quality concerns. Second, for multidimensional indicators, we used dimension scores rather than summary indicator scores to exploit all of the information contained in the PEFA scores. This decision allowed us to avoid the downward bias introduced by the M1 scoring methodology, whereby summary indicators are based on the lowest-scoring dimension or "weakest link." Third, we converted the letter scores included in PEFA reports into numerical scores, with higher scores denoting better performance (from A = 4 to D = 1).

In addition to measuring the aggregate PFM system, we also computed measures of specific elements of the PFM system to shed light on which components

---

Hypothesis 1:
A well-functioning PFM system will increase the credibility of the budget if and only if the country is not fragile.

Hypothesis 2:
A well-functioning PFM system will improve fiscal outcomes (that is, lower budget deficits and debt ratios) if and only if the country is not fragile.

TABLE 4.1 **Summary of hypothesized links with specific public financial management (PFM) elements**

PFM ELEMENT	HYPOTHESIZED LINK WITH FISCAL DISCIPLINE AND BUDGET CREDIBILITY
Comprehensiveness and transparency	A comprehensive budget reduces the risk that public spending outside the budget could redirect resources from the approved budget, while budgetary transparency makes the common-pool problem and the agency problem less likely by increasing the degree of accountability felt by public officials.
Policy-based budgeting	The more public expenditure is well aligned with public goals, the higher the probability that the budget will respect the originally approved allocations as well as the fiscal and macroeconomic framework defined by government.
Predictability and control in budget execution	Orderly execution of the budget may strengthen fiscal management by facilitating appropriate in-year adjustment to the budget totals in accordance with the fiscal framework. Strong control arrangements may also prevent expenditures from deviating from what was planned and from leading to higher deficit or debt levels.
Accounting, recording, and reporting	Timely, adequate information on expenditure flows and debt levels strengthens the capacity of government to decide and control budget totals as well as manage long-term fiscal sustainability and affordability of policies.
External scrutiny and audit	Scrutiny of government's budget and its implementation by parliamentarians and by external audit agencies may motivate a better quality of budgetary execution as well as increase the pressure on government to consider long-term fiscal sustainability issues and to respect its targets.

of budget institutions may be most relevant for good budget execution and fiscal discipline (summarized in table 4.1), following earlier work by Dabla-Norris et al (2010) and based on the underlying hypotheses of the PEFA framework (PEFA Secretariat 2011).

Although not as comprehensive and transparent as PEFA, we used the World Bank's Country Policy and Institutional Assessment indicator 13 (CPIA-13) averaged over the period 2012–15 to test the robustness of our results. CPIA-13 measures the quality of budgetary and financial management on a six-point scale along three dimensions: (a) a comprehensive and credible budget, linked to policy priorities; (b) effective financial management systems to ensure that the budget is implemented in a controlled and predictable way; and (c) timely and accurate accounting and fiscal reporting, including audits.

Measuring fragility

Fragility is a broad term whose definition is highly contested because of its complex, multidimensional nature. Given that a key feature of fragile situations is the risk or presence of conflict, we start with a very narrow definition of fragility based on the number of battle-related deaths—a country is considered fragile if it had more than 100 battle-related casualties (Fragile 1) in any year between 2012 and 2015. We then use a broader definition of fragility (Fragile 2) and consider the countries included in the World Bank's list of fragile states between 2012 and 2015. For a given year, this list classifies countries as fragile either based on their macroeconomic administrative capacity (the World Bank's CPIA score of 3.2 or lower) or based on their capacity to deliver security (signaled by the presence of a peace-keeping or peace-building operation during the past three years). The CPIA rates countries on a set of criteria grouped in four clusters: economic management, structural reforms, policies for social inclusion and equity, and public sector management. Our choice of CPIA as a measure of fragility comes after considering several indicators of fragility used by different donor agencies and international financial institutions. The benefit given to the CPIA score is that it goes through a rigorous review process, although it reflects a degree of subjective judgment.

FIGURE 4.1

Average quality of the public financial management (PFM) system in fragile and nonfragile countries (Fragile 1)

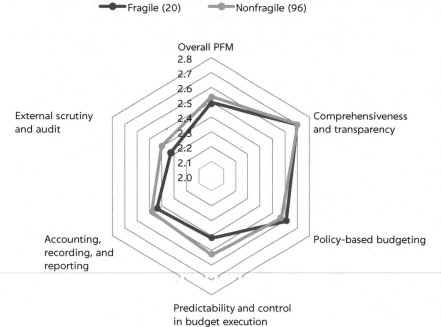

Some basic descriptive analysis of the data set is suggestive of relative strengths and weaknesses in budget institutions across fragile and nonfragile countries. As expected and in line with the findings of others (Andrews 2010), the average quality of the PFM system—both overall and specific components—is generally weaker in fragile states than in nonfragile states (as shown in figures 4.1 and 4.2). The gap between fragile and nonfragile countries is most pronounced when we use the broad definition of fragility, with the difference in means statistically significant at the 1 percent level. In general, the weakest component of the PFM system in both fragile and nonfragile countries is external scrutiny and audit, whereas the strongest component tends to be comprehensiveness and transparency.[6]

Measuring budget credibility

Aggregate budget credibility

In many countries, particularly low-income or fragile states, national budgets are often poor predictors of expenditures. Our first measure of budget credibility is based on PEFA indicator PI-1 and measures whether governments are able to plan aggregate expenditures ex ante and keep to the broad parameter during execution. According to the PEFA methodology, countries in which deviations between actual expenditures and budgeted expenditures were less than 5 percent in the last two or three years receive a score of A or 4. On the other end, countries in which deviations between actual and budgeted expenditures were greater than 15 percent in two or three of the last three fiscal years receive a D or 1.

Compositional budget credibility

Our second measure of budget credibility is based on PEFA indicator PI-2(i), which measures the extent to which reallocations between budget heads during execution have contributed to variance in the composition of expenditures. Countries get a score of A or 4 if the variance in expenditure composition was less than 5 percent in the last two or three years. On the other end, countries for which the variance in expenditure composition exceeded 15 percent in at least two of the last three years get a score of D or 1.

Measuring fiscal outcomes

Consistent with the literature, we consider two measures of fiscal discipline:

1. General government primary net lending or borrowing (percent of GDP)

2. Public external debt (percent of GDP).

We focus on the average primary balance as a preferred measure of the government's fiscal stance because it abstracts from the effect of inflation on interest payments, since interest payments are a function of accumulated debt and not the present fiscal stance. The reason to focus on debt is that primary deficits in some countries may not be driven by a systematic bias but instead may reflect temporary effects. We use official public external debt because the data on total government debt are unavailable for a large number of countries in the sample. We examine the relationship between PFM quality and these fiscal variables during the 2012–15 period, because the fiscal positions in many countries were affected by the food and fuel crisis and subsequently by the global financial crisis between 2008 and 2011.

FIGURE 4.2

Average quality of the public financial management (PFM) system in fragile and nonfragile countries (Fragile 2)

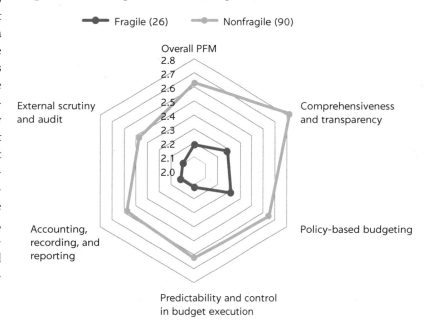

ESTIMATION APPROACH

In this section, we empirically test whether better PFM systems (as measured by PEFA) are associated with better fiscal outcomes and more reliable budgets, after controlling for relevant explanatory variables and differentiating between fragile and nonfragile countries. We estimate cross-sectional multiplicative interaction models because our hypotheses are conditional in nature—that is, we test whether "an increase in X is associated with an increase in Y when condition Z is met, but not otherwise." These interaction models are common in the quantitative social science literature because institutional arguments frequently imply that the relationship between certain inputs and outcomes varies depending on the institutional context (Brambor, Clark, and Golder 2006), or in this case, fragility.

Our model is as follows:

$$Y_i = \beta_0 + \beta_1 X_i + \beta_2 Z_i + \beta_3 X_i Z_i + \varepsilon, \qquad (4.1)$$

where i indexes countries, Y is the dependent variable of interest (average of fiscal balance or public external debt as a percentage of GDP between 2012 and 2015 or our PEFA-based measure of budget credibility), X measures the quality of the overall PFM system or PFM element (based on the country's most recent PEFA assessment), Z is a fragility dummy that equals 1 where a country is fragile and 0 otherwise, and ε is the error term. We estimate this model using ordinary least squares (OLS) because the data are cross-sectional.

It is relatively easy to see that the model presented in equation (4.1) captures the intuition behind our hypothesis. This is because, when the country is nonfragile, that is, when $Z = 0$, equation (4.1) simplifies to:

$$Y_i = \beta_0 + \beta_1 X_i + \varepsilon. \qquad (4.2)$$

In equation (4.1), β_1 captures the effect of a one-unit change in X on Y in a non-fragile state. When the country is fragile, that is, when $Z = 1$, equation (4.1) can be simplified to:

$$Y_i = \left(\beta_0 + \beta_2\right) + \left(\beta_1 + \beta_3\right) X_i + \varepsilon. \qquad (4.3)$$

In constructing these models, we follow good practice (Brambor, Clark, and Golder 2006). First, we include PFM quality (X) and fragility (Z) variables separately alongside the interaction term (XZ) in the model. Second, we do not interpret the coefficients on the constitutive terms (X and Z) as if they were unconditional marginal effects and instead compute substantively meaningful marginal effects and standard errors, that is, we estimate the coefficient on X when $Z = 0$ and when $Z = 1$ in a separate table. This is important because it is possible for the marginal effect of X on Y to be significant for different values of the modifying variable Z even if the coefficient on the interaction term is insignificant. We assume that, like previous studies, β_1 will be positive (negative) when the dependent variable is budget credibility or fiscal balance (public debt), indicating that on average better PFM quality is associated with more credible budgets or favorable fiscal outcomes in nonfragile countries. If fragility offsets this effect, we expect β_3 to have the opposite sign, and $\beta_1 + \beta_3 = 0$.

In this chapter, we also control for a larger number of variables than Fritz, Sweet, and Verhoeven (2014), adding W to equation (4.1). W refers to a series of control variables dictated by the existing literature.

$$Y_i = \beta_0 + \beta_1 X_i + \beta_2 Z_i + \beta_3 X_i Z_i + \beta_4 W_i + \varepsilon. \qquad (4.4)$$

To assess the impact of PFM quality on budget credibility, we identify other factors that may influence a country's budget credibility. On the basis of Addison (2013) and Sarr (2015), these factors include the level of GDP per capita because governments in wealthier countries can pay for better talent and better systems of control than other governments. The quality of public and civil services and the degree of their independence from political pressures can also be expected to have a significant impact on the formulation and implementation of the budget and are proxied by the government effectiveness index. Finally, we include countries' dependency on natural resource revenue and foreign aid because the volatility of these revenue sources can be expected to affect the way in which the budget is implemented.

When fiscal outcomes are the dependent variables, the selection of control variables also draws heavily on the earlier literature (Dabla-Norris et al. 2010), which serves as a benchmark to compare our results. The control variables include real economic growth (Growth) to control for economic circumstances, the log of initial GDP per capita in 2011 (Initial GDP per capita) to control for differences in economic and overall institutional development, a dummy for resource-rich countries (Resource), and a trade variable (Trade). Following Alesina et al. (1999), changes in the terms of trade (Trade) are scaled by the degree of openness of the economy, measured as the sum of exports and imports to GDP. Because in some countries tax revenues are heavily linked to export activities, we expect improvements in the terms of trade to be associated with lower deficits and debt levels and these effects to be more important for economies that are more open to international trade. Growth, terms of trade changes, and openness are measured as annual averages for the period 2012–15 to control for cyclical effects. For the Resource dummy, we use the same definition as IMF (2011), which classifies countries as resource rich if their resource rents exceed 10 percent of GDP. In our debt regressions, we control for two additional variables shown to be important in previous studies: a dummy for highly indebted poor country (HIPC), post-completion-point countries (HIPC dummy), and the initial debt-to-GDP ratio (Initial debt). The HIPC dummy controls for low-income countries that have benefited from official debt relief and, as a result, are expected to have stronger fiscal positions, while initial debt, proxied by external debt in the year prior to the beginning of the sample (2011), is included to focus on the effect of budget institutions on recent fiscal policy settings.

RESULTS

Budget credibility

Table 4.2 shows the results from estimating equation (4.4) using OLS, with aggregate budget credibility as the dependent variable in columns 1 and 2 and compositional budget credibility as the dependent variable in columns 3 and 4. As shown in the first row, we find that better PFM systems are associated with more credible budgets (aggregate and compositional) in nonfragile states, with this effect statistically

TABLE 4.2 **Cross-country ordinary least squares using budget credibility as the dependent variable**

VARIABLE	AGGREGATE BUDGET CREDIBILITY		COMPOSITIONAL BUDGET CREDIBILITY	
	(1)	(2)	(3)	(4)
PFM	0.413*	0.520**	0.520**	0.533*
	(0.208)	(0.236)	(0.218)	(0.272)
PFM* Fragile 1	−0.0314		−0.0657	
	(0.548)		(0.452)	
PFM* Fragile 2		−0.430		−0.0438
		(0.384)		(0.342)
Fragile 1	−0.178		0.00358	
	(1.299)		(0.966)	
Fragile 2		0.946		0.212
		(0.972)		(0.897)
GDP per capita (ln)	−0.226	−0.229	0.0200	0.0222
	(0.170)	(0.166)	(0.135)	(0.134)
Govt. effectiveness	0.328	0.379	0.368*	0.427*
	(0.256)	(0.250)	(0.203)	(0.227)
Resource	−0.593**	−0.601**	−0.224	−0.233
	(0.260)	(0.257)	(0.208)	(0.204)
Aid dependency	−0.00531	−0.00348	−0.00799	−0.00905
	(0.0105)	(0.0118)	(0.00898)	(0.00917)
Constant	4.196**	3.933**	0.780	0.717
	(1.707)	(1.679)	(1.400)	(1.455)
Observations	98	98	93	93
R-squared	0.194	0.196	0.239	0.238

Note: Robust standard errors are in parentheses. PFM = public financial management.
*** p<0.01, ** p<0.05, * p<0.1

significant (at the 5 percent or 10 percent level). Our estimated coefficient implies that nonfragile states that score 1.0 point higher on our measure for the quality of the aggregate PFM system will score 0.4–0.5 higher on the PEFA budget credibility indicators on average (columns 1 to 4). However, the linear combinations of the PFM coefficients calculated in table 4.3 suggest that this effect for credibility at the aggregate level generally weakens in size and loses statistical significance in fragile states (using both definitions of fragility).

However, we do find that a better PFM system is associated with better compositional budget credibility in fragile states using the broad definition of fragility, with a conditional coefficient 0.49 that is statistically significant at the 5 percent level (as shown in table 4.3).[7]

Similarly, although we generally find no significant relationship between aggregate budget credibility and five specific PFM elements in fragile states,[8] table 4.4 provides evidence of a positive and statistically significant relationship between credibility at the sectoral level and three specific elements of the PFM system in fragile states (using the broad definition of fragility, Fragile 2). The effect is largest for predictability and control in budget execution. Other things equal, better systems for ensuring predictability and control in budget execution are associated with a higher level of compositional credibility in fragile states at the 5 percent level or better, irrespective of the definition of fragility used.

TABLE 4.3 **Conditional coefficients for overall public financial management (PFM) quality in fragile states**

VARIABLE	FRAGILE 1	FRAGILE 2
Aggregate budget credibility	0.381	0.090
	(0.456)	(0.319)
Compositional budget credibility	0.455	0.490
	(0.417)	(0.227)**

Note: Conditional coefficients, with conditional standard errors given in parentheses.
** $p < 0.05$

TABLE 4.4 **Conditional coefficients for quality of specific elements of public financial management (PFM) in fragile states with compositional budget credibility as the dependent variable**

PFM ELEMENT	FRAGILE 1	FRAGILE 2
Comprehensiveness and transparency	0.054	0.374
	(0.297)	(0.159)**
Policy-based budgeting	0.301	0.522
	(0.428)	(0.226)**
Predictability and control in budget execution	0.677	0.565
	(0.303)**	(0.201)***
Accounting, recording, and reporting	0.172	0.253
	(0.350)	(0.183)
External scrutiny and audit	−0.349	−0.063
	(0.737)	(0.230)

Note: Conditional coefficients, with conditional standard errors given in parentheses. Regression results shown in annex 4C.
*** $p < 0.01$, ** $p < 0.05$

Fiscal outcomes

Table 4.5 shows the relationship between the quality of the overall PFM system and fiscal outcomes, other things equal. The primary balance is the dependent variable in columns 1 and 2, whereas public external debt is the dependent variable in columns 3 and 4.

As shown in tables 4.5 and 4.6, we find no statistically significant relationship between our PEFA-based measure of overall PFM quality and the fiscal balance in both nonfragile and fragile states.[9] This finding is in stark contrast to the results of most of the studies reviewed in this chapter. Our results are, however, in line with those of Fritz, Sweet, and Verhoeven (2014), despite our larger sample size of 116 observations and wider set of control variables. However, given the poor fit of the model, with an R^2 as low as 0.08 in column 1 of table 4.5 and with only the resource dummy statistically significant, these results should be treated with caution.

TABLE 4.5 **Cross-country ordinary least squares using fiscal outcomes as the dependent variable**

VARIABLE	PRIMARY BALANCE (% OF GDP)		PUBLIC EXTERNAL DEBT (% OF GDP)	
	(1)	(2)	(3)	(4)
PFM	−0.671	0.170	3.081**	0.642
	(0.823)	(0.571)	(1.509)	(1.149)
PFM* Fragile 1	0.824		−4.799**	
	(1.215)		(2.353)	
PFM* Fragile 2		−0.468		3.163
		(1.793)		(4.080)
Fragile 1	−2.289		9.529	
	(3.264)		(6.220)	
Fragile 2		3.668		−12.88
		(4.976)		(10.89)
Initial GDP per capita (ln)	0.305	0.828	1.097	−0.135
	(0.499)	(0.570)	(0.801)	(1.131)
Economic growth (2012–15)	−0.124	−0.0548	−0.493*	−0.593**
	(0.131)	(0.137)	(0.260)	(0.250)
Trade (2012–15)	−0.154	−0.135	−0.129	−0.124
	(0.138)	(0.138)	(0.133)	(0.163)
Resource	−2.336***	−2.638***	−1.178	−0.538
	(0.819)	(0.823)	(1.775)	(1.826)
Initial debt			0.828***	0.833***
			(0.0738)	(0.0733)
HIPC dummy			2.665	2.912*
			(1.725)	(1.626)
Constant	−0.891	−8.322	−10.10	7.390
	(4.924)	(5.508)	(7.796)	(11.76)
Observations	116	116	95	95
R-squared	0.079	0.126	0.792	0.803

Note: Robust standard errors are in parentheses. To reduce the impact of outliers, the coverage of models using debt as the dependent variable in columns 3 and 4 is limited to countries with an average external debt within two standard deviations of the average debt levels for the sample of countries. HIPC = highly indebted poor country; PFM = public financial management.
*** p<0.01, ** p<0.05, * p<0.1

When debt is the dependent variable in column 3, we find a statistically significant relationship (at the 5 percent level) between PFM quality and public external debt ratio, although the sign of the coefficient is in the opposite direction we expected. This suggests that, on average, a better PFM system is associated with higher external debt ratios in nonfragile states. These results are contrary to our hypothesis as well as the findings of previous studies like those of Dabla-Norris et al. (2010), which found that a better PFM system is associated with lower public external debt ratios. Moreover, the conditional coefficient of the PFM variable in fragile states shown in table 4.6 is negative and not significant at conventional levels, suggesting that there is no relationship between debt and PFM quality in fragile states. As shown in table 4C.1 in annex 4C, we also find that better systems for policy-based budgeting and external scrutiny and audit are associated with higher public debt ratios at the 1 percent and 5 percent levels, respectively, in nonfragile states (using the narrow definition of fragility, Fragile 1). This relationship, however, becomes negative and loses statistical significance in fragile states. The economic

TABLE 4.6 Conditional coefficients for public financial management (PFM) quality in fragile and nonfragile states with fiscal outcomes as the dependent variable

VARIABLE	FRAGILE 1	FRAGILE 2
Primary balance (% of GDP)		
Nonfragile states	−0.671	0.170
	(0.823)	(0.571)
Fragile states	0.153	−0.297
	(0.921)	(1.695)
Public external debt (% of GDP)		
Nonfragile states	3.081	0.642
	(1.509)**	(1.149)
Fragile states	−1.718	3.805
	(1.763)	(3.801)

Note: Conditional coefficients, with conditional standard errors given in parentheses.
** $p < 0.05$

TABLE 4.7 Conditional coefficients for public financial management (PFM) quality in fragile and nonfragile states using sovereign credit rating as the dependent variable

VARIABLE	FRAGILE 1	FRAGILE 2
Sovereign credit ratings without controlling for government effectiveness		
Nonfragile states	1.304	1.191
	(0.518)**	(0.467)**
Fragile states	0.602	−0.846
	(0.767)	(2.790)
Sovereign credit ratings with controlling for government effectiveness		
Nonfragile states	0.633	0.504
	(0.614)	(0.537)
Fragile states	−0.315	−1.993
	(0.846)	(3.047)

Note: Conditional coefficients, with conditional standard errors given in parentheses.
** $p < 0.05$

variables—specifically the initial debt ratio and economic growth—are consistently statistically significant at the 1 percent and 10 percent levels, respectively, which is largely in line with a priori assumptions and previous findings.

On the basis of these results, we find no evidence that better PFM systems (as measured by PEFA) go hand in hand with better fiscal outcomes (defined as larger primary balances and lower debt ratios) in nonfragile and fragile states.[10] This is also the case when we look at specific elements of the PFM system in annex 4C, table 4C.1.

However, several potential confounding factors may explain some of our counterintuitive results. We therefore estimate our baseline regressions with additional variables (controlling for having an International Monetary Fund [IMF] program because of concerns about reverse causality in table 4B.1), alternative measures of PFM quality (using de jure PEFA measure in table 4B.2 and CPIA-13 in table 4B.3), a different subset of countries (restricting the sample to PEFA assessments from 2012 onward in table 4B.4), and an alternative dependent variable (using sovereign credit rating in table 4B.5). Overall, our results are largely unchanged and do not seem to suggest a relationship between the quality of budget institutions and fiscal performance in the period following the financial crisis in both nonfragile and fragile states.

Notably, using the sovereign credit rating as the dependent variable in table 4B.5 suggests that the positive relationship between PFM quality and the public external debt ratio in nonfragile countries may be because countries with better PFM systems are more likely to convince the markets about their ability and willingness to repay their debt and as a result are able to borrow more externally relative to the size of their economy. However, this relationship between PFM quality and credit rating in nonfragile states may be spurious, with the PFM variable proxying for quality of the broader institutional environment.[11] We test this possibility by controlling for government effectiveness, which results in the conditional coefficient for PFM quality becoming insignificant in both nonfragile and fragile states, as shown in the last two rows of table 4.7.

DISCUSSION

Overall, we find mixed evidence in support of our hypothesis that fragility impairs the functioning of the PFM system. Contrary to our hypothesis, our results suggest that investing in improving the quality of the PFM system can have a positive impact even in fragile environments (as defined by the World Bank) by increasing the credibility of the budget and reducing the variance in the composition of expenditure. Controlling for other factors, better predictability and control in budget execution appear to have a strong relationship with ensuring that functional or sectoral budget allocations are implemented close to plan in both nonfragile and fragile states. Conversely, at the aggregate level, whereas a stronger PFM system is associated with a more credible budget in nonfragile states, this is not the case in fragile states.

With regard to the effects of PFM quality on fiscal outcomes, we find no evidence that the quality of the PFM system matters for the size of deficits and debt ratios in both fragile and nonfragile states. Resource dependency instead tends to be the main factor associated with larger fiscal deficits. This holds when we look at the quality of more specific elements of the PFM system. Moreover, the statistically significant, but counterintuitive, positive relationship between PFM quality and public external debt ratios found in nonfragile states is potentially because countries with better PFM systems also tend to have stronger institutions more broadly and thus are perceived as having a higher capacity to repay. This, in turn, enables them to access more external financing. We find evidence of this when we use sovereign credit rating as an alternative dependent variable and control for government effectiveness.

Our findings are largely in line with those of previous studies of a more qualitative nature, which concluded that the impact of PFM reforms in fragile states remains less than what might be hoped (World Bank 2012). This finding underscores the need to exercise caution when assuming that the outcomes associated with a well-functioning PFM system in nonfragile states will automatically be realized in conditions of fragility.

Nonetheless, our lack of evidence of a relationship between PFM quality and fiscal outcomes in both nonfragile and fragile states can potentially be attributed to several methodological limitations. The main econometric challenge in establishing a relationship between fiscal outcomes and PFM quality in the models presented above is the problem of reverse causality.[12] Reverse causality refers to the possibility that budget outcomes influence the evolution of fiscal institutions, rather than the other way around, as presumed. Further complicating matters are some limitations with using the PEFA data set to test our hypotheses. PEFA indicators do not adequately measure certain aspects of the PFM system that are perceived as important for fiscal discipline in the literature, such as the fragmentation of budgetary authority and the existence of fiscal rules or expenditure ceilings for line ministries (Dabla-Norris et al. 2010). Another critique of the 2011 PEFA framework that is relevant to this chapter is that its indicators may not be appropriate in different contexts (Andrews 2010). "Best practice for whom?" is the central question. For example, the development of a multiyear budget may not be best or even appropriate in fragile countries where it is very difficult to plan ahead over a longer period of time. A fruitful direction for future research may therefore involve enhancing the PEFA indicators with data that can be extracted from other publicly available data sources and repeating the analysis conducted in this chapter. In addition, there is the possibility that omitted variables will arise from unobservable determinants of the outcomes considered. Despite these limitations, this chapter facilitates a more nuanced understanding of the outcomes of a strong PFM system (as measured by PEFA) in fragile states, while also highlighting the challenges of relying solely on the PEFA data set to explore these complex relationships.

NEXT STEPS

Further research on the outcomes of PFM reforms in fragile environments should focus on outcomes that may be particularly relevant for fragile countries, such as improving budget execution in specific sectors or specific aspects of state building. As noted in this chapter, aggregate outcomes such as fiscal discipline and credibility of the overall budget are good starting points, but a more nuanced analysis that is tailored to the priorities of fragile states is recommended. It would be also worthwhile to focus specifically on the elements of the PFM system that are expected to be most relevant to fragile countries such as cash management. A mixed-methods approach with country case studies is recommended in order to give adequate attention to the contexts and dynamics of specific countries.

ANNEX 4A CROSS-SECTIONAL SAMPLE OF COUNTRIES BY INCOME GROUP AND DEFINITION OF FRAGILITY

TABLE 4A.1 **Cross-sectional sample of 116 countries by income group using the narrow definition of fragility**

LOW-INCOME COUNTRIES	LOWER-MIDDLE-INCOME COUNTRIES	UPPER-MIDDLE-INCOME COUNTRIES	HIGH-INCOME COUNTRIES
Fragile			
Afghanistan	Cameroon	Algeria	None
Burundi	Egypt, Arab Rep.	Colombia	
Congo, Dem. Rep.	India	Lebanon	
Mali	Iraq	Russian Federation	
Myanmar	Nigeria	Turkey	
Yemen, Rep.	Pakistan		
	Philippines		
	Thailand		
	Ukraine		
Nonfragile			
Benin	Armenia	Albania	Antigua and Barbuda
Burkina Faso	Bangladesh	Angola	Bahamas, The
Cambodia	Bhutan	Azerbaijan	Barbados
Comoros	Bolivia	Belarus	Kuwait
Ethiopia	Cabo Verde	Belize	Norway
Gambia, The	Congo, Rep.	Botswana	Oman
Guinea	Côte d'Ivoire	Brazil	Seychelles
Guinea-Bissau	Fiji	Costa Rica	St. Kitts and Nevis
Haiti	Georgia	Dominica	Trinidad and Tobago
Kenya	Ghana	Dominican Republic	
Lao PDR	Guatemala	Ecuador	
Liberia	Guyana	Grenada	
Madagascar	Honduras	Jamaica	
Malawi	Indonesia	Jordan	
Mozambique	Kiribati	Kazakhstan	
Nepal	Kyrgyz Republic	Maldives	
Rwanda	Lesotho	Mauritius	
Sierra Leone	Marshall Islands	Namibia	
Tajikistan	Mauritania	North Macedonia	
Tanzania	Micronesia, Fed. Sts.	Panama	
Togo	Moldova	Paraguay	
Uganda	Mongolia	Peru	
Zimbabwe	Morocco	Serbia	
	Nicaragua	South Africa	
	Papua New Guinea	St. Lucia	
	El Salvador	St. Vincent and the Grenadines	
	São Tomé and Príncipe	Suriname	
	Senegal	Tunisia	
	Solomon Islands	Uruguay	

continued

TABLE 4A.1, *continued*

LOW-INCOME COUNTRIES	LOWER-MIDDLE-INCOME COUNTRIES	UPPER-MIDDLE-INCOME COUNTRIES	HIGH-INCOME COUNTRIES
	Sri Lanka		
	Swaziland		
	Tonga		
	Vanuatu		
	Vietnam		
	Zambia		

Note: Income classification for the year of the most recent Public Expenditure and Financial Accountability assessment.

TABLE 4A.2 **Cross-sectional sample of 116 countries by income group using the broad definition of fragility**

LOW-INCOME COUNTRIES	LOWER-MIDDLE-INCOME COUNTRIES	UPPER-MIDDLE-INCOME COUNTRIES	HIGH-INCOME COUNTRIES
Fragile			
Afghanistan	Congo, Rep.	Angola	None
Burundi	Côte d'Ivoire		
Comoros	Georgia		
Congo, Dem. Rep.	Iraq		
Guinea	Kiribati		
Guinea-Bissau	Marshall Islands		
Haiti	Micronesia, Fed. Sts.		
Liberia	Solomon Islands		
Madagascar			
Malawi			
Mali			
Myanmar			
Nepal			
Sierra Leone			
Togo			
Yemen, Rep.			
Zimbabwe			
Nonfragile			
Benin	Armenia	Albania	Antigua and Barbuda
Burkina Faso	Bangladesh	Algeria	Bahamas, The
Cambodia	Bhutan	Azerbaijan	Barbados
Ethiopia	Bolivia	Belarus	Kuwait
Gambia, The	Cabo Verde	Belize	Norway
Kenya	Cameroon	Botswana	Oman
Lao PDR	Egypt, Arab Rep.	Brazil	Seychelles
Mozambique	Fiji	Colombia	St. Kitts and Nevis
Rwanda	Ghana	Costa Rica	Trinidad and Tobago
Tajikistan	Guatemala	Dominica	
Tanzania	Guyana	Dominican Republic	
Uganda	Honduras	Ecuador	
	India	Grenada	
	Indonesia	Jamaica	
	Kyrgyz Republic	Jordan	

continued

TABLE 4A.2, *continued*

LOW-INCOME COUNTRIES	LOWER-MIDDLE-INCOME COUNTRIES	UPPER-MIDDLE-INCOME COUNTRIES	HIGH-INCOME COUNTRIES
Nonfragile			
	Lesotho	Kazakhstan	
	Mauritania	Lebanon	
	Moldova	Maldives	
	Mongolia	Mauritius	
	Morocco	Namibia	
	Nicaragua	North Macedonia	
	Nigeria	Panama	
	Pakistan	Paraguay	
	Papua New Guinea	Peru	
	Philippines	Russian Federation	
	El Salvador	Serbia	
	São Tomé and Príncipe	South Africa	
	Senegal	St. Lucia	
	Sri Lanka	St. Vincent and the Grenadines	
	Swaziland	Suriname	
	Thailand	Tunisia	
	Tonga	Turkey	
	Ukraine	Uruguay	
	Vanuatu		
	Vietnam		
	Zambia		

Note: Income classification for the year of the most recent Public Expenditure and Financial Accountability assessment.

ANNEX 4B ROBUSTNESS CHECK

Robustness Check Controlling for Having an IMF Program

To address the possibility that fiscal outcomes may influence the quality of the PFM system, we control for a country having an IMF program between 2012 and 2015. It is highly possible that budgetary reforms are tightly linked to IMF programs that are introduced in response to fiscal performance. In that case, the quality of budget institutions could be expected to be endogenous to prior fiscal performance. We tested this possibility by including an IMF program dummy variable in the baseline models. The results are summarized in table 4B.1 and are largely unchanged from those in table 4.5.

Robustness check using quality of de jure PFM elements

To mitigate concerns about reverse causality, the working assumption in earlier papers is that budget institutions are costly to change and should therefore be more stable than fiscal outcomes—at least in the short to medium run. This assumption is likely to be stronger for de jure PFM (or procedural) elements rather than de facto elements because legal frameworks (especially when grounded in the constitution)[13] can take a long time to amend, whereas informal practices can be quickly altered. We therefore repeat the baseline regression models in table 4.1 using this de jure PFM measure, but again we generally find no statistically significant relationship between PFM quality and

TABLE 4B.1 Regression results controlling for having an International Monetary Fund program between 2012 and 2015

VARIABLE	PRIMARY BALANCE (% OF GDP)		PUBLIC EXTERNAL DEBT (% OF GDP)	
	(1)	(2)	(3)	(4)
PFM	−0.602	0.240	2.916*	0.370
	(0.802)	(0.606)	(1.605)	(1.172)
PFM* Fragile 1	0.840		−4.978**	
	(1.177)		(2.297)	
PFM* Fragile 2		−0.402		3.158
		(1.733)		(4.073)
Fragile 1	−2.344		9.986	
	(3.179)		(6.107)	
Fragile 2		3.546		−12.99
		(4.841)		(10.87)
Initial GDP per capita (ln)	0.176	0.692	1.326	0.125
	(0.603)	(0.637)	(0.938)	(1.218)
Economic growth (2012–15)	−0.138	−0.0696	−0.462*	−0.556**
	(0.131)	(0.135)	(0.277)	(0.263)
Trade (2012–15)	−0.165	−0.147	−0.118	−0.111
	(0.134)	(0.132)	(0.136)	(0.163)
Resource	−2.438***	−2.754***	−1.021	−0.326
	(0.824)	(0.824)	(1.855)	(1.874)
IMF program (2012–15)	−0.507	−0.561	0.771	0.973
	(0.876)	(0.865)	(1.185)	(1.172)
Initial debt			0.823***	0.827***
			(0.0722)	(0.0724)
HIPC dummy			2.597	2.815*
			(1.701)	(1.628)
Constant	0.367	−6.978	−12.03	5.392
	(5.983)	(5.962)	(8.677)	(12.49)
Observations	116	116	95	95
R-squared	0.082	0.130	0.793	0.804

Note: Robust standard errors are in parentheses. HIPC = highly indebted poor country; IMF = International Monetary Fund; PFM = public financial management.
*** $p<0.01$, ** $p<0.05$, * $p<0.1$

our two fiscal outcomes in fragile and nonfragile countries, except for a weak, but potentially large, relationship between debt and PFM quality (de jure) in nonfragile countries using the measure for the narrow definition of fragility in column 3 of table 4B.2.

Robustness check using CPIA-13 as an alternative measure of PFM quality

Given the limitations of the PEFA data set, specifically the fact that PEFA assessments are conducted in different years and that some indicator scores may measure improvements in form rather than PFM functionality, we consider an alternative measure of PFM quality, CPIA-13 (table 4B.3). Notably, the PEFA-based measure of overall PFM quality and the CPIA measure are highly correlated (0.7776). Although the results are mostly unchanged, we do find that better PFM quality as measured by CPIA-13 is associated with larger primary balances, although the finding is not statistically significant.

TABLE 4B.2 **Robustness check using de jure measure of public financial management (PFM) quality as the dependent variable**

VARIABLE	PRIMARY BALANCE (% OF GDP)		PUBLIC EXTERNAL DEBT (% OF GDP)	
	(1)	(2)	(3)	(4)
PFM (de jure)	−0.857	0.422	2.729*	0.400
	(1.006)	(0.639)	(1.576)	(1.407)
PFM (de jure)* Fragile 1	0.823		−3.518	
	(1.280)		(2.133)	
PFM (de jure)* Fragile 2		−1.603		2.082
		(1.984)		(3.263)
Fragile 1	−2.522		7.156	
	(3.661)		(6.231)	
Fragile 2		6.614		−10.86
		(5.905)		(9.294)
Initial GDP per capita (ln)	0.308	0.808	1.173	−0.115
	(0.490)	(0.564)	(0.824)	(1.133)
Economic growth (2012–15)	−0.129	−0.0579		−0.579**
	(0.132)	(0.135)	(0.262)	(0.244)
Trade (2012–15)	−0.159	−0.140	−0.152	−0.149
	(0.130)	(0.130)	(0.136)	(0.158)
Resource	−2.408***	−2.577***	−1.153	−0.704
	(0.845)	(0.846)	(1.941)	(1.902)
Initial debt			0.824***	0.831***
			(0.0775)	(0.0747)
HIPC dummy			2.473	2.625
			(1.807)	(1.715)
Constant	−0.171	−8.934	−10.64	7.817
	(5.503)	(5.954)	(8.100)	(12.21)
Observations	116	116	95	95
R-squared	0.083	0.132	0.789	0.800

Note: Robust standard errors are in parentheses. HIPC = highly indebted poor country; PFM = public financial management.
*** p<0.01, ** p<0.05, * p<0.1

Robustness check using PEFA assessments from 2012 onward

Our sample includes countries whose PEFA assessments were undertaken as far back as 2007. Given that these PEFA assessments may not reliably capture the recent quality of the PFM system, especially in fragile states where reversals are common, we restrict our analysis to countries whose most recent PEFA assessments are from the year 2012 onward. Our results in table 4B.4, however, remain largely unchanged when compared with those recorded in table 4.5, with no relationship between PFM quality and primary balance and a positive but weak relationship between PFM quality and public external debt ratio in nonfragile states, but not in fragile states.

Robustness check using sovereign credit rating as dependent variable

Although we do not find a statistically significant relationship between PFM quality and primary balance in table 4.5, the positive relationship between PFM quality and

TABLE 4B.3 Robustness check using Country Policy and Institutional Assessment indicator 13 (CPIA-13) as the alternative measure of overall public financial management (PFM) quality

VARIABLE	PRIMARY BALANCE (% OF GDP)		PUBLIC EXTERNAL DEBT (% OF GDP)	
	(1)	(2)	(3)	(4)
CPIA-13	0.103	0.903	1.881	0.932
	(0.716)	(0.642)	(1.132)	(0.969)
CPIA-13* Fragile 1	0.745		−1.812	
	(0.963)		(1.783)	
CPIA-13* Fragile 2		−1.909		0.415
		(1.184)		(2.932)
Fragile 1	−2.155		3.877	
	(3.762)		(6.540)	
Fragile 2		8.221*		−6.149
		(4.450)		(9.700)
Initial GDP per capita (ln)	−0.315	0.106	0.471	−0.502
	(0.484)	(0.469)	(0.831)	(1.081)
Economic growth (2012–15)	−0.107	−0.0285	−0.437*	−0.551**
	(0.120)	(0.128)	(0.244)	(0.228)
Trade (2012–15)	0.00353	−0.0245	−0.238*	−0.213
	(0.129)	(0.121)	(0.141)	(0.152)
Resource	−2.141**	−2.555***	−1.327	−0.958
	(0.893)	(0.866)	(1.919)	(1.858)
Initial debt			0.851***	0.854***
			(0.0727)	(0.0711)
HIPC dummy			1.793	2.071
			(1.878)	(1.713)
Constant	1.966	−5.198	−4.100	8.396
	(4.014)	(4.055)	(7.911)	(11.38)
Observations	122	122	104	104
R-squared	0.082	0.141	0.803	0.814

Note: Robust standard errors are in parentheses. HIPC = highly indebted poor country.
*** p<0.01, ** p<0.05, * p<0.1

public debt level is large and almost statistically significant in nonfragile states, while it appears to weaken in fragile states using the narrow definition of fragility. This counterintuitive relationship may be due to a supply-side issue—that is, countries with better PFM systems are more likely to convince the markets about their ability and willingness to honor their debt. This relationship should be reflected in better credit ratings,[14] so a logical question to ask is whether countries with better PFM systems have better ratings after controlling for other economic fundamentals.

As shown in table 4B.5, a better PFM system is associated with a higher sovereign credit rating in nonfragile states, with this relationship statistically significant at the 5 percent level using both definitions of fragility. This relationship appears to weaken and lose statistical significance for fragile countries. However, it is likely that the quality of PFM system is proxying for quality of the broader institutional environment. This is confirmed when we include a measure of government effectiveness. Nonetheless, like previous studies, we find that rating assignments are related to economic fundamentals, including initial external debt across all models, and per capita income and growth when we do not control for government effectiveness in columns 1 and 2.

TABLE 4B.4 **Robustness check using baseline models restricted to a sample of countries with Public Expenditure and Financial Accountability (PEFA) assessments from 2012 onward**

VARIABLE	PRIMARY BALANCE (% OF GDP)		PUBLIC EXTERNAL DEBT (% OF GDP)	
	(1)	(2)	(3)	(4)
PFM	−0.524	−0.524	3.419*	0.850
	(0.766)	(0.689)	(1.790)	(1.445)
PFM* Fragile 1	−1.240		−1.773	
	(1.388)		(2.018)	
PFM* Fragile 2		1.012		3.183
		(1.664)		(4.067)
Fragile 1	3.852		1.031	
	(3.408)		(5.169)	
Fragile 2		−0.903		−13.20
		(4.398)		(10.82)
Initial GDP per capita (ln)	−0.260	0.0258	1.238	0.496
	(0.504)	(0.569)	(1.175)	(1.345)
Economic growth (2012–15)	−0.166	−0.134	−0.650*	−0.737**
	(0.163)	(0.154)	(0.338)	(0.304)
Trade (2012–15)	−0.133	−0.127	−0.153	−0.142
	(0.103)	(0.103)	(0.161)	(0.185)
Resource	−3.105***	−3.132***	−0.125	0.547
	(1.015)	(0.983)	(2.549)	(2.573)
Initial debt			0.792***	0.813***
			(0.113)	(0.107)
HIPC dummy			2.086	2.955
			(2.126)	(1.810)
Constant	3.497	0.733	−10.74	2.643
	(4.987)	(5.708)	(10.78)	(13.86)
Observations	92	92	77	77
R-squared	0.139	0.157	0.742	0.762

Note: Robust standard errors are in parentheses. HIPC = highly indebted poor country; PFM = public financial management.
*** p<0.01, ** p<0.05, * p<0.1

TABLE 4B.5 **Robustness check using sovereign credit rating as the dependent variable**

VARIABLE	(1)	(2)	(3)	(4)
PFM	1.304**	1.191**	0.633	0.504
	(0.518)	(0.467)	(0.614)	(0.537)
PFM* Fragile 1	−0.702		−0.947	
	(0.912)		(1.007)	
PFM* Fragile 2		−2.037		−2.497
		(2.945)		(3.149)
Fragile 1	1.688		2.394	
	(2.133)		(2.500)	
Fragile 2		4.315		6.366
		(6.374)		(6.767)
Initial GDP per capita (ln)	1.521***	1.434**	0.903	0.764
	(0.501)	(0.594)	(0.539)	(0.625)

continued

TABLE 4B.5, *continued*

VARIABLE	(1)	(2)	(3)	(4)
Initial debt	–0.0861***	–0.0843***	–0.0972***	–0.0965***
	(0.0295)	(0.0293)	(0.0305)	(0.0302)
Economic growth (2012–15)	0.283*	0.277*	0.209	0.195
	(0.141)	(0.147)	(0.126)	(0.132)
Trade (2012–15)	–0.0139	–0.0230	–0.0509	–0.0585
	(0.0813)	(0.0948)	(0.0847)	(0.0986)
Resource	–0.429	–0.349	–0.0903	–0.0566
	(0.842)	(0.827)	(0.851)	(0.825)
HIPC dummy	0.00549	–0.151	–0.437	–0.707
	(0.671)	(0.825)	(0.727)	(0.839)
Government effectiveness			1.939**	2.160**
			(0.867)	(0.958)
Constant	–6.347	–5.307	2.050	3.714
	(4.786)	(5.609)	(5.551)	(6.345)
Observations	56	56	56	56
R-squared	0.544	0.542	0.587	0.589

Note: Robust standard errors are in parentheses. HIPC = highly indebted poor country; PFM = public financial management.
*** p<0.01, ** p<0.05, * p<0.1

ANNEX 4C REGRESSION RESULTS FOR DISAGGREGATED PUBLIC FINANCIAL MANAGEMENT (PFM) SYSTEM

TABLE 4C.1 Regression results using primary balance (% of GDP) as the dependent variable

VARIABLE	FRAGILE 1	FRAGILE 2
Comprehensiveness and transparency		
PFM 1	–0.394	0.158
	(0.712)	(0.530)
PFM 1* Fragile	0.255	–0.511
	(0.932)	(1.348)
Policy-based budgeting		
PFM 2	–0.363	0.390
	(0.905)	(0.703)
PFM 2* Fragile	0.656	–0.300
	(1.214)	(1.404)
Predictability and control in budget execution		
PFM 3	–0.351	0.201
	(0.721)	(0.559)
PFM 3* Fragile	0.104	–0.413
	(1.252)	(1.626)
Accounting, recording, and reporting		
PFM 4	–0.522	–0.148
	(0.636)	(0.446)

continued

TABLE 4C.1, *continued*

VARIABLE	FRAGILE 1	FRAGILE 2
PFM 4* Fragile	0.952	0.227
	(0.962)	(1.946)
External scrutiny and audit		
PFM 5	−0.425	0.0359
	(0.597)	(0.643)
PFM 5* Fragile	0.485	−0.745
	(1.076)	(1.740)

Note: Robust standard errors are in parentheses. PFM = public financial management.
*** p<0.01, ** p<0.05, * p<0.1

TABLE 4C.2 Regression results using public external debt (% of GDP) as the dependent variable

VARIABLE	FRAGILE 1	FRAGILE 2
Comprehensiveness and transparency		
PFM 1	0.671	−0.965
	(1.123)	(1.027)
PFM 1 * Fragile	−1.518	2.895
	(1.510)	(2.772)
Policy-based budgeting		
PFM 2	3.524***	0.391
	(1.220)	(0.919)
PFM 2 * Fragile	−5.359***	2.144
	(1.687)	(2.611)
Predictability and control in budget execution		
PFM 3	1.490	0.647
	(1.361)	(1.098)
PFM 3* Fragile	−2.074	0.642
	(1.886)	(3.679)
Accounting, recording, and reporting		
PFM 4	1.665	0.776
	(1.138)	(0.705)
PFM 4* Fragile	−1.468	2.622
	(1.506)	(3.756)
External scrutiny and audit		
PFM 5	2.032**	0.687
	(0.796)	(0.748)
PFM 5* Fragile	−5.064**	2.548
	(2.345)	(3.305)

Note: Robust standard errors are in parentheses. PFM = public financial management.
*** p<0.01, ** p<0.05, * p<0.1

TABLE 4C.3 Regression results using a narrow definition of fragility with aggregate budget credibility as the dependent variable

VARIABLE	(1)	(2)	(3)	(4)	(5)
Comprehensiveness and transparency	0.352**				
	(0.158)				
Policy-based budgeting		0.360*			
		(0.198)			
Predictability and control in budget execution			0.299		
			(0.206)		
Accounting, recording, and reporting				0.212	
				(0.162)	
External scrutiny and audit					0.112
					(0.177)
Comprehensiveness and transparency* fragile	−0.297				
	(0.402)				
Policy-based budgeting* fragile		−0.168			
		(0.552)			
Predictability and control in budget execution* fragile			0.0577		
			(0.495)		
Accounting, recording, and reporting* fragile				−0.0844	
				(0.355)	
External scrutiny and audit* fragile					0.891
					(0.630)
Fragile 1	0.531	0.166	−0.126	−0.0230	−2.371
	(0.980)	(1.333)	(1.236)	(0.914)	(1.624)
Log GDP per capita	−0.256	−0.167	−0.235	−0.274	−0.252
	(0.169)	(0.176)	(0.168)	(0.170)	(0.168)
Government effectiveness	0.373	0.353	0.330	0.411*	0.424*
	(0.251)	(0.238)	(0.274)	(0.243)	(0.249)
Resource	−0.620**	−0.584**	−0.603**	−0.635**	−0.576**
	(0.254)	(0.261)	(0.253)	(0.267)	(0.272)
Aid dependency	−0.00512	−0.00269	−0.00652	−0.00788	−0.00747
	(0.0106)	(0.0102)	(0.0110)	(0.0101)	(0.0105)
Constant	4.578***	3.804**	4.583***	5.192***	5.254***
	(1.669)	(1.861)	(1.712)	(1.549)	(1.636)
Observations	98	98	98	98	98
R-squared	0.198	0.192	0.184	0.180	0.181

Note: Robust standard errors are in parentheses.
*** $p<0.01$, ** $p<0.05$, * $p<0.1$

TABLE 4C.4 **Regression results using a broad definition of fragility with aggregate budget credibility as the dependent variable**

VARIABLE	(1)	(2)	(3)	(4)	(5)
Comprehensiveness and transparency	0.304				
	(0.186)				
Policy-based budgeting		0.217			
		(0.268)			
Predictability and control in budget execution			0.389*		
			(0.222)		
Accounting, recording, and reporting				0.309*	
				(0.172)	
External scrutiny and audit					0.271
					(0.201)
Comprehensiveness and transparency* fragile	−0.0272				
	(0.296)				
Policy-based budgeting* fragile		0.281			
		(0.416)			
Predictability and control in budget execution* fragile			−0.441		
			(0.367)		
Accounting, recording, and reporting* fragile				−0.415	
				(0.320)	
External scrutiny and audit* fragile					−0.686
					(0.419)
Fragile 2	−0.0525	−0.860	0.878	0.808	1.447
	(0.782)	(1.195)	(0.922)	(0.782)	(1.002)
Log GDP per capita	−0.248	−0.179	−0.253	−0.292*	−0.210
	(0.169)	(0.170)	(0.164)	(0.169)	(0.174)
Government effectiveness	0.361	0.318	0.369	0.437*	0.446*
	(0.255)	(0.247)	(0.269)	(0.246)	(0.247)
Resource	−0.619**	−0.624**	−0.615**	−0.649**	−0.697***
	(0.257)	(0.262)	(0.247)	(0.255)	(0.249)
Aid dependency	−0.00363	0.00101	−0.00405	−0.00464	−0.00241
	(0.0122)	(0.0121)	(0.0119)	(0.0120)	(0.0109)
Constant	4.623***	4.260**	4.497***	5.094***	4.497**
	(1.653)	(1.861)	(1.627)	(1.551)	(1.748)
Observations	98	98	98	98	98
R-squared	0.190	0.188	0.189	0.189	0.193

Note: Robust standard errors are in parentheses.
*** p<0.01, ** p<0.05, * p<0.1

TABLE 4C.5 Regression results using a narrow definition of fragility with compositional budget credibility as the dependent variable

VARIABLE	(1)	(2)	(3)	(4)	(5)
Comprehensiveness and transparency	0.464***				
	(0.175)				
Policy-based budgeting		0.178			
		(0.201)			
Predictability and control in budget execution			0.593***		
			(0.196)		
Accounting, recording, and reporting				0.396**	
				(0.168)	
External scrutiny and audit					0.0551
					(0.183)
Comprehensiveness and transparency* fragile	−0.410				
	(0.333)				
Policy-based budgeting* fragile		0.123			
		(0.465)			
Predictability and control in budget execution* fragile			0.0034		
			(0.340)		
Accounting, recording, and reporting* fragile				−0.224	
				(0.385)	
External scrutiny and audit* fragile					−0.404
					(0.740)
Fragile 1	0.927	−0.487	−0.419	0.415	0.838
	(0.793)	(1.102)	(0.706)	(0.829)	(1.822)
Log GDP per capita	−0.0185	0.0282	0.0228	−0.0442	−0.0196
	(0.134)	(0.149)	(0.135)	(0.136)	(0.142)
Government effectiveness	0.418**	0.475**	0.259	0.435**	0.550***
	(0.198)	(0.197)	(0.212)	(0.192)	(0.201)
Resource	−0.253	−0.237	−0.205	−0.284	−0.290
	(0.205)	(0.208)	(0.200)	(0.211)	(0.223)
Aid dependency	−0.00759	−0.00865	−0.00979	−0.0110	−0.0106
	(0.00868)	(0.0100)	(0.00937)	(0.00936)	(0.00975)
Constant	1.207	1.644	0.562	1.731	2.441*
	(1.325)	(1.599)	(1.445)	(1.229)	(1.391)
Observations	93	93	93	93	93
R-squared	0.253	0.205	0.272	0.241	0.198

Note: Robust standard errors are in parentheses.
*** $p<0.01$, ** $p<0.05$, * $p<0.1$

TABLE 4C.6 **Regression results using a broad definition of fragility with compositional budget credibility as the dependent variable**

VARIABLE	(1)	(2)	(3)	(4)	(5)
Comprehensiveness and transparency	0.428*				
	(0.224)				
Policy-based budgeting		0.0437			
		(0.264)			
Predictability and control in budget execution			0.612***		
			(0.226)		
Accounting, recording, and reporting				0.410**	
				(0.193)	
External scrutiny and audit					0.0744
					(0.230)
Comprehensiveness and transparency* fragile	−0.0536				
	(0.267)				
Policy-based budgeting* fragile		0.478			
		(0.365)			
Predictability and control in budget execution* fragile			−0.0471		
			(0.282)		
Accounting, recording, and reporting* fragile				−0.157	
				(0.249)	
External scrutiny and audit* fragile					−0.137
					(0.325)
Fragile 2	0.245	−1.219	0.200	0.397	0.341
	(0.744)	(1.042)	(0.710)	(0.622)	(0.834)
Log GDP per capita	−0.00777	0.0220	0.0261	−0.0530	−0.0146
	(0.137)	(0.150)	(0.134)	(0.139)	(0.145)
Government effectiveness	0.462**	0.458**	0.326	0.488**	0.575**
	(0.223)	(0.226)	(0.231)	(0.228)	(0.221)
Resource	−0.239	−0.287	−0.225	−0.275	−0.286
	(0.205)	(0.206)	(0.197)	(0.206)	(0.210)
Aid dependency	−0.00977	−0.00520	−0.0100	−0.0116	−0.0106
	(0.00896)	(0.00944)	(0.00939)	(0.00956)	(0.00969)
Constant	1.199	2.032	0.474	1.773	2.334
	(1.373)	(1.697)	(1.418)	(1.240)	(1.523)
Observations	93	93	93	93	93
R-squared	0.244	0.212	0.268	0.240	0.195

Note: Robust standard errors are in parentheses.
*** p<0.01, ** p<0.05, * p<0.1

NOTES

1. An index of PFM capacity was constructed as an average of the 24 PEFA indicators in dimensions 2 through 6.
2. Controls for drivers of the common-pool behavior as well as political institutions.
3. This transparency is measured using the Open Budget Survey.
4. Controls for GDP per capita, population size, government effectiveness, level of democracy, centralization of the budget process, strength of the legislature, and dependency on oil and foreign aid.
5. The fiscal balance is calculated as a three-year forward average beginning the year of the country's first PEFA score.
6. The exception is fragile countries using the broad definition of fragility, with the average score for policy-based budgeting (average of 2.32) being slightly higher than the average score for comprehensiveness and transparency (average of 2.28).
7. This is not due to the slightly smaller sample size when compositional budget credibility is the dependent variable instead of aggregate budget credibility. We test this by running the models again on the same sample.
8. Results not shown.
9. Our results are unchanged when we include regional dummies as well as a democracy measure.
10. This holds when we exclude three countries (Fiji, Lebanon, and Myanmar) whose PEFA assessments are missing scores for 10 or more dimensions.
11. The relationship between institutional quality and repayment capacity is well established in the literature and is a key assumption underlying the debt sustainability framework of the IMF and World Bank (IMF 2017b).
12. Alesina and Perotti (1996), Knight and Levinson (2000), Perotti and Kontopoulos (2002), and Stein, Talvi, and Grisanti (1999) discuss the difficulties in dealing with this problem of reverse causality.
13. Andrews (2010) made this distinction between de jure and de facto elements of the PFM system.
14. Our credit ratings variable is the most dominant sovereign rating on foreign currency long-term debt between 2012 and 2015. The alphabetical ratings are converted into numerical ratings using a simple alphabetical ranking with D (Default) = 1 and AAA (Aaa for Moody's) = 22, with a higher credit rating indicating a better rating.

REFERENCES

Addison, D. 2013. "The Quality of Budget Execution and Its Correlates." Policy Research Working Paper 6657, World Bank, Washington, DC.

Alesina, A., R. Haussman, R. Hommes, and E. Stein. 1999. "Budget Institutions and Fiscal Performance in Latin America." *Journal of Development Economics* 59 (2): 253–73. https://doi.org/10.1016/S0304-3878(99)00012-7.

Alesina, A., and R. Perotti. 1996. "Budget Deficits and Budget Institutions." NBER Working Paper 5556, May. https://www.nber.org/papers/w5556.

Andrews, M. 2010. "How Far Have Public Financial Management Reforms Come in Africa?" Faculty Research Working Paper, Harvard Kennedy School, Cambridge, MA.

Boyce, J. K., and M. O'Donnell. 2007. "Peace and the Public Purse: Economic Policies for Postwar Statebuilding." Political Economy Research Institute, University of Massachusetts Amherst.

Brambor, T., W. R. Clark, and M. Golder. 2006. "Understanding Interaction Models: Improving Empirical Analyses." *Political Analysis* 14 (1): 63–82.

Dabla-Norris, E., R. Allen, L. F. Zanna, T. Prakash, E. Kvintradze, V. Lledo, I. Yackovlev, and S. Gollwitzer. 2010. "Budget Institutions and Fiscal Performance in Low-Income Countries." IMF Working Paper 10/80, International Monetary Fund, Washington, DC.

Deléchat, C., E. Fuli, D. Glaser, G. Ramirez, and R. Xu. 2015. "Exiting from Fragility in Sub-Saharan Africa: The Role of Fiscal Policies and Fiscal Institutions." IMF Working Paper 15/268, International Monetary Fund, Washington, DC.

Filc, G., and C. Scartascini. 2007. "Budget Institutions." In *The State of Reform*, edited by Eduardo Lora. Stanford University Press.

Fritz, V. 2012. "Strengthening PFM in Postconflict Countries: Lessons for PFM Practitioners and Country Programming Staff." PREM Note 1, World Bank, Washington, DC.

Fritz, V., S. Sweet, and M. Verhoeven. 2014. "Strengthening Public Financial Management: Exploring Drivers and Effects." Policy Research Working Paper 7084, World Bank, Washington, DC. http:// documents.worldbank.org/curated/en/349071468151787835 /Strengthening-public-financial- management-exploring-drivers-and-effects.

Gelbard, E., C. Deléchat, U. Jacoby, M. Pani, M. Hussain, G. Ramirez, R. Xu, E. Fuli, and D. Mulaj. 2015. "Building Resilience in Sub-Saharan Africa's Fragile States." International Monetary Fund, Washington, DC.

Ghani, A., C. Lockhart, and M. Carnahan. 2005. "Closing the Sovereignty Gap: An Approach to State-Building." ODI Working Paper 253, Overseas Development Institute, London.

Gollwitzer, S. 2011. "Budget Institutions and Fiscal Performance in Africa." *Journal of African Economies* 20 (1): 111–52.

Hallerberg, M., R. Strauch, and J. von Hagen. 2004. "The Design of Fiscal Rules and Forms of Governance in European Union Countries." ECB Working Paper 419, European Central Bank, Frankfurt.

Hallerberg, M., and J. von Hagen. 1999. "Electoral Institutions, Cabinet Negotiations, and Budget Deficits within the European Union." In *Fiscal Institutions and Fiscal Performance*, edited by J. Poterba and J. von Hagen, 209–32. Chicago: University of Chicago Press.

Hallerberg, M., and S. Yläoutinen. 2010. "Political Power, Fiscal Institutions, and Budgetary Outcomes in Central and Eastern Europe." *Journal of Public Policy* 30 (1): 45–62. https://www.jstor.org/stable/40783567.

IMF (International Monetary Fund). 2011. *Regional Economic Outlook: Sub-Saharan Africa*. Washington, DC: International Monetary Fund.

——. 2017a. "Building Fiscal Capacity in Fragile States." IMF Policy Paper, International Monetary Fund, Washington, DC.

——. 2017b. "Review of the Debt Sustainability Framework in Low-Income Countries: Proposed Reforms." IMP Policy Paper, International Monetary Fund, Washington, DC.

Knight, B., and A. Levinson. 2000. "Fiscal Institutions in U.S. States." In *Institutions, Politics, and Fiscal Policy*, edited by R. R. Strauch and J. von Hagen, 167–87. Part of the ZEI Studies in European Economics and Law book series (ZEIS, volume 2). Boston: Springer.

Levi, M. and A. Sacks. 2009. "Legitimating Beliefs: Sources and Indicators." *Regulation and Governance* 3: 311–33.

Ljungman, G. 2009. "Top-Down Budgeting: An Instrument to Strengthen Budget Management." IMF Working Paper 09/243, International Monetary Fund, Washington, DC.

PEFA (Public Expenditure and Financial Accountability) Secretariat. 2011. *Public Financial Management Performance Measurement Framework*. Washington, DC: PEFA Secretariat. https://pefa.org/sites/default/files/PMFEng-finalSZreprint04-12_1.pdf.

Perotti, R., and Y. Kontopoulos. 2002. "Fragmented Fiscal Policy." *Journal of Public Economics* 86 (2): 191–222.

Persson , T., and G. Tabellini. 2000. *Political Economics: Explaining Economic Policy*. Cambridge, MA: MIT Press.

Prakash, T., and E. Cabezón. 2008. "Public Financial Management and Fiscal Outcomes in Sub-Saharan African Heavily-Indebted Poor Countries." IMF Working Paper 08/217, International Monetary Fund, Washington, DC.

Pritchett, L., and F. de Veijer. 2011. "Fragile States: Stuck in a Capability Trap?" Background paper for the *World Development Report 2011*, World Bank, Washington, DC.

Sarr, B. 2015. "Credibility and Reliability of Government Budgets: Does Fiscal Transparency Matter?" IBP Working Paper, International Budget Partnership, Washington, DC.

Schick, A. 1998. *A Contemporary Approach to Public Expenditure Management*. Washington, DC: World Bank.

Stein, E., E. Talvi, and A. Grisanti. 1999. "Institutional Arrangements and Fiscal Performance: The Latin American Experience." In *Fiscal Institutions and Fiscal Performance*, edited by J. M. Poterba and J. von Hagen, 103–34. National Bureau of Economic Research.

Vlaicu, R., M. Verhoeven, F. Grigoli, and Z. Mills. 2014. "Multiyear Budgets and Fiscal Performance: Panel Data Evidence." *Jounal of Public Economics* 111 (March): 79–95.

von Hagen, J. 1992. *Budgeting Procedures and Fiscal Performance in the European Communities.* Economic Paper 96, Commission of the European Communities, Directorate-General for Economic and Financial Affairs.

von Hagen, J., and I. Harden. 1996. "Budget Processes and Commitment to Fiscal Discipline." IMF Working Paper 96/78, International Monetary Fund, Washington, DC.

Weingast, B., K. Shepsle, and C. Johnsen. 1981. "The Political Economy of Benefits and Costs: A Neoclassical Approach to Distributive Politics." *Journal of Political Economy* 89 (4): 642–64.

Wildavsky, A., and N. Caiden. 1980. *Planning and Budgeting in Poor Countries.* Piscataway, NJ: Transaction Publishers.

Williamson, T. 2015. *Change in Challenging Contexts: How Does It Happen?* London: ODI.

World Bank. 2011a. "Liberia: Integrated Public Financial Management Reform Project." World Bank, Washington, DC.

——. 2011b. *World Development Report 2011: Conflict, Security, and Development.* Washington, DC: World Bank.

——. 2012. *Public Financial Management Reforms in Post-Conflict Countries: Synthesis Report.* Washington, DC: World Bank.

5 PFM and Perceptions of Corruption

CATHAL LONG

International development institutions frequently prescribe improving public financial management (PFM) as part of the response to lowering corruption levels in low- and middle-income countries. But to date there has been little cross-country analysis on whether better PFM is associated with lower levels of corruption. This chapter investigates the relationship between PFM and corruption using the most widely available cross-country measures of both. We use measures from Public Expenditure and Financial Accountability (PEFA) assessments to construct indexes for transparency and controls in public expenditure. We find statistically significant relationships between all of our indexes and perceptions-based measures of corruption, but stronger relationships and more evidence for controls. We also find that the estimated relationships are small compared with other determinants of corruption, particularly economic growth. This finding is in line with the findings of others.

INTRODUCTION

Perspectives on corruption vary. For many, particularly those working in international development, corruption is a constraint on economic growth and development because it results in the inefficient allocation of a country's own resources and limits the quantity of resources that the country can attract from abroad, either through foreign aid or through investment. This view frequently leads to a policy prescription of institution building. As a result, aid agencies have spent large sums supporting the betterment of PFM institutions in low- and middle-income countries, based on an understanding that this institutional development will increase government transparency and accountability, reduce opportunities for corruption, and allow for more and better spending, ultimately resulting in development progress. Domestic actors also frequently include improving PFM as part of their anticorruption strategies. The fact that countries with higher measured PFM performance have lower measured corruption is often used as evidence to support this view and justify an institution-building approach to international development (Dorotinsky and Pradhan 2007). However, it is equally plausible that causation runs in the opposite direction. Some scholars hypothesize that development progress itself, through the emergence of a market-based economy, gives rise to demands for better institutions, leading to declining levels of measured corruption. Others point to a coevolutionary process in which markets and institutions mutually adapt to one another (Ang 2017).

Moreover, measures of both corruption and PFM are hotly disputed. Various problems are associated with measuring corruption, most notably the fact that it is difficult to observe and therefore measures tend to be based on perceptions. Measures of PFM are also the subject of much criticism, for sometimes emphasizing the measurement of form over function (see chapter 2 for further discussion). Regardless, both sets of measures remain influential, particularly with respect to developing donor-funded programs of technical assistance for institution building. This chapter reviews some of the hypothesized links between PFM and corruption and whether they are borne out empirically, using data from PEFA assessments and various corruption indexes and controlling for other determinants of corruption. Our findings suggest that expenditure controls are more important for combating corruption than PFM reforms related to transparency in budgeting, reporting, and audit.

The chapter proceeds as follows. We begin by reviewing the literature on PFM and corruption, developing hypotheses for testing, and providing an overview of the data on corruption and PFM and their empirical relationships. We then outline the methodology for estimating the relationship between corruption and PFM using these data, discuss other determinants of corruption to be used in the model, and present the results from our estimation models. We conclude with further discussion and conclusions regarding our results.

LITERATURE REVIEW

The most widely accepted definition of corruption is "the abuse of public office for private gain" (IMF Staff Team 2016). However, this definition is very broad. Andvig and Fjeldstad (2000) distinguish between "bureaucratic corruption"[1] and "political corruption." Nevertheless, even within the category of bureaucratic corruption, activities may range from the solicitation of bribes by police officers to the embezzlement of large sums of money by government officials through creative accounting.[2] Although activities are illegal in most countries, political corruption can encompass both illegal and legal activities (Khan 2006). In the extreme case of state capture, the law-making process itself can become perverted (IMF Staff Team 2016). More common examples of legal corruption include the allocation of rents to political constituencies through the budget process in the form of pork-barrel projects (Ware et al. 2007) or through preferential regulation and land allocation (Khan 2006). Political corruption is also distinguishable from bureaucratic corruption in its relationship with campaign financing (Tanzi 1998).

In many countries, public spending and the public sector are synonymous with corruption. The PFM system itself presents opportunities for corruption (Dorotinsky and Pradhan 2007). As a result, many low- and middle-income countries and donors view strengthening the PFM system as an anticorruption strategy (Fritz, Verhoeven, and Avenia 2017).

The PFM system provides opportunities for corruption

Most corruption takes place during the budget execution stage of the budget cycle, where resources actually flow and assets change hands (Dorotinsky and

TABLE 5.1 **Examples of corruption, by type of government expenditure**

CATEGORY	EXAMPLES OF CORRUPTION
Wages	Ghost employees, nepotism, absenteeism
Goods and services	Contract steering, collusion, fraudulent invoices, payment for goods and services not received, theft of government supplies
Capital expenditures	Favoritism in payments or contract awards, use of substandard materials or practices in construction, collusive pricing, underpricing of bids and use of change orders to raise cost, theft of stocks
Transfers	Transfers to unauthorized, fictitious, or deceased individuals, transfers of less than approved levels and pocketing of the difference, kickbacks, favoritism in approving eligibility

Source: Dorotinsky and Pradhan 2007.

Pradhan 2007). One way of thinking about corruption in public expenditure is to consider the types of expenditure and the corrupt practices associated with each (table 5.1). But what happens at the budget formulation stage also matters for corruption.[3] Weak budget formulation allows for the development of faulty practices, such as open-ended budgeting, which present problems for budget execution and opportunities for corruption later in the budget cycle (Schiavo-Campo and Tomasi 1999).

In contrast, the reporting and audit stages of the budget cycle are frequently held up as effective anticorruption strategies because they increase the probability of detection and therefore act as disincentives to engage in corruption in the first instance (see, for example, Johnsøn, Taxell, and Zaum 2012; Rocha Menocal and Taxell 2015). Accounting and reporting do not generally offer direct opportunities for engaging in corruption,[4] but lack of accurate and timely reports on revenue and expenditure reduce the probability of detecting it. Similarly, delays or political interference in external audit and oversight limit the possibilities for detecting and punishing corruption.

Strengthening PFM as an anticorruption strategy

Although strengthening PFM as an anticorruption strategy has some sound theoretical underpinnings, the evidence base is limited (French 2013). Reform of the PFM system can reduce opportunities for corruption in two broad ways: directly, by introducing controls that reduce opportunities for corruption (often by minimizing the discretion of politicians and bureaucrats), or indirectly, by increasing the probability of detection and punishment (often by increasing transparency). We discuss each in turn and develop testable hypotheses for the relationships between PFM and corruption.

"Sunlight is said to be the best of disinfectants"

The oft-quoted statement, by U.S. Supreme Court Justice Louis D. Brandeis, captures the essence of the argument for greater transparency in public finances: transparency enables citizens to hold governments accountable. The International Monetary Fund (IMF) considers fiscal transparency—which it defines as "the comprehensiveness, clarity, reliability, timeliness, and relevance of public reporting on the past, present, and future state of public finances"—as "critical for effective fiscal management and accountability."[5] Similarly, the PEFA Secretariat (2011) considers transparency to be a desirable cross-cutting feature of the PFM system and budget cycle. From an anticorruption perspective, it is useful to consider transparency in budget preparation, transparency in the reporting of budget execution, and transparency in the auditing of public expenditures.

Transparency in budget preparation

There is relatively little evidence to support the hypothesized link between budget transparency and corruption, particularly with respect to low- and middle-income countries (French 2013). Moreover, what studies exist tend to establish a statistically significant association rather than a causal link (de Renzio and Wehner 2015). Furthermore, they tend to focus on budget transparency with respect to the entire PFM cycle rather than on budget preparation specifically. Finally, they estimate the relationship between transparency and perceptions-based measures of corruption rather than actual corruption. The problems associated with using perceptions-based measures of corruption are discussed in the next section.

Hameed (2005) finds that fiscal transparency has a positive and statistically significant effect on controlling corruption.[6] However, the effect is quite small following the introduction of other controls,[7] and the sample size is small (56 countries) and limited in coverage for low- and middle-income countries. Moreover, further estimations using four subindexes of the composite fiscal transparency indicator find that only the indicator for medium-term budgeting is statistically significant, whereas the subindex more closely related to budget transparency is not. Bastida and Benito (2007) find a negative relationship between budget transparency and corruption, but their sample is limited to 41 predominantly higher-income countries. Martí and Kasperskaya (2015) find that the correlation between budget transparency and corruption[8] decreases in size and is statistically insignificant once segmented by economic development. They conclude, "Countries with similar governance perception scores show different patterns of PFM practices, suggesting that there is no one-size-fits-all approach," although they acknowledge the limitations of their sample size (49 countries).

Bellver and Kaufmann (2005) use an institutional transparency index to estimate a statistically significant effect on reducing corruption[9] that is robust to the inclusion of other controls[10] for a large sample (104) of countries. However, although their measure of institutional transparency includes measures of budget transparency,[11] it also includes numerous other measures of transparency. Using the same measure of transparency as Bellver and Kaufmann (2005), Lindstedt and Naurin (2010) find that the effects of transparency on corruption are conditional on press freedom and democracy.

Building on this literature, our first hypothesis tests whether a cross-country relationship exists between transparency in budget preparation and corruption.

Transparency in budget execution reporting

Of course, governments may say they are going to do one thing and then do another. Budgets in poor countries are characterized by a lack of credibility (Simson and Welham 2014). Martinez-Vazquez, Boex, and Arze del Granado (2004) note that corruption is particularly prevalent when oversight by the legislature and civil society is limited.

Perhaps more than any other study, Reinikka and Svensson (2011) make the case for the effect on corruption of transparency in budget execution reporting. Their study established a plausible causal effect of increased transparency—in the form of reporting disbursements to primary schools through newspapers—on a reduction of funds captured by local government bureaucrats. The study simultaneously made the case for Public Expenditure Tracking Surveys (PETSs) and likely influenced the

---

Hypothesis 1:
Countries with a more transparent and orderly budget process will have lower levels of corruption.

inclusion of the PI-23 indicator, which measures the availability of information on resources received by service delivery units, in the PEFA framework.

However, this is something of a special case, whereby the link between government spending (by local officials) and those affected (pupils, their parents, and head teachers) was very tangible. More common forms of budget execution reporting are in-year budget reports (measured by PI-24) and annual financial statements (measured by PI-25), which tend to be less specific in nature and may be less digestible to broad groups of stakeholders.[12] Using a transparency index that measures the frequency with which governments update economic data that they make available to the public, Islam (2006) finds that countries with better information flows also govern better.[13]

Our second hypothesis builds on this latter strand of literature by examining whether a cross-country relationship exists between transparency in budget execution reporting and corruption.

Hypothesis 2:
Countries with more transparent budget execution reporting will have lower levels of corruption.

Transparency in external auditing

Of course, whether transparency creates the necessary accountability between government and citizens depends on the latter using the information to hold government to account. According to Heald (2006), "For transparency to be effective, there must be receptors capable of processing, digesting, and using the information. . . . It is possible for an organization to be open about its documents and procedures yet not be transparent to relevant audiences if the information is perceived as incoherent." He further notes, "The expected benefits [may] not materialize because the receptors have been disabled by overload and/or government spin." One way in which this "transparency illusion" might be bridged is through more specialized surveillance—namely, through an independent audit function.

Ex post review through external audit is a means by which institutions with technical expertise can hold government accountable for its performance and use of resources. Generally, this role is carried out by a supreme audit institution,[14] which typically reports to the legislature. The theoretical link between auditing and corruption is straightforward. Audits increase the probability that corruption will be detected, thereby increasing the ex ante cost of engaging in corrupt activities, assuming that corrupt practices are sanctioned. However, the evidence for the impact of audit on corruption is context specific. In contrast to most of the cross-country literature on PFM and corruption discussed thus far, studies on the impact of audit on corruption generally take the form of researchers focusing on a particular sector in a specific country and using a measure of actual corruption, similar to the study by Reinikka and Svensson (2011).

Di Tella and Schargrodsky (2003) find that a large increase in audit intensity, during an anticorruption crackdown, was associated with a 15 percent decline in input prices paid by hospitals in Buenos Aires.[15] Lagunes (2017) finds that Peruvian districts subject to monitoring by both civil society and the supreme audit institution spent 51.39 percent less in the execution of public works than comparable districts that were less scrutinized. This contrasts with the findings of Olken (2007), who finds that grassroots monitoring of corruption has limited impact on corruption in Indonesian village road projects, but that increasing the probability of external audits from 4 percent to 100 percent reduced missing expenditures[16] by 8.5 percentage points, from 27.7 percent to 19.2 percent. He suggests that the effect was not larger because 100 percent probability of audit does not translate into 100 percent probability of detection and punishment and further suggests that providing audit results to the public, who can then use them in making their electoral choices, may be a useful complement to formal punishments.

A study by Ferraz and Finan (2008) examines the effect on municipal electoral outcomes when something much like Olken's suggestion was implemented in Brazil. They find that the dissemination of audit reports revealing corrupt practices to the general media reduced the likelihood of incumbent mayors being reelected. Two and three violations associated with corruption reduced the likelihood of reelection by 7 percent and 14 percent, respectively. Furthermore, they find that, in the presence of a local radio station, the effect on incumbents' likelihood of reelection was reduced further in the presence of corruption and increased in the absence of corruption. The random nature of the timing of the audits, both before and after the elections, allowed them to establish a plausible causal link between the revelations of corruption in the reports and the election outcomes.

In contrast to the more precise nature of these studies, PEFA indicators of the audit function tend to be more broad based. Nevertheless, they are sufficient to construct a hypothesis around the relationship between a more transparent audit function and corruption.

> **Hypothesis 3:**
> Countries with more transparent external audit institutions will have lower levels of corruption.

Controls limit discretion and reduce opportunities for corruption

Weak regulatory and control environments offer the best opportunities for corruption in public spending (Dorotinsky and Pradhan 2007). It is therefore not surprising that sequencing strategies for PFM reform such as the "platform approach" recommend establishing the integrity of very basic data and control systems (such as payroll and procurement) before undertaking more complex reforms (Brooke 2003).

Ware et al. (2007) describe public procurement as "a perennial challenge" from a corruption standpoint because of its specific characteristics. Public procurement expenditures, such as public investments or contracts for the supply of goods and services, are typically low-volume but high-value transactions. This characteristic makes public procurement an attractive arena for corrupt individuals, because bribes are generally extracted as a percentage of the contract. Furthermore, public procurement is frequently characterized by high levels of discretion, both in terms of politicians' discretion over the location of investments and bureaucrats' discretion over the award and management of the related contracts. Moreover, these problems are exacerbated further in low- and middle-income countries where the private sector is more dependent on public procurement. Using PEFA indicators and firm-level survey responses, Knack, Biletska, and Kacker (2017) find that firms pay less in kickbacks in countries with better procurement systems.

Although payroll and welfare abuses present potentially lower monetary incentives for corruption, human resource systems in low- and middle-income countries are frequently plagued by nepotism, ghost workers, and absenteeism. Reforms in this area are typically related to creating better links between personnel systems, social welfare systems, and payment systems, which is often the equivalent of enforcing data sharing across government entities. Gupta et al. (2017) present evidence from case studies in Ghana on the number of ghost workers and in India on the power of digitalization to reduce corruption in welfare benefits.

> **Hypothesis 4:**
> Countries that more closely adhere to best practice in budget execution controls will have lower levels of corruption.

Our final hypothesis considers the relationship between budget execution controls and corruption.

In the next section, we outline the data we use to test these hypotheses and discuss their strengths and limitations with respect to investigating the relationships between PFM and corruption.

DATA AND ANALYSIS

As with previous research on the determinants of corruption, our study is constrained by the absence of comparable cross-country data on actual corruption. Like others, we rely on perceptions-based indicators of corruption. The primary data source we use for our dependent variable is from the World Bank's Worldwide Governance Indicators for control of corruption (hereafter the WGI_COC). Our data on PFM performance come from PEFA assessments. Both data sets have important limitations with respect to how well they represent the hypotheses outlined in the previous section. We discuss these limitations in more detail below.

The WGI_COC "captures perceptions of the extent to which public power is exercised for private gain, including both petty and grand forms of corruption, as well as 'capture' of the state by elites and private interests."[17] It is constructed using 16 questions from 7 representative sources and 27 questions from 15 nonrepresentative sources. Sources include surveys of households and firms such as the Afrobarometer survey and the Gallup World Poll and expert opinions from commercial providers of business information (for example, the Economist Intelligence Unit), nongovernmental organizations (for example, Freedom House), and public sector organizations (for example, the African Development Bank). Questions vary with respect to their direct relevance to PFM. For example, although the WGI_COC indicator includes a measure related to the diversion of public funds (from World Economic Forum 2017), it also includes more general questions, for example, on whether corruption among government officials is perceived to be widespread (from the Gallup World Poll). This perception has implications for our hypotheses. If improvements in PFM are correlated with improvements in components of the WGI_COC that are wholly unrelated to improvements in PFM, then we may find support for our hypotheses in spurious relationships.

More generally, perceptions-based indexes of corruption are the subject of criticism. Cobham (2013) is particularly critical of the use of expert opinion surveys within Transparency International's corruption perceptions index, which, he says, "embeds a powerful and misleading elite bias in popular perceptions of corruption, potentially contributing to a vicious cycle." As noted, the WGI_COC uses expert opinion surveys, although it also uses citizen perceptions surveys. Donchev and Ujhelyi (2013) highlight particular biases within perceptions indexes with respect to measurement errors for low- and middle-income countries and large countries. Furthermore, microlevel data on actual corruption suggest that perceptions of corruption may be off the mark in either direction by a wide margin (Olken and Pande 2012). These criticisms again raise concerns about measurement error in our dependent variable.

A related problem is that improvements in PFM, particularly those related to increased transparency, may result in revelations that actually lead to a worsening in perceptions of corruption. As noted in the discussion of the findings of Ferraz and Finan (2008), information about corrupt practices revealed by transparency in budgets, reporting, and audits could have the opposite effect of our hypotheses regarding their relationships with perceptions of corruption. Indeed, Fisman and Golden (2017) point out that, since the commencement of President Xi Jinping's crackdown on corruption, China's ranking on Transparency International's corruption perceptions index has actually worsened, lending credence to the notion that perceptions are driven more by revelations than by corruption itself. As such, our hypotheses that transparency in budgeting, reporting, and auditing is associated with lower levels of corruption may be compromised by using perceptions of corruption as a proxy for actual corruption.

However, the WGI_COC also has advantages. Chief among them is its cross-country coverage with respect to countries that have also undertaken a PEFA assessment. Moreover, Treisman (2000) makes a strong case for the usefulness of corruption perceptions indexes, noting high correlations between different indexes across countries, within indexes over time, and between surveys of business people and citizens. Moreover, as a composite of numerous corruption surveys or a poll of polls, the WGI_COC includes a measurement error term. This inclusion allows for analysis that places greater weight on composite scores where the various surveys produce similar scores. Nevertheless, the previously noted problems remain pertinent. In particular, perceptions of corruption may not correlate with actual corruption and may be driven by the type of revelations that sometimes come with improvements in PFM. We consider these factors further when interpreting our results in the concluding section.

WGI_COC scores are based on a scale from −2.5 to 2.5, with higher scores indicating better outcomes. For comparison with other indexes and easier interpretation, we rescale the index from 0 to 100.[18] For comparison with backward-looking PEFA assessments, we also calculate our dependent variable as the moving average of the WGI_COC score corresponding to the year of the PEFA assessment and the two preceding years. For the 99 countries in our sample (annex 5B, table 5B.1), the scoring

Distribution and correlation of the Public Expenditure and Financial Accountability (PEFA) and control of corruption (WGI_COC) scores

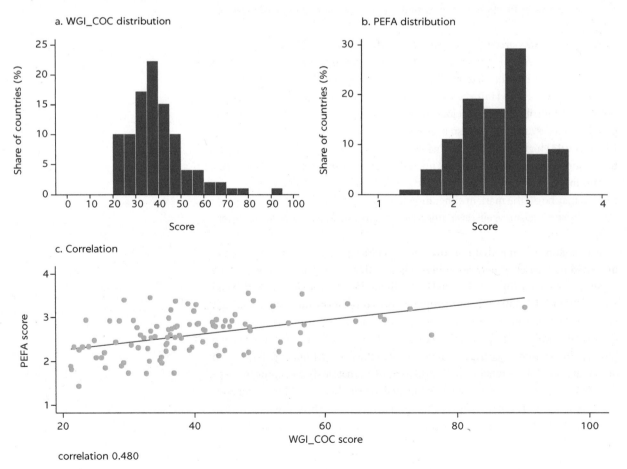

a. WGI_COC distribution

b. PEFA distribution

c. Correlation

correlation 0.480

distribution is skewed left, with most countries having a WGL_COC score between 20 and 60 (figure 5.1, panel a). This distribution is not surprising given that low- and middle-income countries dominate the sample. The mean score for the sample is 39.8, corresponding most closely to the score of Peru in 2015. The highest score is 90.2, for Norway in 2008, while the lowest is 21.2, for Myanmar in 2012. The WGL_COC scores are also strongly correlated with both the Transparency International and the International Country Risk Guide (ICRG) country risk indexes.[19]

PEFA scores are also prone to criticism. A common complaint is that some PEFA indicators emphasize the measurement of form over function. There is also debate around which indicators matter most, particularly when it comes to designing PFM reforms.[20] Our aim in this chapter is to select the indicators that may matter most for corruption and examine whether these relationships are observable in the data. We therefore construct indexes that best match the hypotheses outlined in the previous section. PEFA scores are converted to numeric values using the methodology outlined in chapter 2 of this report.

Compared with the distribution of the WGL_COC scores, the distribution of the overall PEFA scores is skewed right, with 75 percent of countries scoring 2 or higher, despite the lower-income bias in the sample (figure 5.1, panel b). Nevertheless, an observable relationship exists between the two measures (figure 5.1, panel c), with a correlation coefficient of close to 0.5. At the same time, panel c also shows quite a number of outliers, particularly with respect to countries that have performed well on PEFA assessments but have poor WGL_COC scores.

To test hypothesis 1—countries with a more transparent and orderly budget process will have lower levels of corruption—we construct an index of the former (TRANS1) using indicators PI-5, PI-6, PI-11, PI-12, and PI-27 of the PEFA framework (table 5.2). The TRANS1 index is calculated as the average score for each of the dimensions underlying these indicators. However, we exclude PI-12(ii) (on debt sustainability analysis) because the link to corruption is more ambiguous and PI-12(iv) (on in-year amendments) because this budget execution control issue is included in the relevant index for budget execution controls. The distribution of scoring on this

TABLE 5.2 Public Expenditure and Financial Accountability (PEFA) indicators for transparency in budget preparation (TRANS1)

NUMBER	INDICATOR	HYPOTHESIZED LINK
PI-5	Classification of the budget—calls for the use of a standardized chart of accounts in line with government financial statistics	The use of a standardized chart of accounts makes it easier for other stakeholders to understand and engage with budget documents, increasing the probability that corrupt allocations are detected.
PI-6	Comprehensiveness of information included in budget documentation—calls for the inclusion of nine types of budget documentation	The more information is provided, the more other stakeholders can engage with the budget process, increasing the probability that corrupt allocations are detected.
PI-11	Orderliness and participation in the annual budget process—calls for a timely and structured budget process, using a budget calendar, call circulars, and timely submissions and reviews	An orderly and timely budget preparation process should limit the opportunities for corruption in the budget formulation process by introducing a structured set of checks and balances into the preparation process and reduce discretionary practices (such as open-ended budgeting).
PI-12[a]	Multiyear perspective in fiscal, planning, expenditure policy, and budgeting—calls for a longer-term perspective in planning and budgeting	Better information on future allocations increases the probability that corrupt allocations are detected.
PI-27[b]	Legislative scrutiny of the annual budget law—calls for the legislature to have a clearly defined and time-bound role in the scrutiny of the annual budget law	Legislative oversight increases the probability that corrupt allocations are detected.

Source: Based on French 2013.
a. Excludes second subdimension.
b. Excludes fourth subdimension.

FIGURE 5.2

Distribution of scores for subindexes of transparency of budget execution reporting

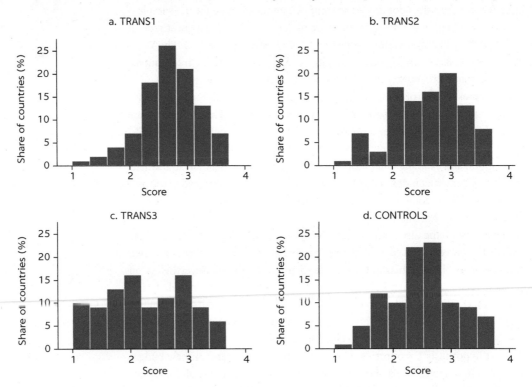

FIGURE 5.3

Correlations between subindexes and control of corruption (WGI_COC)

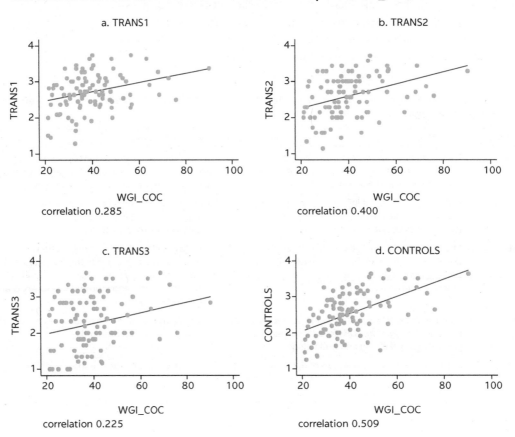

index is skewed to the right, similar to the overall PEFA index (figure 5.2, panel a) and is weakly correlated with the WGL_COC index (figure 5.3, panel a).

To test hypothesis 2—countries with more transparent budget execution reporting will have lower levels of corruption—we construct an index (TRANS2) based on the dimensions of indicators PI-23, PI-24, and PI-25 (see table 5.3). Indicators PI-24 and PI-25 measure the quality and timeliness with which the government prepares standard financial reports. PI-23 is more of a special case that obliges central government to take steps to ensure that resources are reaching schools and health facilities.[21] The TRANS2 index is distributed more normally and correlated more strongly with the WGL_COC than the TRANS1 index (figure 5.2, panel b; figure 5.3, panel b). These are indicators of internal transparency in budget execution reporting. Whether they are made publicly available is measured separately under PI-10. However, the PI-10 indicator does not provide enough precision to determine whether budget execution reporting is made publicly available.[22] Nevertheless, the fact that they are produced makes it more plausible that they will make it into the public sphere.

In contrast, TRANS3, which was constructed to test hypothesis 3—countries that have more transparent audit institutions will have lower levels of corruption—shows the greatest variation in its distribution and the weakest relationship with the WGL_COC (figure 5.2, panel c; figure 5.3, panel c, respectively). Most notable is the level of variation in scoring on the TRANS3 index across those countries that score below the mean of approximately 40 on the WGL_COC (figure 5.3, panel c). The index is constructed as the average of the dimensions under PI-26 and PI-28 (table 5.4). Our hypothesis is that adherence to best practice in auditing increases the probability of detection and that placing audit reports before the legislature increases the probability of sanction.

Our final subindex (CONTROLS) is a composite of indicators PI-18, PI-19, and PI-20 and the fourth dimension of PI-27 (table 5.5), constructed to test our fourth hypothesis—countries that adhere more closely to best practice in budget execution controls will have lower levels of corruption. Our hypothesis is that these types of

TABLE 5.3 Public Expenditure and Financial Accountability (PEFA) indicators for transparency in budget executing reporting (TRANS2)

NUMBER	INDICATOR	HYPOTHESIZED LINK
PI-23	Availability of information on resources received by service delivery units	Increases the accountability of politicians and bureaucrats to the citizenry
PI-24	Quality and timeliness of in-year budget reports	Increases the probability of detection
PI-25	Quality and timeliness of annual financial statements	Increases the probability of detection

Source: Based on French 2013.

TABLE 5.4 Public Expenditure and Financial Accountability (PEFA) indicators for transparency in audit (TRANS3)

NUMBER	INDICATOR	HYPOTHESIZED LINK
PI-26	Scope, nature, and follow-up of external audit—calls for comprehensive scope of audits, timely submission to the legislature, and evidence that issues raised have been followed up	Increases the probability that corruption will be detected and sanctioned
PI-28	Legislative scrutiny of external audit reports—calls for timely scrutiny of audit reports, in-depth hearings on qualified or adverse audit opinions, and evidence that the legislature's recommendations on action have been implemented by the executive	Increases the probability that corruption will be sanctioned

Source: Based on French 2013.

TABLE 5.5 **Public Expenditure and Financial Accountability (PEFA) indicators for budget execution controls (CONTROLS)**

NUMBER	INDICATOR	HYPOTHESIZED LINK
PI-18	Effectiveness of payroll controls—calls for links between the payroll and personnel systems that are audited annually	Reduces the opportunity and incentive for ghost workers
PI-19	Competition, value for money, and controls in procurement—calls for open competition in contracting, justification for the use of less competitive methods, and the existence of a complaints mechanism	Reduces the opportunity and incentive for corruption by reducing the level of discretion of public officials and politicians
PI-20	Effectiveness of internal controls for nonsalary expenditure—calls for compliance with commitment controls and other documented payment procedures	Reduces the opportunity and incentive for corruption by reducing the level of discretion of public officials and politicians
PI-27(iv)	In-year amendments—calls for clear rules on in-year budget amendments that are respected	Reduces the opportunity for and incentive for corruption through budget reallocations

Source: Based on French 2013.

TABLE 5.6 **Spearman correlation coefficients for public financial management (PFM) subindexes**

	PEFA	TRANS1	TRANS2	TRANS3	CONTROLS
PFFA	1				
TRANS1	0.7621	1			
TRANS2	0.7217	0.3897	1		
TRANS3	0.6323	0.368	0.4146	1	
CONTROLS	0.7494	0.4661	0.5699	0.2905	1

controls are associated with lower levels of corruption on the basis that they limit opportunities and incentives for specific types of corruption. The fact that they are in place may also demonstrate political commitment to budget priorities. Of our four indexes, the CONTROLS index has the most normal distribution and is correlated most strongly with the WGL_COC (figure 5.2, panel d; figure 5.3, panel d, respectively).

All of our subindexes are positively correlated with one another. TRANS2 and CONTROLS have the highest correlation of 0.57, while the other subindexes are weakly correlated with one another (table 5.6). All of the subindexes are strongly correlated with the overall PEFA index.

The analysis in this section has served to establish relationships between various parts of the PFM system and corruption based on the hypotheses outlined in the previous section. However, this analysis comes with the important caveat that our data on corruption, the WGL_COC, is a perceptions-based indicator rather than a measure of actual corruption. Furthermore, our measurement of components of the PFM system using aggregated PEFA scores may not perfectly reflect our hypotheses. The implications for the interpretation of the observed relationships are revisited in the concluding discussion. In the next section, we describe our approach to estimating these relationships when controlling for other determinants of corruption.

ESTIMATION APPROACH

Following the example of Treisman (2000), we take a two-step approach to estimating the relationship between our PFM indexes and the WGL_COC. We use linear regression as the estimation technique rather than maximum likelihood estimation because the dependent variable is closer to being a continuous variable than a categorical variable. As a first step, in equation (5.1) we employ weighted least squares (WLS) to estimate the relationship in levels:

$$Y_i = \alpha + \beta X_i + \gamma Z_i + \varepsilon_i, \tag{5.1}$$

where Y_i is the WGL_COC, X_i is the relevant PFM index for country i, Z_i is a matrix of country-level controls, and ε_i is our error term. The equation is estimated using data for country i's most recent PEFA assessment, which covers the period from 2005 to 2017 for the 99 countries in our sample (see annex 5B, table 5B.1). Following Treisman (2000), observations are weighted using the inverse of WGL_COC variance between surveys, which gives less emphasis to countries with wide variations in the components making up the WGL_COC.

Our control variables are based on the findings of similar studies on the determinants of corruption (table 5.7). Countries with large natural resource endowments are more susceptible to rent seeking and corruption, whereas openness to trade is associated with less corruption (Ades and Di Tella 1999). We use natural resource rents as a percentage of gross domestic product (GDP) to control for the former and trade as a percentage of GDP to control for the latter. Higher-income countries tend to have lower perceptions of corruption, which we control for using the log of GDP per capita. Following the example of Treisman (2000), we use lagged values for each of these first three controls in recognition that current levels of corruption and development are likely to be jointly determined. Specifically, we use the four-year moving average of the year of the PEFA assessment lagged by five years (for example, for a PEFA assessment score of 2015, the natural resource endowments variable will be the average of *natural resource rents as % of GDP* for the four years 2011, 2010, 2009, and 2008).

We also control for country size using the log of population because of its association with political structures such as federalism, although the effects on corruption are ambiguous (Treisman 2000). And again, following the example of Treisman (2000), we control for both democracy and press freedom using indexes of each and differences in region and colonial origin using dummy variables. Finally, following Knack, Biletska, and Kacker (2017), we employ year dummies for the year in which the PEFA assessment was carried out, because this varies across our sample.

The model outlined in equation (5.1) suffers from obvious endogeneity concerns, particularly simultaneity bias arising from the likelihood that corruption and its determinants (including PFM performance) may be jointly determined (Olken

TABLE 5.7 **Control variables**

CONTROL	MEASUREMENT	SOURCE
Natural resource endowments	Natural resource rents as % of GDP	World Development Indicators
Openness to trade	Imports and exports as a % of GDP	World Development Indicators
Economic development	Log GDP per capita	World Development Indicators
Population	Log population	World Development Indicators
Democracy	Polity index	Quality of Governance Data set
Press freedom	Press freedom index	Quality of Governance Data set
Geography	Regional dummy variables (10)	Quality of Governance Data set
Colonial origin	Colonial origin dummy variables (10)	Quality of Governance Data set

and Pande 2012), measurement error (because both our dependent and independent variables may not accurately reflect actual corruption and PFM performance, respectively), and omitted variable bias arising from unobservable determinants of corruption, for example, culture. Overcoming the endogeneity issues related to the former two is beyond the scope of this chapter, which aims to investigate relationships rather than establish causal mechanisms. The second step of our two-step approach is aimed at addressing some of the concerns regarding omitted variable bias. In this second estimation, we exploit the repeat assessments within the PEFA data set to estimate the relationship using the fixed-effects estimator for panel data in equation (5.2):

$$Y_{it} = \alpha_i + \beta X_{it} + \gamma Z_{it} + \varepsilon_{it}. \tag{5.2}$$

This model estimates the relationship between changes in the WGL_COC (Y) and changes in our PFM indexes (X) in country i over a period of time t, also controlling for changes in our other controls (Z) and nonobservable, nonchanging country fixed effects (α_i). However, if the model fails to specify important determinants of corruption that do change over time, the problem of omitted variable bias remains. This discussion is taken up further in our conclusions later in the chapter. Not every country that has undertaken a first PEFA assessment has undertaken a second, which reduces our sample size for estimating equation (5.2) to 60 countries (see annex 5B, table 5B.2). The next section discusses the results from our estimations.

RESULTS

Table 5.8 outlines the estimates of our model using WLS estimation. We find that our overall PEFA index (PEFA) as well as the three subindexes for transparency (TRANS1–3) and our subindex for controls (CONTROLS) have a positive relationship with the control of corruption index (WGL_COC) after controlling for other factors. Furthermore, these relationships have a statistical significance of 5 percent or better. Our results suggest that scoring 1 point higher on the PEFA index scale of 1–4 is associated with a score that is 10.7 points higher on the WGL_COC index scale of 0–100 on average (column 1). The results are lower for each of our subindexes, but our CONTROLS index has a stronger relationship than our TRANS1–3 indexes (columns 2–5). Moreover, when each of the subindexes competes in the same model (column 6), the effect of the CONTROLS index dominates the effect of the transparency indexes, which suggests that controls are a more important determinant of perceptions of corruption than transparency.

With respect to our control variables, our findings are largely in line with theory and previous empirical findings. We find that a natural resource base (NAT_RES) that is 1 percent of GDP higher on average is associated with a WGL_COC score that is 0.3 point lower on average and that GDP per capita (LOGINCOMEPC) that is 1 percent higher on average is associated with a WGL_COC score that is 5.5–6.5 points higher on average. Country size is a significant determinant of WGL_COC in our model. Countries whose population (LOGPOP) is on average 1 percent larger have WGL_COC scores that are on average 2–3 points lower. We also find a small effect for press freedom (PRESS). A 1-point improvement in the press freedom index is associated with a 0.2-point improvement in the WGL_COC score.[23] For trade openness (TRADE) and democracy (POLITY), we find small negative associations with the WGL_COC. This is the opposite of what is predicted by theory and contradicts

TABLE 5.8 **Weighted least squares estimates for Public Expenditure and Financial Accountability (PEFA) indicators and control of corruption**

VARIABLE	(1)	(2)	(3)	(4)	(5)	(6)
PEFA	10.70***					
	(2.671)					
TRANS1		4.614**				1.877
		(2.263)				(2.320)
TRANS2			3.808**			−0.439
			(1.794)			(2.168)
TRANS3				3.897***		2.279*
				(1.329)		(1.365)
CONTROLS					7.012***	5.790**
					(1.987)	(2.270)
NAT_RES	−0.281***	−0.346***	−0.355***	−0.362***	−0.270***	−0.267***
	(0.0883)	(0.0983)	(0.0977)	(0.0853)	(0.0804)	(0.0873)
TRADE	−0.721	−0.446	−0.181	−0.400	−0.0580	−0.496
	(1.260)	(1.332)	(1.261)	(1.322)	(1.358)	(1.459)
LOGINCOMEPC	5.461***	6.577***	6.383***	6.316***	5.796***	5.507***
	(1.449)	(1.552)	(1.562)	(1.371)	(1.367)	(1.413)
LOGPOP	−2.788***	−2.406***	−2.142***	−2.082**	−2.205***	−2.438***
	(0.784)	(0.871)	(0.772)	(0.785)	(0.747)	(0.808)
POLITY	−0.225	−0.202	−0.222	−0.291	−0.231	−0.243
	(0.238)	(0.255)	(0.254)	(0.252)	(0.240)	(0.258)
PRESS	−0.203**	−0.211**	−0.228**	−0.270***	−0.211**	−0.218**
	(0.0959)	(0.105)	(0.0978)	(0.0966)	(0.0975)	(0.107)
Constant	12.01	13.47	12.10	26.89	7.903	10.32
	(18.34)	(20.56)	(19.95)	(19.74)	(18.32)	(18.44)
Observations	99	99	99	99	99	99
R-squared	0.762	0.716	0.710	0.724	0.746	0.761

Note: Robust standard errors are in parentheses. Dummy variables for regions, colonial origins, and years are not reported.
*** $p<0.01$, ** $p<0.05$, * $p<0.1$

the findings of others, although we do not find either relationship to be statistically significant within our model.

As a robustness check, we reestimate our model excluding the top and bottom 5 percent of observations for the WGL_COC.[24] Our results remain broadly similar (annex 5C, table 5C.1). The estimated coefficients of our PFM indexes are slightly lower, with the exception of TRANS1, which is found to be slightly higher. TRANS2 is no longer found to be statistically significant; neither are population size (LOGPOP) and press freedom (PRESS). As a second robustness check, we estimate the model using the ICRG index instead of the WGL_COC. This reduces the sample size from 99 countries to 76. Our estimated coefficients are smaller, and the coefficients for TRANS1 and TRANS2 are no longer found to be statistically significant, but we again find the CONTROLS index to have the largest and most statistically significant effects (annex 5C, table 5C.2).

The panel results in table 5.9 broadly corroborate our core findings from the WLS estimates. Again, we find positive relationships between our PFM indexes and the WGL_COC. We find the largest effect for the overall PEFA index, where

TABLE 5.9 **Panel estimates for the relationship between Public Expenditure and Financial Accountability (PEFA) indicators and control of corruption**

VARIABLE	(1)	(2)	(3)	(4)	(5)	(6)
PEFA	3.005*					
	(1.793)					
TRANS1		1.971				1.446
		(1.700)				(2.396)
TRANS2			0.00342			−1.292
			(1.151)			(1.420)
TRANS3				0.147		−0.482
				(0.956)		(1.086)
CONTROLS					2.638**	2.704*
					(1.251)	(1.453)
NAT_RES	−0.186	−0.190	−0.236	−0.231	−0.235	−0.218
	(0.162)	(0.171)	(0.170)	(0.155)	(0.148)	(0.151)
TRADE	0.828	1.235	1.126	1.074	−0.152	−0.210
	(2.832)	(2.815)	(2.863)	(2.887)	(2.954)	(2.744)
LOGINCOMEPC	4.725*	5.429**	6.421**	6.319**	6.283**	6.561**
	(2.375)	(2.427)	(2.875)	(2.621)	(2.819)	(2.996)
LOGPOP	−8.416	−7.946	−4.495	−4.781	−7.724	−8.119
	(6.885)	(7.071)	(7.059)	(7.351)	(6.316)	(6.747)
POLITY	0.495**	0.506**	0.414*	0.417*	0.352*	0.346*
	(0.227)	(0.240)	(0.207)	(0.224)	(0.188)	(0.183)
PRESS	−0.0131	−0.00750	−0.0265	−0.0265	−0.0368	−0.0281
	(0.0686)	(0.0688)	(0.0679)	(0.0699)	(0.0609)	(0.0609)
Constant	123.1	110.3	54.88	60.07	106.4	110.5
	(104.8)	(105.8)	(110.2)	(111.8)	(97.01)	(104.0)
Observations	120	120	120	120	120	120
R-squared	0.296	0.264	0.225	0.225	0.349	0.379
Number of id	60	60	60	60	60	60

Note: Robust standard errors are in parentheses. Dummy variables for regions, colonial origins, and years are not reported.
*** $p<0.01$, ** $p<0.05$, * $p<0.1$

the estimated coefficient suggests that a 1-point improvement on the PEFA index 1–4 scale is associated with an improvement of 3 points along the WGL_COC index 0–100 scale (table 5.9, column 1). Also consistent with the WLS estimates are the weaker estimated relationships for the transparency subindexes (columns 2–4) compared with the controls index (column 5). Again, we find that, when forced to compete in the same model, the controls index dominates the effects of the other indexes in both magnitude and statistical significance. Moreover, we find the estimates of overall PEFA and controls indexes to be statistically significant at the 10 percent and 5 percent levels, respectively, but we do not find the estimates of the transparency indexes to be statistically significant.

However, our estimates of the relationship between improvements in our PFM indexes and improvements in the WGL_COC index are quite small. When one considers first that Organisation for Economic Co-operation and Development (OECD) countries do not score perfectly on a range of these indicators[25] and the amount of time it took for them to get to that point, a movement of one score—from an average PEFA index score of B to A, C to B, or D to C—would require a lot of effort to achieve a 3-point improvement on the WGL_COC index. In contrast, our estimates for the relationship between increases in income per capita and increases in the WGL_COC index are substantially higher, ranging between a 5-point to a 6-point increase in the WGL_COC index for a 1 percent increase in GDP per capita (LOGINCOMEPC). We also find a statistically significant relationship between democracy (POLITY) and the WGL_COC index, with a 1-point improvement in the score of the former corresponding to a 0.4-point to a 0.5-point improvement in the latter. We do not find statistically significant relationships between changes in the natural resource base, trade openness, country size, or press freedom and the control of corruption index.

Our panel estimate results are sensitive to the inclusion of the top and bottom 5 percent of countries in terms of absolute change in WGL_COC scores (annex 5C, table 5C.3).[26] Once those countries are excluded, we no longer find any of our PFM indexes to be statistically significant. The estimated coefficients for changes in income (LOGINCOMEPC) and democracy (POLITY) remain statistically significant at the 10 percent and 5 percent levels, respectively.

We also try to replicate similar results using the ICRG index for a smaller sample of 44 countries (annex 5C, table 5C.4). In this instance, we do not find statistically significant relationships for any of our PFM indexes individually and actually find negative coefficients for TRANS2 and TRANS3. We again find the largest coefficient for the CONTROLS index, and when we include all four indexes, the effect of CONTROLS is positive and statistically significant at the 5 percent level. However, we also find negative effects for the TRANS2 and TRANS3 indexes in this specification. The negative signage of the estimated effects for TRANS2 and TRANS3 provides some weak evidence for the alternative hypothesis that improvements in PFM that increase transparency lead to revelations that worsen the perceptions of corruption.

DISCUSSION

PFM reform often forms part of a low- or middle-income country's anticorruption strategy, frequently with external support from its development partners in the form of funding and technical assistance. It is therefore important for the governments of both donor and recipient countries, as well as PFM practitioners, to consider whether there is evidence that PFM reforms have an impact on corruption. The literature that tries to establish a causal link between PFM reforms and corruption tends to have a reform niche and country focus. Cross-country examination of the relationship is limited to higher-income countries. This chapter tries to fill the gap in the literature by looking at the relationship for a large sample of predominantly lower-income countries. We also try to provide a more nuanced examination of the relationship by testing four hypotheses related to PFM reforms regarding transparency in budgeting, reporting, and auditing and in expenditure controls. Our analysis provides evidence that there is a relationship between "better" PFM, particularly expenditure controls, and lower levels of corruption. But these results come with important caveats.

Our estimation of the cross-country relationship in levels shows a statistically significant correlation between our four measures of PFM performance and perceptions of corruption after controlling for other determinants of the latter. Compared with greater transparency in budgeting, reporting, and auditing, we find a stronger correlation between lower perceptions of corruption and "better" expenditure controls. Moreover, when allowed to compete in the same model, the effect of our expenditure controls index dominates the effects of our transparency indexes. To address potential omitted variable bias concerns, we also estimate the relationship between PFM performance and perceptions of corruption over time. Using a fixed-effects estimator, we once again find a statistically significant correlation between "better" expenditure controls and lower perceptions of corruption, but our estimates of the relationship between transparency in budgeting, reporting, and auditing and in perceptions of corruption are no longer found to be significant.

We interpret these findings as supporting the idea that expenditure controls are likely to be useful in an environment characterized by political commitment to budget credibility. We find weaker evidence of a relationship between transparency in budgeting, reporting, and auditing and in perceptions of corruption. But we do not find evidence to support an alternative hypothesis that greater transparency leads to revelations that worsen perceptions of corruption. We also note that, compared with the effect of economic growth, PFM performance has a very limited impact on perceptions of corruption.

However, our analysis has important limitations. Robustness checks show that our results are sensitive to changes in sample size and alternative measures of corruption. But more fundamentally, our estimation technique suffers from endogeneity issues and our data are far from perfect. These weaknesses were largely insurmountable for this research and may lead to possible interpretations of our results.

A causal interpretation suggests that improvements in PFM performance lead to improvements in perceptions of corruption. However, several endogeneity concerns lead us to caution against this interpretation. The first is reverse causality. Our estimation technique cannot rule out the possibility that causality flows in the opposite direction—that is, that lower levels of corruption allow for improved PFM performance. However, our results fit with the general theory outlined in our hypotheses as well as the results of previous studies.

A larger concern is omitted variable bias. Although our panel estimation controls for nonvarying determinants of corruption, PFM reforms do not occur in a vacuum. Often the more salient political issue is corruption. Politicians rarely campaign on the promise of PFM reform, but they frequently campaign on an anticorruption platform. PFM reform tends to be part of a package of wider anticorruption reforms. Because our estimations do not include controls for other anticorruption strategies, our results may be biased. As such, we cannot rule out the possibility that our results are picking up a co-movement in improvements in PFM performance and corruption perceptions that are not directly related. This possibility becomes more of a concern given the potential for measurement error. As noted throughout, perceptions of corruption and actual corruption may diverge, while our measures of PFM performance may be unrelated to the types of corruption that are driving our perceptions of corruption indicator. Wages paid to civil servants may also be an important determinant of corruption,[27] but the paucity of a comprehensive source of data on wages across countries meant that controlling for wages was beyond the scope of this paper.

Further research in this area should focus on identifying more specific cross-country measures of corruption that can be linked to more specific PFM reforms. This chapter has outlined the relationships between the most commonly used measures of both PFM and corruption. Our findings suggest that, during windows of opportunity when there is strong high-level commitment to combatting corruption, the focus of support for PFM reform should be on improving expenditure controls.

ANNEX 5A PEFA INDICATORS: 2011 FRAMEWORK

TABLE 5A.1 **Performance indicators in the 2011 Public Expenditure and Financial Accountability (PEFA) framework**

A. PFM OUTTURNS: CREDIBILITY OF THE BUDGET	
PI-1	Aggregate expenditure outturn compared to original approved budget
PI-2	Composition of expenditure outturn compared to original approved budget
PI-3	Aggregate revenue outturn compared to original approved budget
PI-4	Stock and monitoring of expenditure payments arrears
B. KEY CROSS CUTTING ISSUES: COMPREHENSIVENESS AND TRANSPARENCY	
PI-5	Classification of the budget
PI-6	Comprehensiveness of information included in budget documentation
PI-7	Extent of unreported government operations
PI-8	Transparency of intergovernmental fiscal relations
PI-9	Oversight of aggregate fiscal risk from other public sector entities
PI-10	Public access to key fiscal information
C. BUDGET CYCLE	
C(i) Policy-based budgeting	
PI-11	Orderliness and participation in the annual budget process
PI-12	Multiyear perspective in fiscal planning, expenditure policy, and budgeting
C(ii) Predictability and control in budget execution	
PI-13	Transparency of taxpayer obligations and liabilities
PI-14	Effectiveness of measures for taxpayers registration and tax assessment
PI-15	Effectiveness in collection of tax payments
PI-16	Predictability in the availability of funds for commitment of expenditures
PI-17	Recording and management of cash balances, debt, and guarantees
PI-18	Effectiveness of payroll controls
PI-19	Competition, value for money, and controls in procurement
PI-20	Effectiveness of internal controls for nonsalary expenditure
PI-21	Effectiveness of internal audit
C(iii) Accounting, recording, and reporting	
PI-22	Timeliness and regularity of accounts reconciliation
PI-23	Availability of information on resources received by service delivery units
PI-24	Quality and timeliness of in-year budget reports
PI-25	Quality and timeliness of annual financial statements
C(iv) External scrutiny and audit	
PI-26	Scope, nature, and follow-up of external audit
PI-27	Legislative scrutiny of the annual budget law
PI-28	Legislative scrutiny of external audit reports
D. DONOR PRACTICES	
D-1	Predictability of direct budget support
D-2	Financial information provided by donors for budgeting and reporting on project and program aid
D-3	Proportion of aid that is managed by use of national procedures

Source: PEFA Secretariat 2011.

ANNEX 5B ESTIMATION SAMPLES

TABLE 5B.1 **Sample of 99 countries for the weighted least squares (WLS) estimation**

LOW-INCOME COUNTRIES	LOWER-MIDDLE-INCOME COUNTRIES	UPPER-MIDDLE-INCOME COUNTRIES	HIGH-INCOME COUNTRIES
Benin	Armenia	Albania	Kuwait
Burkina Faso	Bangladesh	Algeria	Norway
Burundi	Bhutan	Angola	Oman
Cambodia	Bolivia	Azerbaijan	Trinidad and Tobago
Central African Republic	Cabo Verde	Belarus	
Chad	Cameroon	Botswana	
Comoros	Congo, Rep.	Brazil	
Congo, Dem. Rep.	Côte d'Ivoire	Colombia	
Gambia, The	Egypt, Arab Rep.	Costa Rica	
Guinea	El Salvador	Dominican Republic	
Guinea-Bissau	Eswatini	Ecuador	
Kenya	Fiji	Gabon	
Lao PDR	Georgia	Jamaica	
Liberia	Ghana	Jordan	
Madagascar	Guatemala	Kazakhstan	
Malawi	Honduras	Lebanon	
Mali	India	Mauritius	
Mozambique	Indonesia	Montenegro	
Myanmar	Kyrgyz Republic	Namibia	
Nepal	Lesotho	North Macedonia	
Niger	Mauritania	Panama	
Rwanda	Moldova	Paraguay	
Sierra Leone	Mongolia	Peru	
Tajikistan	Morocco	Russian Federation	
Tanzania	Nicaragua	Serbia	
Togo	Nigeria	South Africa	
Uganda	Pakistan	Suriname	
Yemen, Rep.	Philippines	Tunisia	
Zimbabwe	Senegal	Turkey	
	Sri Lanka	Uruguay	
	Sudan		
	Thailand		
	Timor-Leste		
	Uzbekistan		
	Vietnam		
	Zambia		

Note: Income classification at the time of the most recent Public Expenditure and Financial Accountability (PEFA) assessment.

TABLE 5B.2 **Sample of 60 countries for the panel estimation**

LOW-INCOME COUNTRIES	LOWER-MIDDLE-INCOME COUNTRIES	UPPER-MIDDLE-INCOME COUNTRIES	HIGH-INCOME COUNTRY
Benin	Armenia	Albania	Trinidad and Tobago
Burkina Faso	Bhutan	Algeria	
Burundi	Cabo Verde	Azerbaijan	
Central African Republic	Congo, Rep.	Belarus	
Comoros	El Salvador	Botswana	
Congo, Dem. Rep.	Eswatini	Colombia	
Gambia, The	Guatemala	Costa Rica	
Guinea	Indonesia	Dominican Republic	
Liberia	Kenya	Ecuador	
Madagascar	Kyrgyz Republic	Fiji	
Malawi	Lao PDR	Georgia	
Mali	Mauritania	Jamaica	
Mozambique	Moldova	Mauritius	
Nepal	Morocco	Montenegro	
Niger	Pakistan	Namibia	
Rwanda	Philippines	North Macedonia	
Senegal	Tajikistan	Paraguay	
Sierra Leone	Timor-Leste	Peru	
Uganda	Tunisia	South Africa	
	Zambia	Suriname	

ANNEX 5C ROBUSTNESS CHECKS

TABLE 5C.1 **Weighted least squares (WLS) estimation—robustness check 1—for control of corruption excluding the top and bottom 5 percent of sample**

VARIABLE	(1)	(2)	(3)	(4)	(5)	(6)
PEFA	10.10***					
	(2.759)					
TRANS1		5.106**				3.041
		(2.231)				(2.147)
TRANS2			2.975			−0.786
			(1.870)			(2.346)
TRANS3				3.085*		1.853
				(1.562)		(1.592)
CONTROLS					6.205***	5.363**
					(2.238)	(2.596)
NAT_RES	−0.278***	−0.321***	−0.326***	−0.346***	−0.279***	−0.281***
	(0.0748)	(0.0868)	(0.0901)	(0.0833)	(0.0716)	(0.0779)
TRADE	3.713	3.282	1.871	2.918	2.991	4.391
	(3.125)	(3.041)	(3.279)	(3.327)	(3.110)	(3.302)
LOGINCOMEPC	4.500***	5.429***	5.420***	5.323***	4.843***	4.518***
	(1.245)	(1.365)	(1.388)	(1.199)	(1.170)	(1.225)

continued

TABLE 5C.1, *continued*

VARIABLE	(1)	(2)	(3)	(4)	(5)	(6)
LOGPOP	–1.388*	–1.044	–0.940	–0.797	–1.190	–1.244
	(0.766)	(0.821)	(0.739)	(0.774)	(0.726)	(0.784)
POLITY	–0.174	–0.130	–0.144	–0.211	–0.142	–0.164
	(0.203)	(0.220)	(0.228)	(0.231)	(0.211)	(0.224)
PRESS	–0.143*	–0.132	–0.142	–0.189**	–0.137	–0.150
	(0.0808)	(0.0904)	(0.0873)	(0.0900)	(0.0896)	(0.0957)
Constant	–21.32	–17.25	–5.427	–8.623	–10.14	–21.04
	(22.09)	(22.14)	(21.78)	(22.13)	(21.12)	(22.14)
Observations	89	89	89	89	89	89
R-squared	0.695	0.641	0.614	0.627	0.665	0.696

Note: Robust standard errors are in parentheses. Dummy variables for regions, colonial origins, and years are not reported.
*** p<0.01, ** p<0.05, * p<0.1

TABLE 5C.2 Weighted least squares (WLS) estimation—robustness check 2—using the International Country Risk Guide (ICRG) index

VARIABLE	(1)	(2)	(3)	(4)	(5)	(6)
PEFA	5.721*					
	(2.858)					
TRANS1		0.893				–1.892
		(2.257)				(2.531)
TRANS2			3.066			0.103
			(2.211)			(2.647)
TRANS3				3.652**		3.201*
				(1.667)		(1.802)
CONTROLS					5.448***	4.706**
					(2.010)	(2.207)
NAT_RES	–0.152	–0.185*	–0.160	–0.172*	–0.113	–0.111
	(0.0999)	(0.0986)	(0.103)	(0.102)	(0.0900)	(0.0964)
TRADE	–1.305	–0.745	–0.862	–1.452	–1.174	–1.582
	(1.921)	(2.035)	(1.945)	(1.845)	(1.942)	(1.894)
LOGINCOMEPC	2.884	3.296*	2.890	3.068*	2.939*	2.883*
	(1.786)	(1.801)	(1.829)	(1.669)	(1.543)	(1.572)
LOGPOP	–0.924	–0.416	–0.415	–0.576	–0.502	–0.412
	(0.886)	(0.943)	(0.843)	(0.821)	(0.720)	(0.709)
POLITY	–0.455	–0.457	–0.434	–0.550*	–0.464*	–0.556*
	(0.301)	(0.292)	(0.315)	(0.300)	(0.267)	(0.299)
PRESS	–0.330***	–0.353***	–0.342***	–0.388***	–0.327***	–0.372***
	(0.107)	(0.108)	(0.108)	(0.106)	(0.105)	(0.111)
Constant	16.31	16.90	13.64	19.18	9.229	10.50
	(21.30)	(21.14)	(20.29)	(20.49)	(17.78)	(18.61)
Observations	76	76	76	76	76	76
R-squared	0.714	0.690	0.704	0.719	0.727	0.746

Note: Robust standard errors are in parentheses. Dummy variables for regions, colonial origins, and years not reported.
*** p<0.01, ** p<0.05, * p<0.1

TABLE 5C.3 Panel estimates—robustness check 1—for control of corruption excluding the top and bottom 5 percent of sample

VARIABLE	(1)	(2)	(3)	(4)	(5)	(6)
PEFA	1.411					
	(1.423)					
TRANS1		0.572				0.348
		(1.312)				(2.181)
TRANS2			0.340			−0.160
			(0.992)			(1.123)
TRANS3				−0.260		−0.581
				(0.833)		(1.063)
CONTROLS					1.471	1.559
					(1.236)	(1.480)
NAT_RES	−0.120	−0.130	−0.140	−0.150	−0.153	−0.164
	(0.0977)	(0.105)	(0.100)	(0.0947)	(0.0958)	(0.110)
TRADE	−0.223	−0.163	−0.164	−0.142	−0.431	−0.169
	(2.616)	(2.586)	(2.596)	(2.719)	(2.728)	(2.671)
LOGINCOMEPC	3.178	3.585*	3.615*	3.976*	4.252*	4.650*
	(1.995)	(1.870)	(1.858)	(1.980)	(2.279)	(2.585)
LOGPOP	−4.624	−3.647	−2.911	−2.053	−4.943	−4.514
	(5.766)	(5.957)	(6.159)	(6.477)	(5.845)	(5.982)
POLITY	0.379**	0.368**	0.356**	0.334*	0.313*	0.305*
	(0.178)	(0.178)	(0.174)	(0.176)	(0.165)	(0.167)
PRESS	−0.0255	−0.0253	−0.0295	−0.0306	−0.0376	−0.0361
	(0.0629)	(0.0609)	(0.0636)	(0.0626)	(0.0586)	(0.0578)
Constant	84.27	67.45	56.54	41.58	82.25	71.71
	(86.20)	(87.77)	(90.48)	(96.98)	(86.55)	(92.89)
Observations	108	108	108	108	108	108
R-squared	0.204	0.185	0.183	0.182	0.229	0.239
Number of id	54	54	54	54	54	54

Note: Robust standard errors are in parentheses. Dummy variables for regions, colonial origins, and years are not reported.
*** $p<0.01$, ** $p<0.05$, * $p<0.1$

TABLE 5C.4 Panel estimates—robustness check 2—using the International Country Risk Guide (ICRG) index

VARIABLE	(1)	(2)	(3)	(4)	(5)	(6)
PEFA	2.597					
	(7.953)					
TRANS1		4.438				6.634
		(7.284)				(7.020)
TRANS2			−3.127			−8.413*
			(3.136)			(4.395)
TRANS3				−0.982		−4.797
				(3.648)		(3.684)
CONTROLS					5.019	7.748**
					(3.849)	(3.403)
NAT_RES	−0.615	−0.728	−0.642	−0.642	−0.705	−1.192**
	(0.483)	(0.462)	(0.480)	(0.501)	(0.467)	(0.455)

continued

TABLE 5C.4, *continued*

VARIABLE	(1)	(2)	(3)	(4)	(5)	(6)
TRADE	4.807	6.349	3.023	4.523	2.707	2.271
	(8.486)	(8.340)	(10.05)	(9.479)	(9.205)	(8.189)
LOGINCOMEPC	15.57	16.71*	17.27*	17.01	17.95**	26.50**
	(9.625)	(9.252)	(9.844)	(10.75)	(8.452)	(10.36)
LOGPOP	2.789	0.835	7.800	6.600	−1.840	1.064
	(17.25)	(17.24)	(12.34)	(14.42)	(15.53)	(13.99)
POLITY	−0.571	−0.445	−0.725	−0.665	−0.702	−0.960
	(0.942)	(0.974)	(0.855)	(0.959)	(0.885)	(0.884)
PRESS	−0.477	−0.487	−0.422	−0.454	−0.473	−0.401
	(0.420)	(0.414)	(0.404)	(0.396)	(0.386)	(0.347)
Constant	−144.2	−133.2	−217.6	−207.8	−84.45	−189.3
	(276.2)	(254.4)	(191.8)	(245.5)	(241.8)	(222.8)
Observations	82	82	82	82	82	82
R-squared	0.177	0.197	0.204	0.171	0.244	0.440
Number of id	41	41	41	41	41	41

Note: Robust standard errors are in parentheses. Dummy variables for regions, colonial origins, and years are not reported.
***$p<0.01$, ** $p<0.05$, * $p<0.1$

NOTES

1. Bureaucratic corruption is sometimes called "routine" corruption because it often plays out in the form of bribes for government services by junior to midlevel officials. It is also sometimes referred to as "survival" corruption because of the low wages received by those extracting bribes (Fjeldstad 2005).
2. With Malawi being just the most recent example of how this can occur. See https://www.economist.com/baobab/2014/02/27/the-32m-heist.
3. This chapter focuses solely on the expenditure side of the PFM system. The revenue side also provides ample opportunity and incentives for corruption. For a review, see Fjeldstad (2005).
4. Although anecdotal evidence suggests that clean audits are for sale in some countries.
5. See https://www.imf.org/external/np/fad/trans/.
6. Fiscal transparency was constructed from IMF Reports on the Observance of Standards and Codes, and corruption was based on the Worldwide Governance Indicators (WGI) control of corruption index.
7. These other controls include controls for the log real gross domestic product (GDP), a dummy for high-income economies, dummies for geographic location, dummies for legal origin, trade openness, fractionalization, and education.
8. Using the International Budget Partnership's open budget index score and Transparency International's corruption perceptions index.
9. Using the WGI control of corruption index and the World Economic Forum Executive Opinion Survey.
10. Including income per capita and administrative regulations.
11. Using data from the International Budget Partnership and the Organisation for Economic Co-operation and Development (OECD) on budget transparency.
12. These PEFA indicators of transparency in budget execution reporting do not measure whether information is made publicly available, only that the relevant analysis is prepared. Public dissemination is measured separately through PI-10 (public access to key fiscal information), although it is not a perfect measure of transparency in budget execution reporting alone, because it also includes publication of budget documents, audit reports, and procurement contracts.
13. As measured by the WGI for government effectiveness, regulatory burden, and control of corruption.
14. Usually referred to as the auditor general in Anglophone contexts.

15. They further find that wages played no role in reducing corruption when audit intensity was at its peak but did have an effect on lowering corruption when audit intensity returned to normal levels in the aftermath of the crackdown.

16. As measured by the difference between actual project cost and estimates of engineers.

17. For a list of the surveys and sources used to compile the WGI_COC, see https://info.worldbank.org/governance/wgi/pdf/cc.pdf.

18. The transformation is as follows: [cc_est– (–2.5)] * [100 – (0)]/[2.5 – (–2.5)] + 0.

19. Spearman correlation coefficients for the WGI_COC with these indexes are 0.92 (98 observations) and 0.71 (76 observations), respectively.

20. See Hadley and Miller (2016) for a review of the arguments.

21. It is notable that in its PEFA assessment Norway scored a D on this indicator and decided that it was not a problem that needed rectifying, arguing that it was an issue to be taken up at the subnational level if at all (Hadley and Miller 2016).

22. The PI-10 indicator calls for the publication of six types of documents: three related to budget execution reporting and three related to budget documents, procurement contracts, and audit reports.

23. The press freedom index runs counterintuitively—that is, negative scores are better.

24. As a result, Angola (2016), Bhutan (2016), Botswana (2013), Cabo Verde (2016), Chad (2009), Guinea-Bissau (2014), Myanmar (2012), Norway (2008), Uruguay (2012), and Zimbabwe (2012) are omitted from the sample.

25. Norway is the only OECD country to have undertaken a PEFA assessment, scoring 3.2 out of 4 on our overall PEFA index.

26. This translates to the omission of the Democratic Republic of Congo (2008–13), El Salvador (2009–13), Georgia (2008–13), Madagascar (2006–14), Rwanda (2008–15), and Suriname (2011–15) from the sample.

27. Whereas Van Rijckeghem and Weder (2001) find a strong cross-country association between higher wages and lower levels of corruption, Foltz and Opoku-Agyemang (2015) find that a doubling in police salaries in Ghana actually resulted in highway police officers seeking larger bribes.

REFERENCES

Ades, A., and R. Di Tella. 1999. "Rents, Competition, and Corruption." *American Economic Review* 89 (4): 982–93. http://www.people.hbs.edu/rditella/papers/AERRentsCorruption.pdf.

Andvig, J. C., and O.-H. Fjeldstad, with I. Amundsen, T. Sissener, and T. Søreide. 2000. *Research on Corruption: A Policy Oriented Survey*. Final Report commissioned by Chr. Michelsen Institute and Norwegian Institute of International Affairs, Bergen. http://www.icgg.org/downloads /contribution07_andvig.pdf.

Ang, Y. 2017. *How China Escaped the Poverty Trap*. Cornell University Press.

Bastida, F., and B. Benito. 2007. "Central Government Budget Practices and Transparency: An International Comparison." *Public Administration* 85 (3): 667–716. doi:10.1111/j.1467-9299. 2007.00664.x.

Bellver, A., and D. Kaufmann. 2005. "Transparenting Transparency: Initial Empirics and Policy Applications." Preliminary draft discussion paper presented at the International Monetary Fund conference on transparency and integrity, Washington, DC, July 6–7. http://www.gsdrc.org /document-library/transparenting-transparency-initial-empirics-and-policy-applications/.

Brooke, P. 2003. "Study of Measures Used to Address Weaknesses in Public Financial Management Systems in the Context of Policy-Based Support." Final report prepared for PEFA Secretariat, Washington, DC. https://pefa.org/sites/default/files/asset/study_document/Brookes -PFMReformPlatformapproach.pdf.

Cobham, A. 2013. "Corrupting Perceptions: Foreign Policy." *Foreign Policy* (blog), July 22. http://foreignpolicy.com/2013/07/22/corrupting-perceptions/.

de Renzio, P., and J. Wehner. 2015. "The Impacts of Fiscal Openness: A Review of the Evidence." Incentives Research, Global Initiative for Fiscal Transparency. http://www.fiscaltransparency.net/resourcesfiles/files/20150704112.pdf.

Di Tella, R., and E. Schargrodsky. 2003. "The Role of Wages and Auditing during a Crackdown on Corruption in the City of Buenos Aires." *Journal of Law and Economics* 46 (1): 269–92. doi:10.1086/345578.

Donchev, D., and G. Ujhelyi. 2013. "What Do Corruption Indices Measure?" *Economics and Politics* 26 (2): 309–31. http://www.uh.edu/~gujhelyi/corrmeasures.pdf.

Dorotinsky, W., and S. Pradhan. 2007. "Exploring Corruption in Public Financial Management." In *The Many Faces of Corruption: Tracking Vulnerabilities at the Sector Level,* edited by J. E. Campos and S. Pradhan, 267–94. Washington, DC: World Bank. https://openknowledge.worldbank.org /bitstream/handle/10986/6848/399850REPLACEM101OFFICIAL0USE0ONLY1.pdf.

Ferraz, C., and F. Finan. 2008. "Exposing Corrupt Politicians: The Effects of Brazil's Publicly Released Audits on Electoral Outcomes." *Quarterly Journal of Economics* 123 (2): 703–45. doi:10.1162/qjec .2008.123.2.703.

Fisman, R., and M. A. Golden. 2017. *Corruption: What Everyone Needs to Know.* New York: Oxford University Press. https://lccn.loc.gov/2016042678.

Fjeldstad, O.-H. 2005. "Revenue Administration and Corruption." U4 Issue 2, Chr. Michelsen Institute, Bergen. https://www.cmi.no/publications/file/2558-revenue-administration-and -corruption.pdf.

Foltz, J. D., and K. A. Opoku-Agyemang. 2015. "Do Higher Salaries Lower Petty Corruption? A Policy Experiment on West Africa's Highways." Interational Growth Centre, London. https://www.gov.uk/dfid-research-outputs/do-higher-salaries-lower-petty -corruption-a-policy-experiment-on-west-africa-s-highways.

French, B. 2013. "The Impact of Public Financial Management Interventions on Corruption." Governance and Social Development Resource Centre, University of Birmingham, Birmingham, U.K. http://www.gsdrc.org/wp-content/uploads/2016/06/The Impact of -PFM-Interventions-on-Corruption-v7-FINAL-2.pdf.

Fritz, V., M. Verhoeven, and A. Avenia. 2017. "Political Economy of Public Financial Management Reforms: Experiences and Implications for Dialogue and Operational Engagement." World Bank, Washington, DC. https://pefa.org/sites/default/files/asset/study_document/121436-15-11 -2017-18-52-15-NTDofPFMReformsReportWeb.pdf

Gupta, S., M. Keen, A. Shah, and G. Verdier. 2017. *Digital Revolutions in Public Finance.* Washington, DC: International Monetary Fund. http://www.elibrary.imf.org/doc/IMF073/24661 -9781484323823/24661-9781484323823/Other_formats/Source_PDF/24661-9781484324516.pdf.

Hadley, S., and M. Miller. 2016. *PEFA: What Is It Good For? The Role of PEFA Assessments in Public Financial Management Reform.* ODI Discussion Paper. London: Overseas Development Institute. https://www.odi.org/sites/odi.org.uk/files/resource-documents/10484.pdf.

Hameed, F. 2005. *Fiscal Transparency and Economic Outcomes.* Washington, DC: International Monetary Fund. https://www.imf.org/external/pubs/ft/wp/2005/wp05225.pdf.

Heald, D. 2006. "Varieties of Transparency." In *Transparency: The Key to Better Governance?* edited by C. Hood and D. Heald, 25–43. Proceedings of the British Academy 135. Oxford: Oxford University Press for the British Academy. doi:http://dx.doi.org/10.5871/bacad/9780197263839.003.0002.

IMF (International Monetary Fund) Staff Team from the Fiscal Affairs Department and the Legal Department. 2016. "Corruption: Costs and Mitigation Strategy." IMF Staff Discussion Note SDN/16/05, International Monetary Fund, Washington, DC. https://www.imf.org/en/Publications /Staff-Discussion-Notes/Issues/2016/12/31/Corruption-Costs-and-Mitigating-Strategies-43888.

Islam, R. 2006. "Does More Transparency Go Along with Better Governance?" *Economics and Politics* 18 (2): 121–67. doi:10.1111/j.1468-0343.2006.00166.x.

Johnsøn, J., N. Taxell, and D. Zaum. 2012. "Mapping Evidence Gaps in Anti-Corruption: Assessing the State of the Operationally Relevant Evidence on Donors' Actions and Approaches to Reducing Corruption." U4 Issue 7, Chr. Michelsen Institute, Bergen. http://www.cmi.no /publications/publication/?4624=mapping-evidence-gaps-in-anti-corruption.

Khan, M. H. 2006. "Determinants of Corruption in Developing Countries: The Limits of Conventional Economic Analysis." In *International Handbook on the Economics of Corruption,* edited by S. Rose-Ackerman. Cheltenham, U.K.: Edward Elgar. http://eprints.soas.ac.uk/9850 /1/Drivers_Corruption_in_Developing_Countries_SRA_edits.pdf.

Knack, S., N. Biletska, and K. Kacker. 2017. "Deterring Kickbacks and Encouraging Entry in Public Procurement Markets: Evidence from Firm Surveys in 88 Developing Countries." Policy Research Working Paper 8078, World Bank, Washington, DC. https://openknowledge.worldbank.org /bitstream/handle/10986/26950/WPS8078.pdf?sequence=1&isAllowed=y.

Lagunes, P. F. 2017. "Guardians of Accountability: A Field Experiment on Corruption and Inefficiency in Peru's Local Public Works." International Growth Centre, London. https://www.theigc.org/blog /guardians-accountability-field-experiment-corruption-inefficiency-perus-local-public-works/.

Lindstedt, C., and D. Naurin. 2010. "Transparency Is Not Enough: Making Transparency Effective in Reducing Corruption." *International Political Science Review* 31 (3): 301–22. doi:10.2307/25703868.

Martí, C., and Y. Kasperskaya. 2015. "Public Financial Management Systems and Countries' Governance: A Cross-Country Study." *Public Administration and Development* 45 (May): 165–78. doi:10.1002/pad.

Martinez-Vazquez, J., J. Boex, and J. Arze del Granado. 2004. "Corruption, Fiscal Policy, and Fiscal Management." In *Fighting Corruption in the Public Sector,* edited by J. Martinez-Vazquez, J. Boex, and J. Arze del Granado. Contributions to Economic Analysis 284. Bingley Ward, U.K.: Emerald Group Publishing. http://pdf.usaid.gov/pdf_docs/Pnadh101.pdf.

Olken, B. 2007. "Monitoring Corruption: Evidence from a Field Experiment in Indonesia." *Journal of Political Economy* 115 (2, April): 200–49. http://www.jstor.org/stable/10.1086/517935.

Olken, B. A., and R. Pande. 2012. "Corruption in Developing Countries." Massachusetts Institute of Technology, Cambridge, MA. https://economics.mit.edu/files/7589.

PEFA (Public Expenditure and Financial Accountability) Secretariat. 2011. *Public Financial Management Performance Measurement Framework.* Washington, DC: PEFA Secretariat. https://pefa.org/sites/default/files/PMFEng-finalSZreprint04-12_1.pdf.

Reinikka, R., and J. Svensson. 2011. "The Power of Information in Public Services: Evidence from Education in Uganda." *Journal of Public Economics* 95 (7–8): 956–66. doi:10.1016/j. jpubeco.2011.02.006.

Rocha Menocal, A., and N. Taxell, with J. Stenberg Johnsøn, M. Schmaljohann, A. Guillan Montero, F. De Simone, K. Dupuy, and J. Tobias. 2015. "Why Corruption Matters: Understanding Causes, Effects, and How to Address Them." Evidence Paper, Department for International Development, London. https://www.gov.uk/government/uploads/system/uploads/attachment_data/file /406346/corruption-evidence-paper-why-corruption-matters.pdf.

Schiavo-Campo, S., and D. Tomasi. 1999. *Managing Government Expenditure.* Manila: Asian Development Bank. https://www.adb.org/publications/managing-government-expenditure.

Simson, R., and B. Welham. 2014. "Incredible Budgets: Budget Credibility in Theory and Practice." ODI Working Paper 400, Overseas Development Institution, London. https://www.odi.org /sites/odi.org.uk/files/odi-assets/publications-opinion-files/9103.pdf.

Tanzi. 1998. "Corruption around the World: Causes, Consequences, Scope, and Cures." IMF Working Paper 98/63, International Monetary Fund, Washington, DC.

Treisman, D. 2000. "The Causes of Corruption: A Cross-National Study." *Journal of Public Economics* 76 (3): 399–457.

Van Rijckeghem, C., and B. Weder. 2001. "Bureaucratic Corruption and the Rate of Temptation: Do Wages in the Civil Service Affect Corruption, and by How Much?" *Journal of Development Economics* 65 (2): 307–31. doi:10.1016/S0304-3878(01)00139-0.

Ware, G. T., S. Moss, E. Campos, and G. Noone. 2007. "Corruption in Public Procurement: A Perennial Challenge." In *The Many Faces of Corruption: Tracking Vulnerabilities at the Sector Level,* 295–334. Washington, DC: World Bank. doi:10.1596/978-0-8213-6830-5.

World Economic Forum. 2017. *The Global Competitiveness Report 2017–2018.* Geneva: World Economic Forum.

6 Revenue Administration Performance and Domestic Resource Mobilization

GUNDULA LÖFFLER, CATHAL LONG, AND ZAC MILLS

In this chapter, we estimate the cross-country relationship between penalties for noncompliance and tax collection. Our central hypothesis is that more consistent administration of penalties for noncompliance is a proxy for the type of political commitment required to increase domestic resource mobilization (DRM) in low- and middle-income countries. We find that countries that score higher on the measure of penalties for noncompliance in Public Expenditure and Financial Accountability (PEFA) assessments have ratios of tax to gross domestic product (GDP) that are 1.3 percent higher on average after controlling for other established determinants of cross-country variation in tax collection. We also find that improvements regarding penalties for noncompliance are associated with increases in the tax-to-GDP ratio over time. We further discuss the plausibility of a causal interpretation of these results. Although our results come with some caveats, we conclude that the credible administration of penalties for noncompliance is potentially a much better indicator of the commitment of low- or middle-income countries to DRM than those indicators currently in use. Unfortunately, the measure was discontinued in the updated 2016 PEFA framework without being assimilated into the frameworks of other international financial institutions that assess public administration.

INTRODUCTION

With the advent of the Sustainable Development Goals (SDGs) and the related Addis Ababa Financing for Development Agreement, domestic resource mobilization is again a hot topic in international development circles (Long and Miller 2017). The Addis Ababa agreement states that the international community "welcome[s] efforts by countries to set nationally defined domestic targets and timelines for enhancing domestic revenue as part of their national sustainable development strategies and will support developing countries in need in reaching these targets" (United Nations

2015a). But with this renewed focus on DRM came a renewed focus on revenue targets. Indeed, in the runup to the conference in Addis Ababa, the setting of revenue-to-GDP targets was hotly debated, with the zero draft of the document proposing that countries with "government revenue below 20 percent of GDP agree to progressively increase tax revenues, with the aim of halving the gap toward 20 percent by 2025" (United Nations 2015b). However, many took issue with these targets, and they were ultimately abandoned (Moore et al. 2015).

Nevertheless, they remain pervasive. The standard recommendation of the International Monetary Fund (IMF) is that low-income countries should target a tax-to-GDP ratio of 15 percent. And, though dropped as a target, the revenue-to-GDP ratio was retained as an indicator under SDG 17, the rationale being that it "enables easy comparisons across countries, . . . facilitate[s] transparent policy dialogue, and provide[s] policy makers with an important tool to assess alternative fiscal reforms and to undertake relevant policy actions."[1] Donors are often overly focused on these types of targets (European Court of Auditors 2016). This is not surprising given that they are accountable to their taxpayers to achieve results. Arguably, of most interest for donors supporting DRM reforms are indicators of the political will required "to collect taxes efficiently and effectively without fear or favor" (Bird 2015), so that they can program their financial support where it will add most value.

In this chapter, we argue that, for low- and middle-income countries, more coercive measures of tax administration, specifically the credible administration of penalties for noncompliance, are potentially a good indicator for the type of political will necessary to generate higher revenue. In the next section, we review the literature on tax compliance and note a gap in the literature with respect to cross-country analysis of the use of penalties for noncompliance, particularly in low- and middle-income countries. Then we present some initial analysis of the relationship between tax collection and indicators of revenue administration using data from PEFA assessments and discuss why we think that development agencies should pay more attention to the indicator of penalties for noncompliance. Next, we outline our methodology for examining the relationship between revenue outcomes and penalties for noncompliance in the presence of other explanatory factors of the former. We conclude by presenting and discussing our findings.

LITERATURE REVIEW

Getting citizens to comply with their tax obligations and liabilities is central to increasing DRM. Early theorists, most prominently Allingham and Sandmo (1972), looked at tax compliance as a question of rational choice, where taxpayers weigh the benefit of the additional income they get to keep if they do not pay taxes against the cost of being caught for not doing so. The latter was considered a function of the likelihood of being caught and the severity of punishment. Rational actors were expected to evade their taxes if the benefits they gain from the retained income outweigh the probability of being caught and having to pay a penalty. Accordingly, the original deterrence model emphasized tax enforcement, which identified effective tax administration as the key ingredient to improving compliance.

A rich empirical literature began emerging from this theoretical concept, relying mostly on findings from laboratory experiments that largely confirmed the stipulated mechanism (see, for example, Andreoni, Erard, and Feinstein 1998; Cowell 1990; Friedland, Maital, and Rutenberg 1978; Smith and Stalans 1991; Spicer and

Hero 1985; Thomas and Spicer 1982 for a review of this literature). However, much of this empirical research routinely found compliance levels to be significantly higher than what the deterrence model would predict (Andreoni, Erard, and Feinstein 1998; Cowell 1990; Cummings et al. 2009; Torgler 2007). This realization prompted research on tax compliance to evolve into two lines of thinking.

The first line of thinking is based on the role of uncertainty regarding the likelihood of detection. Empirical findings from both lab experiments and field research made it increasingly clear that, in the real world, taxpayers are unsure about their chances of getting audited, and this has a considerable effect on their compliance decision (Andreoni, Erard, and Feinstein 1998; Beck, Davis, and Jung 1991; Kleven et al. 2011; Slemrod, Blumenthal, and Christian 2001; Spicer and Hero 1985; Thomas and Spicer 1982). Uncertainty with regard to the risk of facing a penalty for evasion tends to make taxpayers overly cautious, resulting in increasing compliance (Mascagni 2017).

The second line of thinking, which has dominated the more recent research in this area, explores the role of nonmonetary motivations for compliance, sometimes referred to as the positive incentives for tax compliance (Smith and Stalans 1991). The literature in this area incorporates a wide range of factors that enhances people's tax morale—that is, their intrinsic motivation to comply with their tax obligations and liabilities (Alm and Martinez-Vazquez 2003; Alm, Martinez-Vazquez, and Torgler 2010; Cummings et al. 2009; Feld and Frey 2002; Smith and Stalans 1991; Torgler 2007). The factors affecting tax morale include people's understanding that they pay taxes in return for receiving public services—contractual taxation or fiscal exchange (Ali, Fjeldstad, and Sjursen 2014; Fjeldstad and Semboja 2001; Luttmer and Singhal 2014; Moore 2004, 2007; Tilly 1985); the social norms dominating their reference group—social influence theory (Ali, Fjeldstad, and Sjursen 2014; Fjeldstad and Semboja 2001; Levi 1988; Torgler 2007); and their perceptions of vertical and horizontal equity—comparative treatment (Ali, Fjeldstad, and Sjursen 2014; D'Archy 2011; Luttmer and Singhal 2014). This research on tax morale has dominated much of the more recent research, which predominantly conducts field experiments or exploits natural experiments to measure the effect of changes in people's tax morale or perceptions of taxation on their compliance behavior.

This shift in attention away from deterring noncompliance and toward encouraging voluntary compliance has led to an increased focus on the ability of tax authorities to engage in taxpayer education and communication and generally to be more transparent and accountable to taxpayers. Although this may result in positive outcomes in terms of tax morale and people's attitudes toward taxation, it has shifted attention away from the core enforcement functions of tax authorities. But in low- and middle-income countries where the use of third-party information to make evasion more difficult is less common, a "healthy fear" of the tax authority is still an important way to get people to comply with their tax obligations and liabilities. Furthermore, the focus on individual-level data of taxpayers has limited cross-country comparisons, resulting in only a small number of studies exploring the determinants of tax compliance across countries (Ali, Fjeldstad, and Sjursen 2014; Riahi-Belkaoui 2004; Richardson 2006).

This chapter seeks to address this gap, while focusing on the specific area of penalties for noncompliance. We test the following hypothesis.

Our contention is that countries that do this well provide political support to their tax administrations, resulting in higher tax-to-GDP ratios on average. In the next section, we outline our motivations for this hypothesis using data from PEFA assessments.

Hypothesis 1:
More consistent administration of penalties that are set sufficiently high to deter noncompliance is a proxy for the type of political will required for higher levels of taxation.

DATA AND ANALYSIS

Our data on penalties for noncompliance come from PEFA assessments in 112 predominantly low- and middle-income countries over the period 2005–15 (see annex 6A)—specifically, indicator 14, dimension 2 (hereafter PI-14(ii)) of the 2011 PEFA framework.[2] The advantages of using penalties for noncompliance as a proxy for political will are that penalties are considered a more functional measure of revenue administration than other dimensions; scoring on the relevant dimension has a more distinct relationship with revenue outcomes than other dimensions; scoring on the dimension is distributed more normally than other dimensions; and the relationship between dimension scores and revenue outcomes is less susceptible to reverse causality concerns than other dimensions. Some endogeneity concerns exist with respect to measurement error, and these concerns are discussed further below.

An important distinction to be made between the dimensions is whether they measure the form or the function of the revenue administration. In an analysis of the PEFA framework, Andrews (2011) distinguishes between de jure dimensions that measure form and de facto dimensions that measure function (see chapter 2 for further discussion). Table 6.1 outlines Andrews's categorization of the nine dimensions of the PEFA assessment concerned with revenue administration. Of the nine dimensions, he considers just four to be de facto measures of revenue administration, including PI-14(ii). In line with our hypothesis, we would expect that scoring on de facto measures would require political will for the revenue administration to be more functional. Therefore, we might expect to see stronger relationships between revenue outcomes and better scoring on these dimensions.

PEFA dimensions are measured on a scale from A to D, with As indicating the achievement of "good practice," Bs and Cs representing some progress toward good practice, and Ds representing lack of effort. As shown in table 6.2, to score an A on PI-14(ii), a country must show evidence that penalties are set sufficiently high to deter noncompliance and are administered consistently. In the guidance material (PEFA Secretariat 2012), assessors are expected to consider the following questions: Are there penalties for noncompliance with registration and tax declaration in existing legislation or current administrative procedures? If the answer is yes, are they sufficient to affect compliance, or are changes needed? How do the penalties work in practice? Are they enforced? Between its first assessment in 2008 and its second in 2015, Nepal moved from a C score to an A score on PI-14(ii). In the 2008 report, the most notable justification given for the C score was that penalties for

TABLE 6.1 De jure versus de facto measures of revenue administration

DIMENSION	TYPE
PI-13(i)—Clarity	De jure
PI-13(ii)—Information	De jure
PI-13(iii)—Appeals	De jure
PI-14(i)—Controls	De jure
PI-14(ii)—Penalties	De facto
PI-14(iii)—Audit	De jure
PI-15(i)—Arrears	De facto
PI-15(ii)—Collection	De facto
PI-15(iii)—Reconciliation	De facto

Source: Based on Andrews 2011.

TABLE 6.2 **PI-14(ii)—penalties for noncompliance—scoring methodology**

SCORE	MINIMUM REQUIREMENTS OR SCORING METHODOLOGY
A	Penalties for all areas of noncompliance are set sufficiently high to act as deterrence and are consistently administered.
B	Penalties for noncompliance exist for most relevant areas but are not always effective because of insufficient scale or inconsistent administration.
C	Penalties for noncompliance generally exist, but substantial changes to their structure, levels, or administration are needed for them to have a real impact on compliance.
D	Penalties for noncompliance are generally nonexistent or ineffective (that is, set far too low to have an impact or rarely imposed).

Source: PEFA Secretariat 2011.

TABLE 6.3 **Tax administration assessment indicators and dimensions in the 2011 Public Expenditure and Financial Accountability (PEFA) framework**

DIMENSION	DESCRIPTION
PI-13	*Transparency of taxpayer obligations and liabilities*
(i)	Clarity and comprehensiveness of tax liabilities
(ii)	Taxpayer access to information on tax liabilities and administrative procedures
(iii)	Existence and functioning of a tax appeals mechanism
PI-14	*The effectiveness of measures for taxpayer registration and tax assessment*
(i)	Controls in the taxpayer registration system
(ii)	Effectiveness of penalties for noncompliance with registration and declaration obligations
(iii)	Planning and monitoring of tax audit and fraud investigation programs
PI-15	*The effectiveness in collection of tax payments*
(i)	Collection ratio for gross tax arrears, being the percentage of tax arrears at the beginning of a fiscal year, which was collected during that fiscal year (average of the last two fiscal years)
(ii)	Effectiveness of transfer of tax collections to the treasury by the revenue administration
(iii)	Frequency of complete accounts reconciliation between tax assessments, collections, arrears records, and receipts by the treasury

noncompliance existed for most relevant taxes, but they were not always effective because of inconsistent administration (Nepal PEFA Secretariat 2008).

In contrast, in the 2015 report, the most notable point made in favor of the A score was that Nepal's Inland Revenue Department investigated 373 cases of tax evasion in fiscal 2012 and found NPR 1.75 billion in payables (tax and fines). In fiscal 2013, it investigated 737 cases and found NPR 2.09 billion in payables (Nepal PEFA Secretariat 2015).

PI-14(ii) is one of nine dimensions that measure good practice in tax administration under the 2011 PEFA framework. PI-13, PI-14, and PI-15 each has three dimensions measuring the transparency of taxpayer obligations and liabilities, effectiveness of measures for taxpayer registration and tax assessment, and effectiveness in the collection of tax payments, respectively. Table 6.3 lists each of the dimensions by indicator.

Our data on tax collection come from the Government Revenue Dataset (GRD) of the International Centre for Tax and Development (ICTD) and the United Nations University World Institute for Development Economics Research (UNU WIDER).[3] The GRD provides the best coverage of revenue collection and its disaggregates for low- and middle-income countries. Of the 124 countries that carried out at least one PEFA assessment between 2006 and 2015, the GRD holds revenue time series for 112 (see annex 6A). For this chapter, we use taxes excluding social contributions as a percentage of GDP (hereafter tax-to-GDP ratio). The option to exclude social contributions is useful because social contributions exist in some countries but not in others. However, according to notes accompanying the GRD, for some countries they are not easily separated, raising concerns about potential measurement error. For the purposes of comparison with PEFA scores, we use a three-year moving average of the tax-to-GDP ratio throughout the chapter to reflect the fact that PEFA is a backward-looking assessment.

Figure 6.1 shows the trends for the mean tax-to-GDP ratio by dimension score for PI-13, PI-14, and PI-15. The trends are indicative of the potential importance of some tax administration functions for increasing the tax-to-GDP ratio.

The evidence for the dimensions under PI-13 is mixed. There seems to be no relationship of note for PI-13(i) (clarity and comprehensiveness of tax liabilities) and PI-13(ii) (taxpayer access to information on tax liabilities and administrative procedures). However, a more distinct positive relationship is evident between the average tax-to-GDP ratio and PI-13(iii) (existence and functioning of a tax appeals mechanism), but its correlation coefficient is among the weakest (table 6.4). Similarly, we find mixed evidence for the dimensions under indicator PI-15. There is no clear relationship for PI-15(i) (collection ratio for gross tax arrears)[4] and PI-15(iii) (frequency of complete accounts reconciliation between tax assessments, collections, arrears records, and receipts by the treasury). The average tax-to-GDP ratio is higher for countries scoring an A on PI-15(ii) (effectiveness of transfer of tax collections to

FIGURE 6.1

Mean tax-to-GDP ratio, by dimension score for Public Expenditure and Financial Accountability (PEFA) indicators PI-13, PI-14, and PI-15

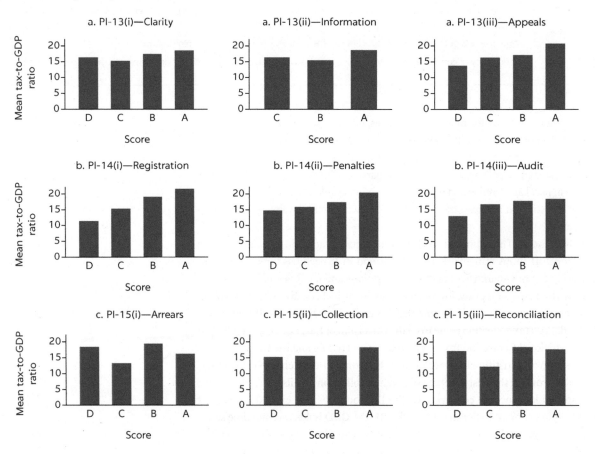

Note: Figure reflects 112 observations for all dimensions, except for PI-15(i) (92), PI-15(ii) (110), and PI-15(iii) (111).

TABLE 6.4 **Spearman correlation coefficients for tax-to-GDP ratio and dimensions under Public Expenditure and Financial Accountability (PEFA) indicators PI-13, PI-14, and PI-15**

	TAX/GDP	PI-13(i)	PI-13(ii)	PI-13(iii)	PI-14(i)	PI-14(ii)	PI-14(iii)	PI-15(i)	PI-15(ii)	PI-15(iii)
Tax/GDP	1.000	0.222	0.240	0.198	0.468	0.264	0.197	−0.170	0.261	0.092
PI-13(i)	0.222	1.000	0.421	0.352	0.332	0.325	0.470	−0.110	0.128	0.334
PI-13(ii)	0.240	0.421	1.000	0.455	0.495	0.387	0.443	0.073	0.260	0.429
PI-13(iii)	0.198	0.352	0.455	1.000	0.298	0.408	0.441	0.004	0.104	0.369
PI-14(i)	0.468	0.332	0.495	0.298	1.000	0.442	0.494	0.188	0.305	0.483
PI-14(ii)	0.264	0.325	0.387	0.408	0.442	1.000	0.369	0.030	0.166	0.415
PI-14(iii)	0.197	0.470	0.443	0.441	0.494	0.369	1.000	0.109	0.168	0.432
PI-15(i)	−0.170	−0.110	0.073	0.004	0.188	0.030	0.109	1.000	0.028	0.196
PI-15(ii)	0.261	0.128	0.260	0.104	0.305	0.166	0.168	0.028	1.000	0.283
PI-15(iii)	0.092	0.334	0.429	0.369	0.483	0.415	0.432	0.196	0.283	1.000

the treasury by the revenue administration), but no notable difference is evident between the average tax-to-GDP ratios associated with scoring a B, C, or D.

In contrast, PI-14(i) (controls in the taxpayer registration system) displays a clear trend of stepped increases in the average tax-to-GDP ratio along the PEFA scale from D to A and has the strongest correlation with the tax-to-GDP ratio (table 6.4). PI-14(ii) and PI-14(iii) (planning and monitoring of tax audit programs)[5] display less obvious trends and have weaker correlations.

The distribution of scores is also revealing (see figure 6.2). We observe more normal distributions for the dimensions under PI-14 as well as PI-13(i) and PI-13(iii), with most countries scoring a B or C. Most countries perform well on PI-13(ii) and PI-15(ii) and poorly on PI-15(i) (for the 92 countries where it was even possible to assess the dimension), whereas performance on PI-15(iii) is at the extremes, with most countries scoring either an A or a D. These findings fit with the discussion in chapter 2—namely, that some indicators measure form over function and are susceptible to isomorphic mimicry and gaming, with countries focusing on those measures that are easier to change in order to satisfy external funders (Hadley and Miller 2016). Andrews (2011) puts forward evidence that countries tend to perform better on measures of de jure reforms (that is, legal and procedural changes) than on measures of de facto reforms (that is, actual changes in practice). Of the nine dimensions, he considers only PI-14(ii) and the three dimensions under PI-15 to be de facto reforms. This supports our hypothesis that PI-14(ii) serves as a good proxy for the political will required to improve tax performance.

PI-14(ii) is also less susceptible to critiques that the relationship with the tax-to-GDP ratio is endogenous because of simultaneity or reverse causality. Many of the reforms related to the nine dimensions are associated with having market-based economies and higher levels of income, which are also associated with higher tax-to-GDP ratios. For example, it is likely to be difficult to perform well on PI-14(i), which requires rather sophisticated links between government and financial market databases to score an A, unless the government can retain software engineers, who are often in short supply in low- and middle-income countries. Similarly, scoring well on PI-14(iii) likely requires the retention of a well-paid cadre of tax auditors, which is often not possible in lower-income countries. As a result, low- and middle-income countries frequently receive support to overhaul their tax administrations in the form of technical assistance, which might improve PEFA scores without improving tax performance.

FIGURE 6.2

Frequency distribution (number), by dimension score for Public Expenditure and Financial Accountability (PEFA) indicators PI-13, PI-14, and PI-15

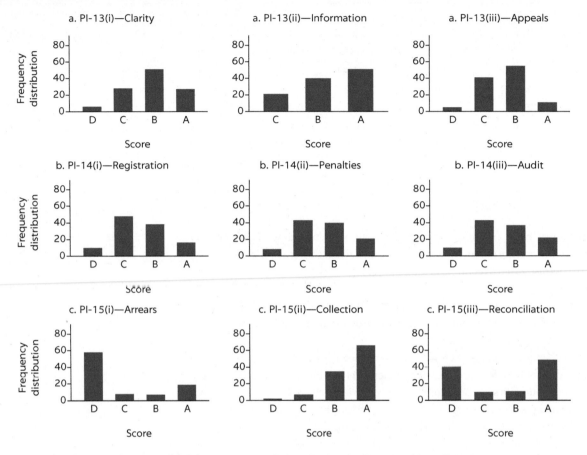

Note: Figure reflects 112 observations for all dimensions, except for PI-15(i) (92), PI-15(ii) (110), and PI-15(iii) (111).

This is because there are limits to what can be achieved through technical assistance. With respect to PI-14(ii), it seems plausible that external advisers could assist with setting credible penalties for noncompliance, but they are unlikely to be able to do much about the administration of penalties in the absence of political will.

Figure 6.3, which shows similar variation in scoring for PI-14(ii) across income levels, provides some evidence in this respect, in contrast to the distribution of scoring for other dimensions. As such, our contention is that the relationship between the tax-to-GDP ratio and PI-14(ii) is a more plausible measure of the political will required to improve tax performance than other measures, because politicians at all income levels may be motivated to raise more taxation or to stymie efforts to do the same. The case against a causal interpretation is that the enforcement of penalties for noncompliance is expensive, and therefore higher scores can only be achieved in countries that have resources. However, the countries that score an A on PI-14(ii) are spread relatively evenly across income groups.

Potentially larger endogeneity concerns are measurement error and omitted variable bias. Concerns about measurement error apply to both our dependent variable (the tax-to-GDP ratio) and our independent variable (PI-14(ii)). As previously stated, our data for the tax-to-GDP ratio is from the GRD, which for 30 countries in our sample of 112 uses general rather than central government data on tax revenues. The justification for this is simple: ICTD and UNU WIDER use general

FIGURE 6.3

Distribution of scores, by dimension and income group for Public Expenditure and Financial Accountability (PEFA) indicators PI-13, PI-14, and PI-15

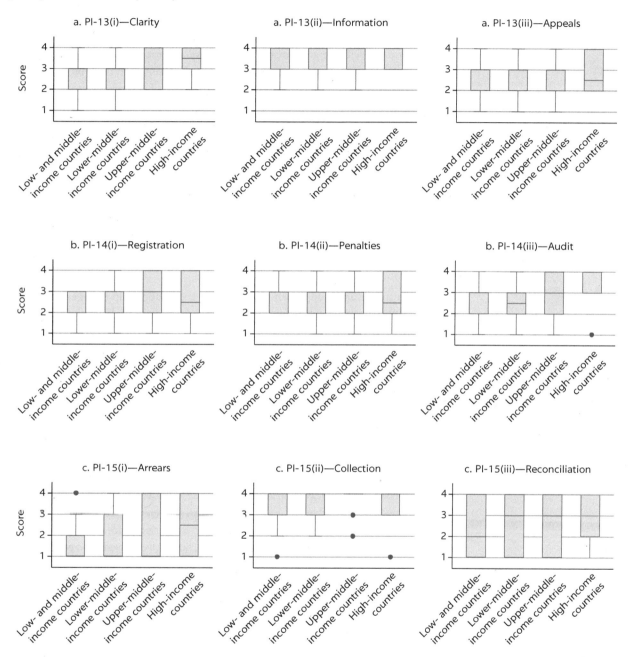

Note: Figure reflects 112 observations for all dimensions, except for PI-15(i) (92), PI-15(ii) (110), and PI-15(iii) (111).

government data where they are available, which is generally the case for larger or federal states, and are less concerned about using government data for unitary or highly centralized states where local taxation is often negligible, particularly in smaller lower-income countries (Prichard, Cobham, and Goodall 2014). But PEFA assessments are carried out at the central government level, so this presents a potential problem for our hypothesis, unless we can assume that penalties for noncompliance are set and administered similarly at both the central and lower levels of government in nonunitary states. The ability to account for subnational revenues may indicate a certain level of coherence that makes this assumption plausible. Nevertheless, we consider this potential source of measurement error in more detail in the sections that follow.

Potential sources of measurement error in PI-14(ii) include the bias of assessors and a mismatch between the report date and reporting period. Many PEFA assessments are self-assessments carried out by government officials themselves, including the example of Nepal cited above. Although the PEFA Secretariat provides quality assurance, some countries choose not to avail of this offer. Unfortunately, the data set does not provide sufficient detail to distinguish or control between self-assessments and more independent assessments. There are also potential mismatches between the date of the assessment report in the PEFA data set and the actual time period covered due to publication lags. The example of Nepal's 2008 report is a case in point. Although the date in the database is 2008, the document clearly states that it covers the year ended 2005/06. These concerns as well as omitted variable bias are discussed in more detail in the next section.

ESTIMATION APPROACH

Our preliminary approach is to estimate the relationship between the tax-to-GDP ratio and penalties for noncompliance using ordinary least squares (OLS) in equation (6.1):

$$Y_i = \alpha + \beta X_i + \gamma Z_i + \varepsilon_i, \tag{6.1}$$

where Y_i is the tax-to-GDP ratio, X_i is PI-14(ii) as measured by the PEFA assessment for country i, Z_i is a matrix of country-level controls, and ε_i is our error term. Our control variables are based on the findings of similar studies on the cross-country determinants of tax collection (table 6.5). Variables from PEFA assessments enter the equation with an ordinal assignment of A = 4, B = 3, C = 2, and D = 1, which has been in common use in research papers since de Renzio, Andrews, and Mills (2011). For our sample of 112 countries, we use the latest PEFA assessment available over the period 2007–15 (table 6.6).

There is a standard approach to modeling tax performance using proxies for the tax base and the structure of the economy. Those proxies used most commonly for low- and middle-income countries for this purpose are the share of agriculture in GDP as a proxy for the size of the informal economy, international trade as a share of

TABLE 6.5 **Cross-sectional sample**

YEAR	MOST RECENT ASSESSMENT
2007	2
2008	4
2009	12
2010	13
2011	9
2012	14
2013	23
2014	17
2015	18
Total	**112**

TABLE 6.6 **Control variables**

CONTROL	MEASUREMENT	SOURCE
Informal economy	Agriculture as a % of GDP	World Development Indicators
Openness to trade	Imports and exports as % of GDP	World Development Indicators
Natural resources	Natural resource rents as % of GDP	World Development Indicators
Economic development	Log GDP per capita	World Development Indicators
Democracy	Voice and accountability score	Worldwide Governance Indicators

GDP as a measure of the openness of the economy, and GDP per capita (Morrissey et al. 2017). We expect tax performance to be negatively associated with the share of agriculture in GDP because the sector is difficult to tax and, in the case of subsistence agriculture, does not generate taxable income. In contrast, trade taxes are easier to collect, so we expect a positive association between the trade share of GDP and tax performance. GDP per capita, a proxy for the level of economic development, is expected to be positively correlated with tax performance, but other studies have often found the opposite (Morrissey et al. 2017).

When modeling the determinants of tax collection in low- and middle-income countries, natural resources are often considered. For example, Gupta (2007) uses dummy variables for oil-producing and mineral-exporting countries. We control for the share of natural resource rents in GDP but are ambiguous about the relationship. Natural resource government revenues are included in revenue-to-GDP ratios, but not in tax-to-GDP ratios. However, taxation on the companies that generate these revenues is included. Therefore, there is the potential for a negative association where natural resource rents deter tax effort, but also a positive association where taxation on the activities of extractive industries mechanically generate more taxation (Bornhorst, Gupta, and Thornton 2009). In keeping with the literature on tax morale, we use the Worldwide Governance Indicators (WGI) for voice and accountability as a proxy for democracy.[6] We expect democracy to be positively correlated with the tax-to-GDP ratio in line with the literature on fiscal contracting.

We also employ dummy variables for regions as defined by the World Bank and include a dummy variable to account for the presence of 24 small island developing states (SIDS) within the sample (table 6.7) and for Botswana, Lesotho, Namibia, and Swaziland (BLNS), which are members of the Southern Africa Customs Union and subject to the peculiarities of its revenue-sharing formula (Basdevant 2012). To account for potential measurement error between the assessment date in the data set and the period covered by the report, the dependent and control variables in table 6.6 enter the equation as a three-year moving average of the year of the assessment and the two preceding years. And for potential measurement associated with the use of general government data, as discussed above, we employ a dummy variable for federal states for which the tax-to-GDP ratio is for general government in the ICTD and UNU WIDER data set.

Our secondary approach is to control for omitted variable bias. Omitted variable bias is a concern for cross-sectional estimation using OLS in equation (6.1) if tax-to-GDP ratios are determined by unobservable national characteristics, such as culture. If they are, our OLS estimates of the coefficient for PI-14(ii) will be biased. However, if these unobservable variables are fixed over time, then estimation over time allows us to remove this bias. Because the PEFA data set contains repeat assessments, it is possible to estimate over time by estimating equation (6.2):

$$Y_{it} = FE_i + \beta X_{it} + \gamma Z_{it} + \varepsilon_{it}. \tag{6.2}$$

TABLE 6.7 **Sample size, by small island developing states (SIDS) status and region**

REGION	NON-SIDS	SIDS	TOTAL
East Asia and Pacific	8	6	14
Europe and Central Asia	18	0	18
Latin America and the Caribbean	13	13	26
Middle East and North Africa	8	0	8
South Asia	7	1	8
Sub-Saharan Africa	34	4	38
Total	88	24	112

TABLE 6.8 **Unbalanced panel data sample, 2005–15**

YEAR	FIRST ASSESSMENT	MOST RECENT ASSESSMENT	TOTAL
2005	4	0	4
2006	13	0	13
2007	15	0	15
2008	13	0	13
2009	11	1	12
2010	4	4	8
2011	1	6	7
2012	0	7	7
2013	0	14	14
2014	0	16	16
2015	0	13	13
Total	61	61	122

This model estimates the relationship between changes in the tax-to-GDP ratio (Y) and changes in PI-14(ii) (X) in country i over a period of time t, also controlling for changes in our other controls (Z) and country fixed effects (FE_i). Our data set has two time periods: the year of the first assessment and the year of the most recent assessment. But it is unbalanced—that is, countries have undertaken their first and most recent assessments at different times (table 6.8).

Finally, because the estimators in equations (6.1) and (6.2) assume continuous rather than ordinal variables, we also estimate equations (6.1) and (6.2) with the independent PEFA variable, PI-14(ii), entering the equation as a series dummy variable in order to obtain a better estimate of the relationship with the tax-to-GDP ratio.

RESULTS

Table 6.9 shows the results from estimating equation (6.1) using OLS. The sample covers the most recent PEFA assessment for 112 countries spanning the period from 2007 to 2015. Our estimates show a positive relationship between PI-14(ii) and the tax-to-GDP ratio that is statistically significant at the 5 percent level or better across all specifications. Our estimated coefficient implies that countries scoring one score higher on PI-14(ii) have tax-to-GDP ratios that are 2 percent higher on average (columns 1 to 4). When we add PI-14(i) as a control (column 5),[7] this effect declines to 1.3 percent.

This stands to reason, given that we would expect the impact of penalties for non-compliance to wane as registration controls are improved. Because PEFA scores are ordinal and OLS estimation assumes continuous variables, we also estimate equation (6.1) using dummy variables for PI-14(ii) (see annex 6B, table 6B.1). These estimates indicate that A scores drive the results for PI-14(ii) in table 6.9. Countries scoring an A have tax-to-GDP ratios that are 2.7 percent higher on average than countries scoring a B, C, or D, and this estimate is statistically significant at the 5 percent level.[8]

Our estimates of controls for the structure of the economy are largely in line with a priori assumptions and previous findings. We estimate correlations for the size of the agriculture sector, our proxy for the informal economy, and natural resource rents that are negative, as expected. Similarly, our estimate for the trade share in GDP is positive, as expected. Our estimated coefficient for the voice and accountability score—our proxy for democracy—is also positive, as expected. Moreover, all of these estimates are statistically significant at the 10 percent level or better across all specifications. A confounding result is our estimate of the coefficient for income per capita, which is consistently both negative and large and statistically significant at the 10 percent level in our full specification, although this is a common finding in the literature.[9] We estimate that all three of our dummy variables for BLNS countries,

TABLE 6.9 **Ordinary least squares (OLS) estimates for the relationship between performance indicators and the tax-to-GDP ratio**

VARIABLE	(1)	(2)	(3)	(4)	(5)
PI-14(ii)—Penalties	1.948***	1.979***	1.977***	1.879***	1.274**
	(0.583)	(0.549)	(0.534)	(0.537)	(0.562)
Agriculture (% of GDP)		−0.202***	−0.196***	−0.153***	−0.133**
		(0.0624)	(0.0636)	(0.0521)	(0.0532)
Trade (% of GDP)		0.0592***	0.0576***	0.0569***	0.0556***
		(0.0164)	(0.0159)	(0.0138)	(0.0130)
Natural resource rents (% of GDP)		−0.177***	−0.141***	−0.130**	−0.126**
		(0.0519)	(0.0519)	(0.0582)	(0.0548)
Income per capita (log)		0.918	−1.561	−1.936**	−1.793*
		(1.062)	(0.999)	(0.976)	(0.970)
Voice and accountability score			1.941***	1.718**	1.431*
			(0.647)	(0.776)	(0.771)
BLNS dummy				8.519***	8.813***
				(2.984)	(2.691)
SIDS dummy				1.711	1.966
				(1.383)	(1.285)
Federal dummy				5.045*	4.068
				(2.710)	(2.669)
PI-14(i)—Registration					1.550***
					(0.582)
Constant	10.97***	18.19*	24.20***	25.94***	22.60**
	(1.962)	(9.679)	(9.163)	(8.764)	(8.915)
Observations	112	112	112	112	112
R-squared	0.247	0.549	0.581	0.650	0.673

Note: Robust standard errors are in parentheses. Coefficients for dummy variables for six regions are not reported. BLNS = Botswana, Lesotho, Namibia, and Swaziland; SIDS = small island developing states.
*** p<0.01, ** p<0.05, * p<0.1

TABLE 6.10 **Panel estimates for the relationship between performance indicators and the tax-to-GDP ratio controlling for country-specific factors**

VARIABLE	(1)	(2)	(3)
PI-14(ii)—Penalties	1.371**	0.975**	1.190**
	(0.629)	(0.478)	(0.486)
Agriculture (% of GDP)		−0.0692	−0.0245
		(0.0992)	(0.0957)
Trade (% of GDP)		0.0427	0.0341
		(0.0382)	(0.0337)
Natural resource rents (% of GDP)		0.0356	0.0421
		(0.112)	(0.0999)
Income per capita (log)		6.113	7.998*
		(4.276)	(4.550)
Voice and accountability score		−1.698	−2.024
		(1.802)	(1.686)
PI-14(i)—Registration			−1.086
			(0.751)
Constant	13.85***	−39.92	−53.89
	(1.671)	(37.94)	(39.60)
Observations	122	122	122
R-squared	0.115	0.288	0.321
Number of id	61	61	61

Note: Robust standard errors in are parentheses.
*** $p<0.01$, ** $p<0.05$, * $p<0.1$

SIDS, and federal states using general government data are positive, but only the BLNS dummy is statistically significant in our full specification.

The size and statistical significance of estimates using data from PEFA assessments are susceptible to being driven by a small number of observations at the fringes. In annex 6B, table 6B.3, we run the same estimation procedure for smaller sample sizes to test the robustness of our estimates and find that they remain statistically significant after decreasing the sample size by the top and bottom 5–10 percent of tax-to-GDP ratio observations. Another concern is with our dependent variable data. For 30 countries in our sample of 112, the data in the GRD is for general rather than central government. PEFA assessments are carried out at the central government level. This affects our hypothesis if subnational enforcement of penalties and fines for noncompliance are administered differently at the national level. In annex 6B, table 6B.4, we find that our results for PI-14(ii) are robust to (a) dropping the 30 countries with general government data and (b) using central government data from the IMF Government Finance Statistics[10] database for 19 of those countries.

As previously noted, various endogeneity issues are associated with this cross-sectional analysis. Omitted variable bias is a concern if tax-to-GDP ratios are determined by unobservable national characteristics. To control for this potential source of bias, we estimate equation (6.2) for a sample of 61 countries (see annex 6B, table 6B.3) that had repeat PEFA assessments. The results in table 6.10 show a statistically significant relationship between PI-14(ii) and the tax-to-GDP ratio over time. In our full specification in column 3, a one-score improvement in PI-14(ii) is associated with a 1.2 percent increase in the tax-to-GDP ratio that is statistically significant at the 5 percent level.[11]

FIGURE 6.4

Changes in PI-14ii and PI-14i scores between assessments

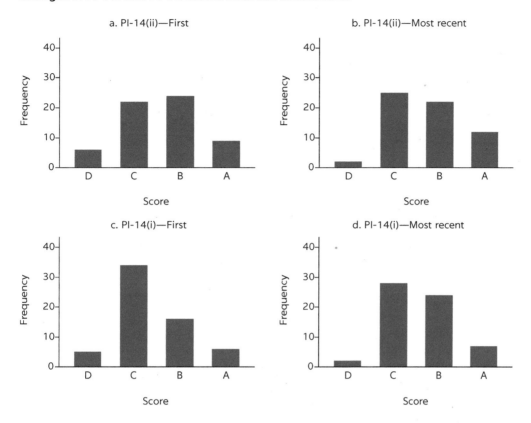

Most of the estimated coefficients of our other controls are not statistically significant. The shares of agriculture, trade, and natural resource rents take on the expected signs, but their estimated coefficients are quite small. In contrast to our cross-sectional models, our estimated coefficient for income per capita is positive and large and statistically significant at the 10 percent level in our full specification. Surprisingly, our democracy control, Worldwide Governance Indicators voice and accountability (WGIVA) score, has a negative estimated coefficient. Our estimated coefficient for PI-14(i) is also counterintuitively negative and statistically insignificant, which contrasts with our cross-sectional results. This may simply be because, in contrast to PI-14(ii), fewer countries have made progress toward an A grade between assessments on PI-14(i) (see figure 6.4). Another reason may be that improvements in de jure indicators do not reflect the political will necessary to increase revenue outcomes in line with our hypothesis. The counterintuitive estimated signage of some of our other controls may be the result of the small sample size, both in terms of the number of countries and length of the time series.

DISCUSSION

Overall our results demonstrate a positive and statistically significant cross-country relationship between the credible enforcement of penalties for noncompliance, as measured by PI-14(ii), and DRM, as measured by the tax-to-GDP ratio, while controlling for a range of other determinants. Our cross-sectional results for 112 countries show that a one-score improvement on the PEFA scale is associated with a tax-to-GDP ratio that is 1.3 percent higher on average, while achieving a "good practice" A score on PI-14(ii) is associated with a tax-to-GDP ratio that is 2.7 percent higher on average. We also address a major endogeneity concern associated with this type of estimation by controlling for unobservable country-specific factors that might influence both a country's PI-14(ii) score and its tax-to-GDP ratio. We do this by including country fixed effects for an unbalanced panel of 61 countries. Our results show that a 1-point improvement on the PEFA scale is associated with a 1.2 percent increase in the tax-to-GDP ratio. Although we find that improving from a C or D to a B or A score on PI-14(ii) is associated with an improvement in the tax-to-GDP ratio of 2.2 percent that is statistically significant, we fail to find a statistically significant effect for improving to a "good practice" A score. This may be due to the fact that our sample period spans the great recession.

Our hypothesis and analysis of the underlying data make a plausible case for a causal interpretation of these findings. However, these results are not without important caveats. Our estimates are based on an unbalanced panel of observations over the period from 2005 to 2015, making interpretation of our coefficient for PI-14(ii) potentially less straightforward; moreover, our panel sample is relatively small and therefore lacking in variation for the independent variable. Although we have addressed issues of measurement error pertaining to the use of general government data, we cannot assuage these concerns fully. Similarly, we cannot account for the potential that the collection of penalties itself is driving increases in the tax-to-GDP ratio, although it seems unlikely. Furthermore, we cannot account for potential bias within the measurement of PI-14(ii) itself arising from self-assessment. Although the PEFA Secretariat provides detailed field guidance to assessors, it is hard to imagine that the assessment is not biased by the judgment of assessors because of the limited availability of data across tax categories and levels of government.

Further research is likely required before developing concrete policy prescriptions. This effort might include attempting to address some of the caveats noted above, taking a more qualitative look at the enforcement of penalties for noncompliance in a sample of countries, and conducting quantitative analysis using the tax administration databases of revenue administrations in low- and middle-income countries. The latter has become a burgeoning industry for experiments in quasi-voluntary compliance but has thus far been relatively silent on more coercive measures of compliance. For example, shedding more light on whether the prescribed measure is the size of the penalty or the credibility of enforcement would be informative for both donors and revenue administrations themselves.

Nevertheless, our empirical findings combined with the theoretical underpinnings we have laid out suggest that PI-14(ii) may provide a much better indicator of the commitment of low- and middle-income countries to DRM under the Addis Ababa Financing for Development Agreement. Compared with the existing practice of simply observing revenue-to-GDP ratios, PI-14(ii) likely requires genuine domestic political commitment. Whereas modern tax systems focus more on voluntary compliance and risk management, donors interested in supporting DRM should not lose sight of the fact that coercive measures may also be an important indicator of the political will necessary to improve revenue outcomes, particularly in lower-income countries. Unfortunately, however, the indicator was not retained in the updated PEFA 2016 framework and appears not to have been assimilated into the Tax Administration Diagnostic Assessment Tool (TADAT). So, if the credible enforcement of penalties for noncompliance is to be monitored going forward, some other institution will have to lead the process of data collection.

ANNEX 6A SAMPLE OF COUNTRIES

TABLE 6A.1 **Cross-sectional sample of 112 countries by income group at time of most recent assessment**

LOW-INCOME COUNTRIES	LOWER-MIDDLE-INCOME COUNTRIES	UPPER-MIDDLE-INCOME COUNTRIES	HIGH-INCOME COUNTRIES
Afghanistan	Armenia	Albania	Antigua and Barbuda
Bangladesh	Bhutan	Azerbaijan	Bahamas, The
Benin	Bolivia	Belarus	Barbados
Burkina Faso	Cabo Verde	Belize	Kuwait
Burundi	Cameroon	Botswana	Norway
Cambodia	Colombia	Brazil	Oman
Central African Republic	Congo, Rep.	Costa Rica	
Chad	Côte d'Ivoire	Dominica	
Congo, Dem. Rep.	Egypt, Arab Rep.	Dominican Republic	
Ethiopia	El Salvador	Ecuador	
Gambia, The	Eswatini	Grenada	
Guinea-Bissau	Fiji	Jamaica	
Kenya	Georgia	Kazakhstan	
Lao PDR	Ghana	Lebanon	
Liberia	Guatemala	Maldives	
Madagascar	Guyana	Mauritius	
Malawi	Honduras	Montenegro	
Mali	India	Namibia	
Mozambique	Indonesia	North Macedonia	
Myanmar	Iraq	Panama	
Nepal	Jordan	Peru	
Niger	Kiribati	Russian Federation	
Rwanda	Kosovo	Serbia	
Sierra Leone	Kyrgyz Republic	Seychelles	
Tajikistan	Lesotho	South Africa	
Tanzania	Mauritania	St. Kitts and Nevis	
Togo	Micronesia, Fed. Sts.	St. Lucia	
Uganda	Moldova	St. Vincent and the Grenadines	
Zimbabwe	Mongolia	Suriname	
	Morocco	Turkey	
	Nicaragua	Uruguay	
	Pakistan		
	Paraguay		
	Philippines		
	Samoa		
	Senegal		
	Sri Lanka		
	Sudan		
	Thailand		
	Tonga		
	Tunisia		

continued

TABLE 6A.1, *continued*

LOW-INCOME COUNTRIES	LOWER-MIDDLE-INCOME COUNTRIES	UPPER-MIDDLE-INCOME COUNTRIES	HIGH-INCOME COUNTRIES
	Ukraine		
	Uzbekistan		
	Vanuatu		
	Vietnam		
	Zambia		

TABLE 6A.2 **Panel sample of 61 countries by income group at time of most recent assessment**

LOW-INCOME COUNTRIES	LOWER-MIDDLE-INCOME COUNTRIES	UPPER-MIDDLE-INCOME COUNTRIES	HIGH-INCOME COUNTRIES
Afghanistan	Armenia	Azerbaijan	Antigua and Barbuda
Benin	Congo, Rep.	Belarus	Barbados
Burkina Faso	El Salvador	Belize	
Burundi	Estwatini	Botswana	
Central African Republic	Fiji	Dominica	
Congo, Dem. Rep.	Georgia	Dominican Republic	
Gambia, The	Ghana	Ecuador	
Kenya	Guatemala	Grenada	
Liberia	Jordan	Jamaica	
Madagascar	Kyrgyz Republic	Maldives	
Mali	Mauritania	Mauritius	
Mozambique	Moldova	Montenegro	
Nepal	Pakistan	Namibia	
Niger	Paraguay	Peru	
Rwanda	Samoa	Serbia	
Sierra Leone	Senegal	Seychelles	
Tajikistan	Tonga	South Africa	
Uganda	Ukraine	St. Kitts and Nevis	
	Vanuatu	St. Lucia	
	Zambia	St. Vincent and the Grenadines	
		Suriname	

ANNEX 6B CROSS-SECTIONAL ESTIMATION

TABLE 6B.1 **Ordinary least squares (OLS) estimates for the relationship between performance indicators and the tax-to-GDP ratio using dummy variables for PI-14(ii) (1 of 2)**

VARIABLE	(1)	(2)	(3)
PI-14(ii) = A	2.699**		
	(1.173)		
PI-14(ii) = A or B		1.464*	
		(0.833)	
PI-14(ii) = A, B, or C			1.358
			(1.637)
Agriculture (% of GDP)	−0.144***	−0.121**	−0.125**
	(0.0537)	(0.0553)	(0.0578)
Trade (% of GDP)	0.0559***	0.0524***	0.0531***
	(0.0135)	(0.0132)	(0.0130)
Natural resource rents (% of GDP)	−0.121**	−0.134**	−0.132**
	(0.0529)	(0.0559)	(0.0547)
Income per capita (log)	−1.927**	−1.652*	−1.635
	(0.953)	(0.995)	(1.008)
Voice and accountability score	1.322*	1.431*	1.360*
	(0.777)	(0.798)	(0.796)
BLNS dummy	8.937***	8.943***	9.014***
	(2.969)	(2.526)	(2.621)
SIDS dummy	1.888	1.901	1.930
	(1.318)	(1.284)	(1.252)
Federal dummy	4.393*	3.813	3.893
	(2.541)	(2.660)	(2.589)
PI-14(i)—Registration	1.792***	1.803***	2.127***
	(0.556)	(0.591)	(0.522)
Constant	26.44***	23.47**	22.11**
	(8.940)	(9.261)	(9.479)
Observations	112	112	112
R-squared	0.674	0.662	0.655

Note: Robust standard errors are in parentheses. Coefficients for dummy variables for six regions are not reported. BLNS = Botswana, Lesotho, Namibia, and Swaziland; SIDS = small island developing states.
*** $p<0.01$, ** $p<0.05$, * $p<0.1$

TABLE 6B.2 **Ordinary least squares (OLS) estimates for the relationship between performance indicators and the tax-to-GDP ratio using dummy variables for PI-14(ii) (2 of 2)**

VARIABLE	(1)	(2)	(3)
PI-14(ii) = A	2.699**	3.093**	3.927*
	(1.173)	(1.267)	(2.201)
PI-14(ii) = B		0.743	1.552
		(0.876)	(1.867)
PI-14(ii) = C			0.928
			(1.821)

continued

TABLE 6B.2, *continued*

VARIABLE	(1)	(2)	(3)
Agriculture (% of GDP)	–0.144***	–0.141***	–0.142***
	(0.0537)	(0.0531)	(0.0536)
Trade (% of GDP)	0.0559***	0.0557***	0.0566***
	(0.0135)	(0.0135)	(0.0134)
Natural resource rents (% of GDP)	–0.121**	–0.122**	–0.121**
	(0.0529)	(0.0541)	(0.0546)
Income per capita (log)	–1.927**	–1.900*	–1.904*
	(0.953)	(0.963)	(0.969)
Voice and accountability score	1.322*	1.371*	1.378*
	(0.777)	(0.777)	(0.771)
BLNS dummy	8.937***	8.880***	8.837***
	(2.969)	(2.888)	(2.912)
SIDS dummy	1.888	1.903	1.943
	(1.318)	(1.326)	(1.329)
Federal dummy	4.393*	4.290	4.305
	(2.541)	(2.594)	(2.621)
PI-14(i)—Registration	1.792***	1.631***	1.588***
	(0.556)	(0.611)	(0.602)
Constant	26.44***	26.14***	25.37***
	(8.940)	(8.995)	(9.111)
Observations	112	112	112
R-squared	0.674	0.676	0.677

Note: Robust standard errors are in parentheses. Coefficients for dummy variables for six regions are not reported. BLNS = Botswana, Lesotho, Namibia, and Swaziland; SIDS = small island developing states.
*** $p<0.01$, ** $p<0.05$, * $p<0.1$

TABLE 6B.3 Ordinary least squares (OLS) estimates for the relationship between performance indicators and the tax-to-GDP ratio for reduced sample sizes

VARIABLE	(1)	(2)	(3)
PI-14(ii)—Penalties	1.274**	1.416***	0.972**
	(0.562)	(0.460)	(0.426)
Agriculture (% of GDP)	–0.133**	–0.142**	–0.112*
	(0.0532)	(0.0567)	(0.0597)
Trade (% of GDP)	0.0556***	0.0484***	0.0421***
	(0.0130)	(0.0142)	(0.0135)
Natural resource rents (% of GDP)	–0.126**	–0.0154	–0.0338
	(0.0548)	(0.0499)	(0.0502)
Income per capita (log)	–1.793*	–1.690*	–1.728*
	(0.970)	(0.880)	(0.884)
Voice and accountability score	1.431*	1.265*	0.837
	(0.771)	(0.685)	(0.703)
BLNS dummy	8.813***	5.739***	5.573***
	(2.691)	(1.448)	(1.676)

continued

TABLE 6B.3, *continued*

VARIABLE	(1)	(2)	(3)
SIDS dummy	1.966	2.618**	3.620***
	(1.285)	(1.199)	(1.216)
Federal dummy	4.068	5.872**	0.811
	(2.669)	(2.332)	(1.020)
PI-14(i)—Registration	1.550***	0.905*	0.908*
	(0.582)	(0.490)	(0.490)
Constant	22.60**	22.59***	23.61***
	(8.915)	(8.190)	(8.308)
Observations	112	102	92
R-squared	0.673	0.619	0.565

Note: Robust standard errors are in parentheses. Coefficients for dummy variables for six regions are not reported. BLNS = Botswana, Lesotho, Namibia, and Swaziland; SIDS = small island developing states.
*** $p<0.01$, ** $p<0.05$, * $p<0.1$

TABLE 6B.4 Ordinary least squares (OLS) estimates for the relationship between performance indicators and the tax-to-GDP ratio using alternative samples for general government data

VARIABLE	(1)	(2)	(3)
PI-14(ii)—Penalties	1.274**	1.107**	1.121**
	(0.562)	(0.554)	(0.464)
Agriculture (% of GDP)	−0.133**	−0.147***	−0.136**
	(0.0532)	(0.0543)	(0.0545)
Trade (% of GDP)	0.0556***	0.0732***	0.0484***
	(0.0130)	(0.0146)	(0.0130)
Natural resource rents (% of GDP)	−0.126**	−0.136***	−0.111**
	(0.0548)	(0.0474)	(0.0499)
Income per capita (log)	−1.793*	−3.693***	−2.408**
	(0.970)	(1.001)	(0.957)
Voice and accountability score	1.431*	1.212	2.173***
	(0.771)	(0.848)	(0.813)
BLNS dummy	8.813***	10.70***	9.804***
	(2.691)	(2.629)	(2.717)
SIDS dummy	1.966	3.900***	3.474***
	(1.285)	(1.363)	(1.183)
Federal dummy	4.068		
	(2.669)		
PI-14(i)—Registration	1.550***	0.794	0.863*
	(0.582)	(0.617)	(0.474)
Constant	22.60**	37.86***	29.12***
	(8.915)	(9.349)	(9.224)
Observations	112	82	101
R-squared	0.673	0.757	0.692

Note: Robust standard errors are in parentheses. Coefficients for dummy variables for six regions are not reported. Column 2 drops observations for 30 countries for which the Government Resources Dataset uses general government data. Column 3 uses International Monetary Fund Government Finance Statistics central government data for 19 countries. BLNS = Botswana, Lesotho, Namibia, and Swaziland; SIDS = small island developing states.
*** $p<0.01$, ** $p<0.05$, * $p<0.1$

NOTES

1. See https://unstats.un.org/sdgs/files/metadata-compilation/Metadata-Goal-17.pdf.
2. Although the Tax Administration Diagnostic Assessment Tool (TADAT) has become the standard for assessing revenue administration in low- and middle-income countries, relatively few countries have submitted themselves to this assessment, and fewer still have made TADAT assessments publicly available. In contrast, 144 countries have undertaken a PEFA assessment, 104 of which have undertaken a repeat assessment (see chapter 2).
3. Version November 2017, which can be downloaded at https://www.wider.unu.edu/project /government-revenue-dataset.
4. The percentage of tax arrears at the beginning of a fiscal year that was collected during that fiscal year (average of the last two fiscal years) (PEFA Secretariat 2011).
5. The minimum requirement for an A on dimension PI-14(i) is that "taxpayers are registered in a complete database system with comprehensive direct linkages to other relevant government registration systems and financial sector regulations." The minimum requirement for an A on dimension PI-14(iii) is that "tax audits and fraud investigations are managed and reported on according to a comprehensive and documented audit plan, with clear risk assessment criteria for all major taxes that apply self-assessment" (PEFA Secretariat 2011).
6. This indicator is highly correlated with actual measures of democracy, including the polity index in the quality of government data set, and provides scores for a larger number of countries that have undertaken PEFA assessments.
7. We include PI-14 on the basis that it has the strongest relationship with the tax-to-GDP ratio
8. An alternative estimation procedure confirms the finding that A scores are driving our results (see annex 6B, table 6B.2).
9. Reasons cited for this result include countries whose economic structures predict higher levels of revenue than they collect as well as multicollinearity leading to imprecise estimates (Morrissey et al. 2017).
10. Available for download at https://data.world/imf/government-finance-statistics-gfs.
11. Because our data are unbalanced, we do not attempt to describe the period over which these estimates are relevant. The average time between assessments in the sample is 66 months, the shortest is 23 months, and the longest is 117 months.

REFERENCES

Ali, M., O. H. Fjeldstad, and I. H. Sjursen. 2014. "To Pay or Not to Pay? Citizens' Attitudes toward Taxation in Kenya, Tanzania, Uganda, and South Africa." *World Development* 64 (December): 828–42. doi:10.1016/j.worlddev.2014.07.006.

Allingham, M. G., and A. Sandmo. 1972. "Income Tax Evasion: A Theoretical Analysis." *Journal of Public Economics* 1 (3–4): 323–38. doi:10.1016/0047-2727(72)90010-2.

Alm, J., and J. Martinez-Vazquez. 2003. "Institutions, Paradigms, and Tax Evasion in Developing and Transition Countries." In *Public Finance in Developing and Transition Countries: Essays in Honor of Richard Bird,* 146–78. Cheltenham, U.K.: Edward Elgar Publishing.

Alm, J., J. Martinez-Vazquez, and B. Torgler. 2010. *Developing Alternative Frameworks for Explaining Tax Compliance.* London: Routledge.

Andreoni, J., B. Erard, and J. Feinstein. 1998. "Tax Compliance." *Journal of Economic Literature* 36 (2): 818–60.

Andrews, M. 2011. "Which Organizational Attributes Are Amenable to External Reform? An Empirical Study of African Public Financial Management." *International Public Management Journal* 14 (2): 131–56. doi:10.1080/10967494.2011.588588.

Basdevant, O. 2012. "Fiscal Policies and Rules in the Face of Revenue Volatility within Southern Africa Customs Union Countries (SACU)." IMF Working Paper 12/93, International Monetary Fund, Washington, DC. doi:10.5089/9781475502831.001.

Beck, P. J., J. S. Davis, and W.-H. Jung. 1991. "Experimental Evidence on Taxpayer Reporting under Uncertainty." *Accounting Review* 66 (3): 535–58.

Bird, R. M. 2015. "Improving Tax Administration in Developing Countries." *Journal of Tax Administration* 1 (1): 23–45. doi:10.1017/CBO9781107415324.004.

Bornhorst, F., S. Gupta, and J. Thornton. 2009. "Natural Resource Endowments and the Domestic Revenue Effort." *European Journal of Political Economy* 25 (4): 439–46. doi:10.1016/j.ejpoleco.2009.01.003.

Cowell, F. A. 1990. *Cheating the Government: The Economics of Evasion.* Cambridge, MA: MIT Press.

Cummings, R. G., J. Martinez-Vazquez, M. McKee, and B. Torgler. 2009. "Tax Morale Affects Tax Compliance: Evidence from Surveys and an Artefactual Field Experiment." *Journal of Economic Behavior and Organization* 70 (3): 447–57. doi:10.1016/j.jebo.2008.02.010.

D'Archy, M. 2011. "Why Do Citizens Assent to Pay Tax? Legitimacy, Taxation, and the African State." Working Paper 126, Afrobarometer. http://afrobarometer.org/sites/default/files/publications/Working%20paper/AfropaperNo126.pdf.

de Renzio, P., M. Andrews, and Z. Mills. 2011. "Does Donor Support to Public Financial Management Reforms in Developing Countries Work? An Analytical Study of Quantitative Cross-Country Evidence." Working Paper, Overseas Development Institute, London. www.odi.org.uk/50years.

European Court of Auditors. 2016. *The Use of Budget Support to Improve Domestic Revenue Mobilisation in Sub-Saharan Africa.* Special Report 35. Luxembourg: European Court of Auditors. https://www.eca.europa.eu/Lists/ECADocuments/SR16_35/SR_REVENUE_IN_AFRICA_EN.pdf.

Feld, L. P., and B. S. Frey. 2002. "Trust Breeds Trust: How Taxpayers Are Treated." *Economics of Governance* 3 (2): 87–99. doi:10.1007/s101010100032.

Fjeldstad, O. H., and J. Semboja. 2001. "Why People Pay Taxes: The Case of the Development Levy in Tanzania." *World Development* 29 (12): 2059–74. doi:10.1016/S0305-750X(01)00081-X.

Friedland, N., S. Maital, and A. Rutenberg. 1978. "A Simulation Study of Income Tax Evasion." *Journal of Public Economics* 10 (1): 107–16.

Gupta, A. Sen. 2007. "Determinants of Tax Revenue Efforts in Developing Countries." IMF Working Paper 07(184), International Monetary Fund, Washington, DC. doi:10.5089/9781451867480.001.

Hadley, S., and M. Miller. 2016. *PEFA: What Is It Good For? The Role of PEFA Assessments in Public Financial Management Reform.* London: Overseas Development Institute. https://www.odi.org/sites/odi.org.uk/files/resource-documents/10484.pdf.

Kleven, H. J., M. B. Knudsen, C. T. Kreiner, S. Pedersen, and E. Saez. 2011. "Unwilling or Unable to Cheat? Evidence from a Tax Audit Experiment in Denmark." *Econometrica* 79 (3): 651–92.

Levi, M. 1988. *Of Rule and Revenue.* Berkley, CA: University of California Press.

Long, C., and M. Miller. 2017. "Taxation and the Sustainable Development Goals: Do Good Things Come to Those Who Tax More?" Briefing Note, Overseas Development Institute, London. https://www.odi.org/sites/odi.org.uk/files/resource-documents/11695.pdf.

Luttmer, E. F. P., and M. Singhal. 2014. "Tax Morale." *Journal of Economic Perspectives* 28 (4): 149–68. doi:10.1257/jep.28.4.149.

Mascagni, G. 2017. "From the Lab to the Field: A Review of Tax Experiments." *Journal of Economic Surveys* 32 (2): 273–301. doi:10.1111/joes.12201.

Moore, M. 2004. "Revenues, State Formation, and the Quality of Governance in Developing Countries." *International Political Science Review* 25 (3): 297–319. doi:10.1177/0192512104043018.

———. 2007. "How Does Taxation Affect the Quality of Governance?" IDS Working Paper 280, Institute of Development Studies, Brighton, U.K.

Moore, M., N. Lustig, R. Bird, N. Birdsall, O.-H. Fjeldstad, R. Manning, and W. Prichard. 2015. "The Sustainable Development Goals—Reject Tax Targeting." *ICTD* (blog), April 16. http://www.ictd.ac/blogs/entry/the-sustainable-development-goals-reject-tax-targeting.

Morrissey, O., C. Von Haldenwang, A. Von Schiller, M. Ivanyna, and I. Bordon. 2017. "Tax Revenue Performance and Vulnerability in Developing Countries." *Journal of Development Studies* 52 (12): 1689–703. doi: 10.1080/00220388.2016.1153071.

Nepal PEFA (Public Expenditure and Financial Accountability) Secretariat. 2008. "Public Expenditure and Financial Acccountability Assessment." PEFA Secretariat, Kathmandu. https://pefa.org/sites/default/files/assements/comments/NP-Feb08-PEFAPFMPMF-Public.pdf.

———. 2015. "Public Expenditure and Financial Accountability (PEFA) Assessment: Nepal PFM Performance Assessment." PEFA Secretariat, Kathmandu. http://www.pefa.gov.np/downloads /pfm_pefa/PEFA-II-Final-Report-May-2015-1.pdf.

PEFA (Public Expenditure and Financial Accountability) Secretariat. 2011. *Public Financial Management Performance Measurement Framework*. Washington, DC: PEFA Secretariat. https://pefa.org/sites/default/files/PMFEng-finalSZreprint04-12_1.pdf.

———. 2012. *Fieldguide*. Washington, DC: PEFA Secretariat. http://siteresources.worldbank.org /PEFA/Resources/PEFAFieldguide.pdf.

Prichard, W., A. Cobham, and A. Goodall. 2014. "The ICTD Government Revenue Dataset." ICTD Working Paper 19, International Centre for Tax and Development, Brighton, U.K. http://www.ictd.ac/publication/the-ictd-government-revenue-dataset/.

Riahi-Belkaoui, A. 2004. "Relationship between Tax Compliance Internationally and Selected Determinants of Tax Morale." *Journal of International Accounting, Auditing, and Taxation* 13 (2): 135–43. doi:10.1016/j.intaccaudtax.2004.09.001.

Richardson, G. 2006. "Determinants of Tax Evasion: A Cross-Country Investigation." *Journal of International Accounting, Auditing, and Taxation* 15 (2): 150–69. doi:10.1016/j. intaccaudtax.2006.08.005.

Slemrod, J., M. Blumenthal, and C. Christian. 2001. "Taxpayer Response to an Increased Probability of Audit: Evidence from a Controlled Experiment in Minnesota." *Journal of Public Economics* 79 (3): 455–83.

Smith, K. W., and L. J. Stalans. 1991. "Encouraging Tax Compliance with Positive Incentives: A Conceptual Framework and Research Directions." *Law and Policy* 13 (1): 35–53.

Spicer, M. W., and R. E. Hero. 1985. "Tax Evasion and Heuristics: A Research Note." *Journal of Public Economics* 26 (2): 263–67.

Thomas, J. E., and M. W. Spicer. 1982. "Audit Probabilities and the Tax Evasion Decision: An Experimental Approach." *Journal of Economic Psychology* 2 (3): 241–45.

Tilly, C. 1985. "Warmaking and State Making as Organized Crime." In *Bringing the State Back In*, edited by P. B. Evans , D. Rueschemeyer, and T. Skocpol, 169–91. Cambridge, U.K.: Bambridge University Press.

Torgler, B. 2007. *Tax Compliance and Tax Morale*. Cheltenham, U.K.: Edward Elgar Publishing.

United Nations. 2015a. *Outcome Document: Addis Ababa Action Agenda of the Third International Conference on Financing for Development*. Addis Ababa: United Nations. www.un.org/esa/ffd.

———. 2015b. *Zero Draft: Addis Ababa Action Agenda of the Third International Conference on Financing for Development*. New York: United Nations. http://www.un.org/esa/ffd/wp-content /uploads/2015/03/1ds-zero-draft-outcome.pdf.